# BEFORE I AM HANGED

# BEFORE I AM HANGED:
## Ken Saro-Wiwa, Literature, Politics, and Dissent

Edited by
## Onookome Okome

**Africa World Press, Inc.**

P.O. Box 1892
Trenton, NJ 08607

P.O. Box 48
Asmara, ERITREA

# Africa World Press, Inc.

P.O. Box 1892
Trenton, NJ 08607

P.O. Box 48
Asmara, ERITREA

Book design: Wanjikũ Ngũgĩ
Cover design: Jonathan Gullery

**Library of Congress Cataloging-in Publication Data**

Before I am Hanged: Ken Saro-Wiwa—literature, politics, and dissent
/ edited by Onookome Okome.
    p. cm.
    Includes bibliographical references and index.
    ISBN 0-86543-744-0. — ISBN 0-86543-745-9 (pbk.)
    1. Saro-Wiwa, Ken, 1941-1995—Criticism and interpretation.
  2. Politics and literature—Nigeria—History—20th century.
  I. Okome, Onookome.
  PR9387.9.S27Z57  1999
    823—dc21                      99-24874
                                         CIP

In the memory of
Claude Ake.


For the poet-nationalist,
Femi Oyebode . . .

# Contents

Introduction
▼▼

# Ken Saro-Wiwa, A Man of Many Tall Parts:
## Literature, Nationhood and Dissent

**Onookome Okome**

## I

Taking stock of the events of the year 1995, *Punch*, the Nigerian independent newspaper based in one of Nigeria's largest cities, Lagos, on November 20th, voted Ken Saro-Wiwa Man of the Year. It is not difficult to see why this man is still so respected, even if his death was inglorious, barbaric, and extremely unprovoked.

Ken Saro-Wiwa was hanged November 10, 1995, with eight other Ogoni Human Rights and Environmental activists by the military government of General Sani Abachi. Ken Saro-Wiwa was born in 1941. He attended the then-prestigious Government College, Umuahia, renowned for producing literary greats such as Chinua Achebe, Christopher Okigbo, Elechi Amadi, and a host of others. He was also at the University of Ibadan where he took his degree just before the Nigerian Civil War began. Ken Saro-Wiwa was a man of many "tall parts," a phrase credited to him out of a minor newspaper squabble with a young journalist who dared to describe him as that "diminutive Ken and his loud mouth." His reply to this journalist was vintage Ken Saro-Wiwa: "The young man does not know my tall parts." Since then this description has stuck. He was also a prolific writer. His writings are mostly political.

Ken Saro-Wiwa's case has been a long running battle with Nigeria's military governments. A writer of immense repute, a man of strong political convictions (one of which is that the military should not have anything to do with politics), he was until his death vocal about the rights of his small Ogoni minority of the Niger Delta area. Trouble with the government in the Ogoni area started much earlier, before Saro-Wiwa took over the mantle of leadership of MOSOP (acroymn for The Movement for the Survival of the Ogoni People). What Saro-Wiwa did to this Movement to save his people from the huge degradation of life and property was to break the rank of the extremely corrupt local chiefs who represented the suffering people in their dealings with the federal government over oil exploration issues. It was probably assumed that once these gullible and insensitive chiefs were placated with loads of money, the government at the center was sure of some measure of peace to carry on oil exploration in the Ogoni area. Shell, the Anglo-Dutch oil company that operated in the Niger Delta, felt secure with government promises to keep the area safe of trouble-makers. Once in a great while, Shell would make some token gesture towards the plight of the people in the Niger Delta. Some roads were built, some lucky villages got electrified, and token bore-holes were sunk for potable water supplies to the Niger Delta that supplies the oil wealth of the nation. To advance these tokenisms, village heads and locals known to be outspoken were elaborately bribed. Today, Shell oil exploration has left the vast agrarian swamps and marshlands of the Niger Delta devastated, uninhabitable. There are often reports of acid rains in this area, and life-expectancy in this country has fallen drastically to an average of 45 years.

Faced with the increasingly restive atmosphere of the people of Ogoniland, the government of General Ibrahim Babangida instituted the OMPADEC (acronym for Oil Mineral Producing Area Development Commission). Rumors are still rife that this Commission was (and still is) essentially a conduit pipe through which large sums of money found their way into private pockets, military and civilian. Several debates were started; the most vehement questioned the basis of a body which was run by a government appointee who cared little for the welfare of the people who suffered directly in the land degradation.

For more than three decades, these deplorable conditions have prevailed, with local chiefs from the Niger Delta aiding and abetting Shell and the government in the gradual but persistent degradation of land and life.

Ken Saro-Wiwa, a man of profound foresight, challenged all this. To be accurate, Ogoniland is not the only part of the Niger Delta that is hard hit. Many ethnic groups live along the coastal line of the Niger Delta. The coastal people comprise Itsekiri, Urhobo, Izon, Kwale, Isoko, and other minorities or "micro-minorities" to borrow a phrase from Bob Nixon's essay on the Ogoni people, "Pipe Dreams: Ken Saro-Wiwa, Environmental Justice, and Micro-Minority Rights," have all suffered a similar fate. In most of the communities, the aquatic life, the mainstay of these rural fishing communities, has been completely destroyed. As one local Chief pointed out to us in a personal conversation, life is now meaningless without the primordial occupation of fishing.

What Ken Saro-Wiwa did was to bring the plight of these people to national and world attention, inspiring and being inspired by the political and cultural ideas of the fictional characters in his published novels such as *Sozaboy* (a novel in rotten English), *Prisoners of Jeb,* and in his collections of short stories such as *Adaku and Other Stories* and *A Forest of Flowers.* The political convictions and social visions of these characters are not altogether fictive. Ken Saro-Wiwa has been part of the growth of the Niger Delta, its ancient and glorious history and culture, and now its gradual but persistent economic and environmental nose-dive from the 1960s onward. These fictive characters are modeled on social types and local events. This explains why some of these characters provoked great and enthusiastic, albeit sometimes ascerbic debate in Nigeria's literary history.

If Saro-Wiwa's literary works generated so much debate here in Nigeria, his political ideas about the Nigerian *Federa-*

*tion* was even more controversial. His book on the Nigerian civil war (*On A Darkling Plain: An Account of The Nigerian Civil War*), carefully conceived around the minority/majority problems of Nigeria's ethnic groups, aroused heated hate-debate, especially among members of the three largest Nigerian ethnic groups. Ken Saro-Wiwa insisted and maintained that a multi-ethnic, multi-religious nation such as Nigeria must respect the rights of the minorities, especially in matters dealing with the distribution of wealth. He nonetheless emphasized his own minority. This, some critics see as parochial.

The news of Ken Saro-Wiwa's death sent shock waves through the entire nation, but it is interesting how individual ethnic groups reacted to the murder of a man of vision fighting for a just cause. Informal talks in the bars, in the classrooms, and elsewhere in Nigeria are often more frank than newspaper reports. Some people could not be bothered about the plight of Ken Saro-Wiwa. Others thought it was a huge breach of individual rights.

The judicial murder of Ken Saro-Wiwa on November 10, 1995 is surely a vindication of this writer's despair so well expressed in his 1992 book, *Genocide in Nigeria: The Ogoni Tragedy:* "Nigeria's rulers have hearts of stone and the brains of millipedes."

Ken Saro-Wiwa was controversial in life, and continues to be so in death. Hanged for his political views and his position in the very touchy debate of the majority/minority discourse in Nigerian politics, his name and his idea have now stood firm in the stream of debates issuing from Nigerian politics. He is reviled by those who find in him an upstart from that region where oil was discovered in the 1930s. For this group of people, Ken Saro-Wiwa is still the epitome of what must be scourged and recycled into the abyss of a forgotten life. Yet his place in the history of this country was never before better consolidated. This group of people who always wanted him dead still do. They have always found ways to make his place in Nigerian history irrelevant. And for those who loved him, Saro-Wiwa is still something of a phenomenon, a symbol of justice and fairplay. He was revered. And now his ideas are. Though dead, he has become a model to many people aggrieved by the current political and economic situation in Nigeria.

Ken Saro-Wiwa was a man who was conscious of his role in his community and in the larger political configuration called Nigeria. He loved history immensely and was constantly reading it and the same passion he showed for the study of history he brought to the creation of history. He often consciously created it and now his life has assumed the historical for us, the living. This fact of his life the most staunch adversary cannot hope to becloud in any way.

It is for this reason that we decided to x-ray his literature for his political thought. This book of essays, the result of our search, is entirely dedicated to his place in Nigeria's entire history in the larger canvas of Nigeria's development from pre-Nigeria through all its many political quakes into the turbulent 1990s when Saro-Wiwa was killed.

## II

In this challenging job of putting together essays on and about the life, literature, and political ideas of Ken Saro-Wiwa, we were immediately confronted with all the political problems of this nation, Nigeria, summed up within the controversial perspective from which Saro-Wiwa viewed and talked about the many national questions which assailed us (and still do). The debates which Ken Saro-Wiwa's life and activism generate inhabit the two extremes of Nigeria's political life. As soon as we set out to "quench the matter" (as Saro-Wiwa's character would have put it), we were confronted with newer problems, some of which are tied to the controversial positions Saro-Wiwa took in the many subjects he dealt with on the idea of nation, nationhood, ethnicity and the minority problem, and—the most difficult of all—the need for and the place of dissent in Nigeria's daily life as a nation. Ken Saro-Wiwa touched upon all of these problems in his life, in his literature, and in his political philosophy in two of his most radically articulated books: *On A Darkling Plain: An Account of The Nigeria Civil War* (Port Harcourt: Saros International Publishers, 1989) and the posthumously published *A Month and A Day: A Detention Diary* (London: Heineman, 1996) as the most eloquent articulations of his political ideas. There are other nonfictional texts, such as the less serious, but equally important book of debate on the state of Nigeria, *Nigeria: The Brink of Disaster* (Port Harcourt: Saros International Publishers, 1991).

The problem of putting together a collection of representative essays on Ken Saro-Wiwa, whose politics elicited the full spectrum of debate in Nigeria, was even more difficult. This volume is the first by any scholar to attempt this sort of enterprise since Saro-Wiwa was judicially murdered on November 10, 1995. Our primary objective was to re-cast the perspective of this man in the light of contemporary Nigerian history, pre-figuring what happened before independence and after as a backdrop against which to re-examine this enigmatic man whose death has become, in a sense, the height of this nation's moral aberration. Since not everyone agrees with the last statement, something which many people are awfully aware of, the primary and important task was for us to select from a huge body of submitted contributions (solicited and unsolicited) a just and fair representation from those who were touched one way or the other by the life and writing of this man. Expectedly, the response was as diverse as possible. In dealing with the subjects on and about Ken Saro-Wiwa, Nigerians are put once more out at the battle-front; sometimes the battles are fought on the plains of pure intellectualism, but more often in the slippery space defined by the discourse of ethnic minority/majority debate and the disbursement of a nation's wealth.

Of the many problems which this project made visible, the easiest to resolve was the one which had to do with the fair representation of the extremes of the debate on Ken Saro-Wiwa's life and times in Nigeria. Simply, essays are selected from both extremes of the discourse-spectrum, allowing the essays rather to speak for themselves. The regret however is that we cannot fully assure our readers that both sides are fully represented in the school of debates which Ken Saro-Wiwa has engendered in Nigerian politics, literature, ethnic *wahala,* and in the right to dissent in a pluri-ethnic society gone berserk. Many of the essays submitted try to stay out of the murky water of this man's controversy by simply relying more on what he wrote about his life and his people in the literary and journalistic texts. It is in this regard that the essay of Azubike Ileoje stands out in this volume as a forthright contribution. While the reader may not agree with all the positions expressed in it, it is important to see the *logic* of the other extreme on the debate about the life and times of Ken Saro-Wiwa. Ileoje's essays stands out for other reasons: its obvious ethnic stance and its almost irreducible desire to re-read the history of Nigeria in the light of of Ken Saro-Wiwa's *On A Darkling Plain*. This essay carries and amplifies this controversial figure as an ethnic bigot.

As any observer of the Nigerian political scene knows, issues of ethnicity and ethnic representation are very tricky matters. Ethnic debates make it obvious that there is hardly a common center, a phenomenon which according to Ernest Renan is essential for the well-being of all plural nation-states:

> A nation is a soul, a spiritual principle. Two things, which in truth are but one, constitute the soul and the spiritual principle. One lies in the past, one in the present. One is the possession in common of a rich legacy of memories; the other is present-day consent, the desire to live together, the will to perpetuate the value of the heritage that one had received in an undivided form. (Renan 1990:9)

Saro-Wiwa's position does provide some headaches to anyone who insists on the shared principle of a historical past as an essential qualification of a nation. His grave insistence that only his Ogoni people must be compensated leaves something of the *selfish* on the palate. What do we do with the other micro-minorities with the same problems? Are they not part of what we have loosely defined as the nation of Nigeria? This question was put to Ken Saro-Wiwa sometime in September 1991 at his publishing office in Surulere, Lagos. His answer was as robust as his sense of history and ethnicity. He said he was beginning at home— charity after all, he said, laughing that full laughter of his, begins at home. "If other people feel as aggrieved as my people, then they should set up a front

such as ours," he continued, "and fight for their rights." Justi-
fied as this position is, it does not wish away the fact that Ken
Saro-Wiwa did not make any attempt to bring all the devastated and marginalised people of the Niger Delta into the forefront of this struggle, thereby opening up his small micro-
minority for the ultimate onslaught from the Federal powers.
Some critics have said that this to a great extent accounts for
why it was so easy to crack down on him.

There is also the other argument: that he personalized the
struggle at the end of his life, so that there were major dissensions even within his own MOSOP (Movement For the Survival of Ogoni People). This also opened up the movement to
outside influence. There was a small group among his own
Ogoni people who actually welcomed his death. In many ways,
therefore, Ken Saro-Wiwa's *tactics* were not good enough to
pull the struggle along a course which embraced the whole
Niger Delta or even the whole Ogoni people. This does not
delegitimate his fight, though. It simply implies that his tactics proved fatal.

At some point one wonders at the apparent carelessness to
the lessons of history which Saro-Wiwa showed. Ken Saro-
Wiwa was a man who loved history, read much of it, domestic
and international, lived it, and even created it when he felt the
need to do so. Why didn't he learn from the story of Isaac
Adaka Boro, a revolutionary from the Niger Delta, who saw
the degradation and mass suffering of the people of the Niger
Delta in the 1960s, a result of oil exploration and the consequent neglect from the Federal Government, and promptly
declared a Republic of the Niger Delta during the Ironsi government? This is how Ken Saro-Wiwa casually reports this
very important political precedent in his *On A Darkling Plain:
An Account of The Nigerian Civil War.*

> Only one event interrupted this honeymoon. The na-
> tion woke up one morning in February to hear of se-
> cession. The late Isaac Boro of the minority Ijaw eth-
> nic group, ex-policeman, ex-University student, had de-
> clared a Niger Delta Republic and had taken up arms
> against his fatherland. (30)

The Nigerian nation was just getting embroiled in its post-Independence politics and this young idealistic man, infused with the ideas of Che Guevera, coupled with a passionate sense of the idea of revolution (though not its practical implication), declared a war on the establishment with only twelve soldiers on his side. He was hopefully idealistic. Quoting another source, Ken Saro-Wiwa tells us in *On A Darkling Plain* that Boro's ideas about the revolution and the new nation were clearly protestations against the degradation of the minority people of the Niger Delta:

> The Niger Delta State is a clear case as the people concerned have a distinct historical silhouette. Such a demand becomes all the more compelling when the area is so viable, yet the people are blatantly denied development and the common necessities of life. If Nigerian governments refuse to do something to drastically improve the lot of the people inevitably a point of no return will be reached. (30)

As far as Boro was concerned, the "point of no-return" was here. He declared the Republic, swearing to "break the Niger Delta Area into a nation and strive to maintain it." Saro-Wiwa goes even further, quoting the opinions of commentators on Boro. Tony Tebekaemi, the editor of Boro's posthumously published pamphlet, *The Twelve-Day Revolution,* is one of the sources that Ken Saro-Wiwa quotes here, yet the salient points of this ill-fated protest failed to influence his position on the subject when he became physically involved. As he himself reports in his book, "The Ironsi regime moved in against Boro and quickly captured him before more harm could be done. The Eastern Nigerian High Court tried and sentenced him to death for treason" (p. 31). Why didn't Saro-Wiwa, a man of history, an acute and critical observer of the Nigerian society in its process of decay, read clearly the consequences of Boro's attempt at calling attention to marginality and minority degradation? For one moment in his struggle to right the wrong which the Nigerian state has perpetuated on minorities, Saro-Wiwa allowed the flight of passion and the sense that the just often triumph to becloud his judgement of tactics. This was a fatal flaw. He died for it. Boro's revolution prefigures the problems that minorities face when confronted with a blatant show of state terror and intimidation.

Conscious of this lack of a discursive center then and now, our criteria for collecting the essays presented here on and about Ken Saro-Wiwa were more or less predicated on discourses of *nationalities* rather than on a discourse of a nationality; ethnicities rather than ethnicity; *political ideas* rather than a political idea, *the uses of* literature rather than the use of literature, dissensions rather than *dissent*, conscious that it is in the intersections of the many discourses of the nation that we can arrive at something meaningful, at least in the intellectual realm if not at the practical sphere of politics.

The essays presented here are discourses of nations and nationalities in a geographical expression that has become obviously rudderless. However antagonistic in their discursive preferences the essays presented here, all of them, even when they deal with the literary and political ideas of Ken Saro-Wiwa, privilege the inescapable sites of political antagonisms in Nigerian life: nation and the idea of ethnicity. In other words, each of the essays seems to ask the questions which Ken Saro-Wiwa often asked in his life-time: Is there a nation here? Or as Soyinka would put it, "When is a nation"? Where is our allegiance weighted? Ethnicity or nationality?

The idea of the nation has been a keen subject of debate since independence from the British in 1960. The notion that this geographical expression was not inaugurated out of a common accent by all the people concerned has been stressed by the horde of specialists and common wo/men who bother to think about the future of this country. This debate has become even more vociferous in recent times, probably because ethnic inequalities and sectional favoritism and nepotism have simply raged on in spite of the articulated detrimental effect of such vices to the nation. Once the idea of the nation comes up, ethnicity is quickly inserted. It is often a complement to all discourses of the nation in Nigeria.

Two recent books which deal with these issues are Wole Soyinka's *The Open Sore of A Continent: A Personal Narrative of*

*The Nigerian Crisis* (Oxford: Oxford University Press, 1996) and Ken Saro-Wiwa's posthumously published book, *A Month and A Day: A Detention Diary* (London: Penguin Books, 1995). Dealing extensively with subjects such as nationhood and dictatorship in Nigeria, both texts not only legitimize that basis for the discourse of dictatorship and nationhood, they also underscore the important place that free and unfettered individual choices can play in a plural country such as the one in question. Let us stop briefly to look at Soyinka's position in this debate, after which we shall attempt to see how the essays represent these matters.

Beginning with the introduction to *The Open Sore of A Continent*, Soyinka makes it clear that he detests military dictatorship in any guise it assumes. He condemns any regime that carries this stigma and, as usual with Soyinka's essays on governance and people, he scornfully pre-empts the moral position and ethical sites of preference which this kind of regime can ever hope to put forward. In "The Last Despot and The End of Nigerian History", the introduction to *The Open Sore of A Continent*, Soyinka writes of the current military regime under whose auspices Ken Saro-Wiwa and eight fellow Ogoni people were hanged on 10 November 1995:

> What Nigeria is confronting today is a species of mimic succession that considers itself innovative. The imposition of a Constitutional Conference in 1994 by General Sani Abacha as a "solution" to the artificial crisis developed from a free and fair election is really a pitiable compliment to I. B. Babangida, who at least played that con game with panache, milking it eventually to death. (10)

This is the state of the nation's problems. And it is not different from what was in the 1960s when Boro and Ojukwu declared "independence" from mainland Nigeria, both of whom were brutally crushed. In other words, Soyinka is telling us that we have not moved from *anywhere* to *anywhere* significant since 1960. We are still floating aimlessly on the sea of ethnic tension, in which *tribal* squabble has allowed a "mimic succession" of "military messiahs." Where would this lead a country such as Nigeria? How do we then define this geographical space called Nigeria in the light of these problems which have remained unsolved (unresolved) for almost half a decade? In the same essay, Soyinka provides a possible way out, but it is still the grim possibilities which both Isaac Adaka Boro and Odumegwu Ojukwu took a couple of years ago:

> The real danger, the very real danger, however, is in the character of this last torchbearer for military demonology, the puny Samson whose arms are wrapped around the pillars, ready to pull down the edifice in his descent into hell. That hell that is Ogoniland today is the perception of nation compatibility of which Abacha's mind is capable . . . In Sani Abachi's self-manifesting destiny as the last despot, we may be witnessing, alas the end of Nigerian history. (16)

This prophetic statement from a man whose life was on the line here in his own country freely talked about everywhere in the streets, in homes, in bars, schools, yet no ruler has cared to do anything about it.

This was the state of affairs in the late 1960s. This is the state in which we live today. This is the state in which Ken Saro-Wiwa lived and died. This is the condition that he found intolerable. This is the political and social context in which we live today in Nigeria. This is the context which has engendered the question, ubiquitous and significant, "When is a nation?" in "A Flawed Origin—But No Worse Than Other," Soyinka's desperate attempt to fully grasp the import of Nigeria's season of anomy. This is also the propelling backdrop against which Ken Saro-Wiwa lived and died. In all his writings, not even the casual observer can hope to escape this web of social confusion and political quagmire. It is *writ large* in our consciousness, in our daily lives, so that our relationships are defined by our ethnic affiliations and the loose class badges that we carry around. Is this not a situation which elicits the renewed prospect of dissent in literature?

What Soyinka refers to as "the end of Nigeria's history" is after all an indirect contemplation of that idea. Coming from a man who has opposed the split of our geography into tiny chiefdoms to be governed by petty chiefs during the 1967 war, this must be a serious matter. The idea of dissent then perpetually stares us in the face every day, demanding from us the need to re-define our nationhood, our very willingness to relocate our national *locus*.

## III

The essays selected and presented here are on and about Ken Saro-Wiwa who was killed on November 10, 1995 after being accused and convicted by a special military tribunal of murder. He was killed with eight other Ogoni men who were also arraigned before this tribunal for this same offence. But the essays are only around and on Ken Saro-Wiwa in so far as they represent the discourse which Ken Saro-Wiwa himself made very visible in the political and cultural history of Nigeria. Far beyond the personality of Saro-Wiwa, the essays discuss Nigeria: the state of its nationhood, ethnicity, its new literature, especially of Ken Saro-Wiwa and the temperament of this literature, the possibility of dissent and the consequence of dissention. The essays speak for themselves, but there is a need to outline some of the features common to all of them. Each of these essays look into one aspect of Nigeria's contemporary existence through a personalized reading of Ken Saro-Wiwa's literature or political ideas. Autonomous and sometimes highly polemical, some of the essays here take sides in the debates about the idea of dissention and the possibilities of a permanent break-up of Nigeria.

All except one is not concerned with the summary and ultimate dismissal of Ken Saro-Wiwa into the world beyond. That essay is the contribution of Azubike Ileoje, "*On A Darkling Plain: The Darksome Lyric of An Outsider*." We will have to dwell a little more on this essay, as it prefigures some very important aspects of the debate on nation/nationhood, ethnicity, and the viability of dissent in contemporary Nigeria.

Ileoje's essay is a critical reading of one of Saro-Wiwa's well known books on Nigeria's dark days, the civil war. Like

Saro-Wiwa's book, *On A Darkling Plain*, this reading is itself based entirely on the defense of an ethnic position before, during, and after the civil strife which engulfed the Nigerian nation from 1967 to 1970. As this author tells us, the premise of this paper is unambiguously "that the significance of *On A Darkling Plain* can be grasped only if it is understood that he [Saro-Wiwa] was an outsider constantly in search of an alternative context that would convert him into an insider." The evidence of this writer's life and in death tells us otherwise. He actually administered one of the oil rich neighboring towns of the Igbo country which Ileoje talks about during Nigeria's darksome days of war. No matter how hard Ileoje tries to prove otherwise, Saro-Wiwa's narrative was (and is, especially in this literature and political ideas) a minority one and as is evident in the politics of this country, nobody can convincingly deny the horrific lessons that minority ethnic groupings have suffered at the hands of the so-called three ethnic majorities, whether in times of war or peace.

Nobody can ever hope to "fully comprehend the issues and forces of contention within and about Nigeria" during those days as Ileoje puts it. So if we do not understand "the issues and forces" at play in those dark, hazy days, how then do we hope to understand what Saro-Wiwa did or does in his book on the subject, *On A Darkling Plain*. Like others who have written about the war, Ken Saro-Wiwa is ethnically tainted. Yet Ileoje tries hard to argue that Saro-Wiwa was an outsider of the war who was perpetually plotting for personal gain. He only gained prominence because he used an ethnic front to his advantage. But if we do not press this superhuman tag on him, then we can, like Harry Garuba or Grace Okereke, begin to see the many coalescing sub-discourse units of Ken Saro-Wiwa's writing and activism into a major micro-minority discourse which was (still is) oppositional to the hegemonized politics of the big three ethnicities—Yoruba, Igbo, and Hausa/ Fulani. Discourses and their formational dialectics are means to the acquisition of power. They are structures constructed to voice preferred positions or counter-positions. This is what Ken Saro-Wiwa's *On A Darkling Plain,* as well as *Nigeria: The Brink of Disaster* and *A Month and A Day* privilege. If we agree that it is otherwise, this is simply because we also know that there are other reasons to question it, reminding ourselves that there is more than one site in the large discourses of nation and nationhood, two subjects which Saro-Wiwa deals with extensively in his political ruminations. Read this way, therefore, the story of Ken Saro-Wiwa, which is the discourse of all micro-ethnicities in this country, becomes a corroding sign on the tableaux of the three major privileged ethnic discourses. This is what makes up what we can loosely identify as the *national center*. Ken Saro-Wiwa's political life questions this, calling attention to all other (un)manned sites of antagonism in Nigeria's nation-building. What is curious is that the (un)manned sites of antagonism also house another very important aspect of our daily life and the *raison d'etre* of our nationhood—oil—the major revenue earner of the country. This partly explains why every attempt to empower the discourse of ethnic minorities becomes something of a national "problem." Ken Saro-Wiwa was a national problem; so too is the narrative of micro-minority marginalization.

But Ileoje's contribution to the debate raised in this book is important. It is frank and upright, witty and sarcastic, and logically attenuated. Often moving beyond the boundaries of the text he examines, this author implicates history and social systems; ethnicity and power relations, and the personalization of historicity in his analysis of Saro-Wiwa's declared and undeclared motives, but it is his own version of a national history. The result is interesting. Without quite making this clear, Ileoje raises the question which our endeavor privileges here: When is a nation? If in 1966 the Igbo nation did not feel that there was a political nation and then opted to declare war on the unity of the imperial geography called Nigeria, wasn't it right to summon this critical anger in 1993 or thereabouts for the same reason? Isn't dissent an inescapable fact of plural society?

Akpan's contribution "Ethnic Minority and The Nigerian State: The Ogoni Struggle After Ken Saro-Wiwa," is a political reading of the Nigerian parlous political state in which is inserted the discourse of dissent, aptly represented by the position expressed by Ken Saro-Wiwa. This paper begins from a reasoned and well established position: pluri-ethnic state cannot hope to avoid ethnic, cultural, and political cleavages. These problems are inescapable. The need is to seek the most democratic means of resolving them. The paper then grinds on to the turbulent position of ethnic minorities in Nigeria.

Akpan situates the premise of his paper on what he terms "the political economy" of Nigeria before oil was suddenly discovered in the Niger Delta area, privileging revenue allocation formulae before the advent of oil wealth. In this presentation which mainly supports the position of the Ogoni struggle, Akpan seems to be saying that "what is good for the goose is also good for the gander," meaning that if the derivation formula favored in the pre-military centralization of political authority was good for the three major ethnic groups, then it should be equally applied in the case of oil. His essay finds it ironic that this did not happen, rather every effort was (and is) being made to re-write or write- over every existing constitution or decree concerning this thorny issue. The result is all too glaring to see—the turbulence in the oil-producing areas of the Niger Delta, the Ogoni case being just one example. But Akpan is quick to point out that it is only with the clause of the Ogoni Bill of Rights dealing with wealth-distribution grievance that other ethnic minorities in the Niger Delta identify with. The question of inter-ethnic relationships among the micro-minorities is left unattended to. This is also a major problem. Azubike Ileoje's paper hints at this, but from a position which tends to vilify the *outsideness* of Ken Saro-Wiwa, the prominent casualty and symbol of minority/majority discourse of power in Nigeria.

Akpan's paper is also interesting in other regards. Coming from a social science base, it is not merely concerned with the Ogoni struggle and the literature it has produced, it is also concerned with what we may term the unwritten social intercourse between oil-producing companies and the communities in which they operate. He details these relationships, showing how oil producing communities took laws into their own hands in the 1990s to redress their own problems arising from oil exploration. His examples of violent clashes between oil producing communities and oil-producing companies are telling. He does not expand on the off-shot of what these encounters portend for the oil companies and for the nation. But let us take two examples. That these communities have forced many oil producing companies to pay some form of compensation points to some social and political problems. Is there still a credible political center? Under whose laws do the oil companies operate? Are the communities who opted to deal directly with the oil companies not flouting the laws of the nation? Is a nation a nation when its laws are recklessly disobeyed by multi-national corporations, as the oil companies have done by dealing directly with the oil-producing communities? Akpan's paper does not address the center of the debates about revenue allocation in Nigeria, the subject of Akpan's paper. *A Month and A Day: A Detention Diary* by Ken Saro-Wiwa and *The Open Sore of A Continent* by Wole Soyinka have posed these questions in many ways, none of them providing satisfactory answers.

Obododimma's essay "The Testament of A 'Penful' Prisoner" is a very cautious one; it denies us any peep into the horrifying brutality of the State actions which this writer went through from his early incarceration to his death by judicial murder. But it does not fail to tell how horrific prison in Nigeria can be, especially for a writer whose mind is constantly looking out for meaning in a meaningless state. This essay takes us through this gruesome terrain, putting us through the transformation which the self-declared radical writer Ken Saro-Wiwa (the writer must be *l'homme engage*) undergoes as a political prisoner from "prison artist" to the "artist prisoner." The difference between the two Obododimma explains this way in Saro-Wiwa's context:

> The "prison artists" were oral performers (of a kind) whose arts were most relevant to their condition in prison, who perform to encourage themselves and hope for (God's) intervention. Saro-Wiwa eventually overcomes the alienation (occasioned by his being an artist-prisoner) to become a (secular) "prison artist."

Through this reading, and the many interesting interventions which Obododimma makes into Saro-Wiwa's last book on his extended and reinvigorated political idea, *A Month and A Day*, the reader is let into the solid and singular uprightness of this writer-politician. For one moment, we are convincingly led to believe that Ken Saro-Wiwa is not simply an Ogoni activist or the diminutive political ideologue who wants a country of his own to assuage his ambition to become the only successful secessionist in Nigeria's turbulent political history as the pro-establishment media have painted him. In *A Month and A Day*, his ideas about this nation, Nigeria, are spelled out unambiguously. Justice is at the center of that political ideology; justice and fair play for those who are denied political power, and his case-study can only be his own people, the Ogoni micro-minority that has been subjected to environmental degradation for more than 50 years. Implicated in this complicity is the multinational oil company, Shell. It was his political ideas that got him into trouble with the military authorities in Abuja, but it was through his literature, his access to the use of the diverse literary genres, that he made his political ideas visible in the troubled landscape of Nigeria's political history. He died for this. Obododimma's paper is about the state of prison which Saro-Wiwa saw before his death. Obododimma goes further in his reading of the Nigerian prison and engaged in the decoding of the many signs which the state of the prison foretell for the state of the nation itself, concluding as Saro-Wiwa did that "You can tell the state of a nation by the way it keeps its prisons" (*A Month and A Day*, 224).

Without getting down into any great detail, Solomon Ediri Ejeke's essay merely touches upon significant details in the life of Ken Saro-Wiwa, emphasizing Saro-Wiwa's moral uprightness and his political vision. This essay positions the judicial murder of this writer-philosopher-political activist in a proper national perspective. Ejeke's essay, "The Socio-Political Dimensions of Ken Saro-Wiwa's Activism," merely introduces the many dimensions of the life and times of Ken Saro-Wiwa.

Harry Garuba's contribution, "Ken Saro-Wiwa's *Sozaboy* and The Logic of Minority Discourse," is a rigorous, albeit theoretically positioned effort to unravel the counter-ideological premise with which Ken Saro-Wiwa confronted the dominant discourse, a dominant discourse governed by the logic of a repressive regime of war perpetually at war with its own people. The narrator in this novel, *Sozaboy*, negotiates this minority position in the nebulous world of a war which is itself the result of unexplained and inexplicable ethnic antagonisms. Garuba's paper moves beyond the boundaries imposed by the text, implicating the life of Ken Saro-Wiwa in a minority/majority discourse similar to that found in *Sozaboy*:

> The construction of a representation relation of coincidence between Sozaboy's story and the structure of the story of the oppressed minorities can in fact be extended to the life of Ken Saro-Wiwa himself. Ken Saro-Wiwa always cut the picture of a small embattled man confronting a material and discursive power far in excess of his ability to overcome. But Ken was born into an awareness of *difference*.

The suggestion in Garuba's paper is obvious: in Mene, Saro-Wiwa's major character in *Sozaboy*, the minority discourse which Saro-Wiwa's political treatise favors in *On A Darkling Plain: An Account of The Nigerian Civil War* and *A Month and A Day: A Detention Diary* is hegomonized. This is, as Garuba puts it, life imitating art and art copying life. For Ken Saro-Wiwa, both are intricately bound together.

Oshita O. Oshita's paper introduces an interesting aspect to the discourse of Ken Saro-Wiwa's narrative as a micro-minority protester for justice and fair play in the distribution of national resource. Ken Saro-Wiwa, he writes, was not the first to have openly protested the degradation of life and environment in the Niger Delta, the young "brilliant officer, Major Isaac Adaka Boro had done so in the 1960s, proclaimed the Niger Delta Republic inspired by the fears of a stolen future of minorities in the post-independent capitalist Nigeria." Oshita points out too that Ken Saro-Wiwa was well aware of this, implying that Saro-Wiwa was only building his own unit upon an existing micro-minority narrative of the Delta. This position establishes an existing narrative without which it is difficult to understand the significance of Ken Saro-wiwa.

Outrightly partisan, it is not difficult at all to see that Oshita O. Oshita speaks and believes the minority discourse. Perhaps he has also been bruised by similar experiences. On these pages, Oshita fights for and on behalf of the ideas of Ken Saro-Wiwa.

Imo Ben Eshiet's essay is a deep textual reading of one of Ken Saro-Wiwa's best known plays, *The Transistor Radio*. This short play has won a number of national and international awards and, as Eshiet points out, this play, a comedy, written with the best satirical wit of this witty man of letter, is set in that inscrutable hub of urban life in Nigeria, Lagos. The concern in this play, Eshiet tells us, is Saro-Wiwa's constant engagement with the poorest of the poor. His investigation into their lives is a way of understanding also how his country has continuously *fringified* a group of people by making them urban scums. This reading, like the many interpretations of Saro-Wiwa's work in this volume, relies on the text, and then jumps across its boundaries to unearth the kind of meaning which Ken Saro-Wiwa always wanted to grasp: the meaning of the ordinary people's lives who live the devastation of Nigeria's morbid political and economic inconsistencies. Eshiet concludes his study with an analysis of another play of Saro-Wiwa, *The Wheel*, dealing exclusively with the "Nigerian political milieu." As with the first play in the volume *Four Farcical Plays*, *The Wheel* is a parody of the idiocy and crass materialistic disposition of the Nigerian ruling elite.

Ahunuwangho's paper, "The Gift of Voice" is a discourse analysis of Saro-Wiwa's most obviously political novel, *Prisoners of Jebs*. This analysis privileges language as a vehicle for Saro-Wiwa's political swipe at Nigeria's political, social, and cultural decay. In it, Ahunuwangho successfully shows us the many levels of meaning in the semantic options utilized by Ken Saro-Wiwa in this work to do this. Essentially the position of the paper is that this novel is a political treatise which uses a medley of narrative strategies ranging from the comic to the biting satire of people and institutions.

David Eka's essay "Aspect of Language in Ken Saro-Wiwa's *Sozaboy*" is yet another dealing with the interesting language issue in the corpus of Saro-Wiwa's writing. Strictly concerned with how nonstandard English is used in *Sozaboy: A Novel in Rotten English* (the subtitle is suggestive of the language formation which the characters parade), Eka takes us through an interesting array of sentence constructions, examining for our benefit how the constructed language is conceived from the dismal education fountain of the main character. His argument is obvious: on the face of it the rule-mangling nonstandard English which these characters speak might appear incomprehensive, but a critical look tells us that it is indeed a well articulated linguistic map which provides a sure way into the inner minds of these characters. In this linguistic zone too, we can faithfully construct the lives of these characters.

Grace Okereke's "The Female Narrative and Ken Saro-Wiwa's Discourse of Change in *A Forest of Flowers*" is a profound feminist(ic) reading of Saro-Wiwa's appropriation of the female gaze and consciousness in a book of poems—*A Forest of Flowers*. The argument is that Saro-Wiwa's appropriation of the female voice, without due activation of the female *self,* is itself another form of gender deprivation common among male writers attempting to enter into the consciousness of female characters. The result, as Okereke puts it, is that "by keeping the female narrator unnamed, Saro-Wiwa robs her of identity and disposses her of some of the power that her vocal status confers on her." What remains in the poems invested with the male voice is the political consciousness of the narrative itself. Clearly Saro-Wiwa is not so very concerned with the issues of gender and *voicing* as the essay makes us believe, but this does not take away much from the very well articulated argument which Okereke puts forward. Saro-Wiwa may be more concerned with the political, yet, as Okereke insinuates, we cannot deny the fact that his *cultural unconscious* becomes obvious in his supplanting of the female narrative in the *voicing* of male narratives. Okereke thinks this follows a tradition of phalocentricism as defined in many, if not all, patriarchal orders. In his study, Grace Okereke concludes that "By keeping the female narrator in the major female narratives in *A Forest of Flowers* unnamed, Ken Saro-Wiwa confers on them a collective female identity." They become an "Every woman" and by so doing "Saro-Wiwa engages society in a discourse on change structured on our basic humanity, harmony and a more enriching relationship between men and women in spite of gender."

## IV

In the preceding pages of this introduction, the reader is let into the content and peculiar discourse spaces of some of the essays presented here. No attempt is made to summarize all the essays. Indeed, the summaries made are only peeps into the rich textual controversies which the essays privilege, in which highlights of some of the controversies are foregrounded. There are many more controversies around and on Ken Saro-Wiwa which the textual evidence of the essays do not privilege here. As is the custom with academic papers, each contributor chooses one (or more in some cases) aspect of the subject and proceeds to examine. There are certain aspects of our unofficial life which rarely find attention in academic discourses such as this one. In his life time, Ken Saro-Wiwa also engendered and energized that area of our public sphere. After all, as Wole Soyinka aptly points out:

> For the majority of Nigerians, Ogoni is only some localized problem, remote from the immediate, overall mission of the rooting out the military from politics, rescuing the nation's wealth from its incontinent hands, and terminating, once and for all, its routine murders of innocent citizens on the streets of Lagos and other visible centres of opposition. (*Open Sore*, 4-5)

It is the public sphere that is so energized by the debate of national problems built around the minority/majority equation that Soyinka talks about here:

> But it is not just in the Nigerian free media that this minority's tyranny is discussed; and perhaps, before it is too late, our nettled general of the occupation forces of the media houses will be made to realize this. Public debate—in such places as bars, bus stops, market, garages, staff and student clubs, government offices

(largely in the south, naturally)—has catapulted the activities of this minority to the heart of the national crisis, resulting in questioning the presumption (and June 12 affirmation) of the nation as a single entity. (8)

What then are some of the contentions in this heated public sphere during the life and after the death of Ken Saro-Wiwa? Let us take only one of the hushed tales built around the diminutive man from the creeks. It is rumored in this public that Ken Saro-Wiwa had greater plans of secession, and that in fact he had designed an Ogoni flag and anthem. The rumor also had it that Saro-Wiwa was only waiting for the right time to declare himself president of a small, oil-rich nation. Tied to this tale is that he had promised the Ogoni youths who murdered the four Ogoni chiefs for which Ken Saro-Wiwa was hanged huge wealth: Mercedes Benz cars, big houses and so on. For this reason, the radical arm of MOSOP was totally committed to him. Since none of these was reported at the trial, we can only rely on what he said of his struggle.

> I am a man of peace, a man of ideas. Appalled by the denigrating poverty of my people who live on a richly endowed land, distressed by their political marginalisation and economic trangulation, angered by the devastation of their land, their ultimate heritage, anxious to preserve their right to life and to a decent living, and determined to usher to this country as a whole a fair and just democratic system which protects everyone and every ethnic group and gives us all a valid claim to human civilization I have devoted all my intellectual and material resources, my very life, to a cause in which I have total belief . . .. Neither imprisonment nor death can stop our ultimate victory. (*ANA Review* 1995:23)

This is not the voice of a man who wanted his country split. This is a voice calling for justice in a land of all kinds of bigotries. The picture is that of a country on trial.

# Works Cited

Renan, Ernest. "What is A Nation?" *Nation and Narration.* London: Routledge, 1990: 9.

Saro-Wiwa, Ken. *A Month and A Day: A Detention Diary.* London: Heineman, 1996.

_____. *Nigeria: The Brink of Disaster.* Port Harcourt: Saros International Publisher, 1991.

_____. *On A Darkling Plain: An Account of The Nigerian Civil War.* Port Harcourt: Saros International Publisher, 1989.

Soyinka, Wole. *The Open Sore of A Continent: A Personal Narrative of The Nigerian Crisis.* Oxford: Oxford University Press, 1996.

1

# The Testament of a "Penful" Prisoner:
## Ken Saro-Wiwa's Literary Dialogue with the Prison

### Obododimma Oha

*Books and all forms of writing have always been objects of terror to those who seek to suppress truth.*
—Wole Soyinka, *The Man Died* (9)

It is difficult and, in fact, misleading, to strictly dichotomize Ken Saro-Wiwa's political career and his literary career. Both careers, as a matter of fact, are intertwined for—as an apostle of the *engage*—Saro-Wiwa used his literary works largely to advance the cause of (ethnic) politics. Making a strong case in this regard in *A Month and a Day*, he says:

> ...Literature in a critical situation such as Nigeria's cannot be divorced from politics.[1] Indeed, literature must serve society by steeping itself in politics, by intervention, and writers must not merely write to amuse or to take a bemused, critical look at society. They must play an interventionist role..., the writer must be *L'homme engage*: the intellectual man of action. He must take part in mass organizations.

...A struggle will necessarily ensue, but that should
conduce to making the writer even better. For we write
best of the things we directly experience, better of what
we hear, and well of what we imagine. (81)

This essay is on one of those subjects which require an inter-
reading of Saro-Wiwa's literary and political ideas. It focuses
on how Saro-Wiwa carried on with his writing while he was
in prison custody: the challenges he faced as an artist, the inevitable dialogue of his art with his condition as a prisoner,
and the impact of his literary career on imprisonment, both
being supposedly instruments of *reformation.*[2]

Our subtitle for this essay, therefore, is a playful evocation
and/or constriction of relationships: pain vs. pen; "penfulness"
as painfulness. The pain of imprisonment flowing through
the barrel of the pen. The pain felt by the powers that construct and use the prison to control "penful" persons. And the
pain we feel, as readers who feel the impact of the patheticizing
rhetoric of the "penful" prisoner-narrator, *et cetera.*

The imprisonment of a man/woman of letters, especially
due to his/her writing, is an attempt to *imprison* the pen, to
subvert writing as social discourse. Also, the artist that is jailed
for the practice of his or her art stands in symbolic reaction to
the art. He or she stands for his or her art, metonymically
speaking. In other words, the "pen" is the art, as the art is the
activist in prison.

Saro-Wiwa's literary career in prison therefore has to be
viewed in relation to Wole Soyinka's observation (our epigraph)
that books and all literary practices are anathema in the (Nigerian) prison culture, and that, as in his own case, efforts made
to ruin the creative being of the artist in prison:— "measures
(were) taken both to contain and destroy my mind in prison"
(*The Man Died,* 9). The major struggle of the writer in prison
thus is to *preserve* his or her mind. Soyinka, in this regard,
writes:

> ... to deny me means of utilizing my mind is torture.
> To feed my body but deny my mind is deliberate dehu-
> manization. To accept this meekly is a form of supine-

ness. To accept this continuously is to accept risks of
an end which even I cannot foretell. I need to exchange
thoughts not merely with myself but within a community of other minds. I cannot circle indefinitely in the
regurgitations of my mind alone. It is evil.
... I must break out of the *mental prison* in which they
have encased me. (*The Man Died* 226; emphasis added)

Solitary confinement, which is supposed to be a reformative
action/state, ironically becomes a destruction of the mind. The
irony appears to be the major character of imprisonment as a
symbolic politico, judicial action, and especially enables the jail-
ing authority in a typical political context to play a double
game: to pretend to be reforming when it is deforming, or
deforming to reform. The paradox in "deforming to reform"
is useful to a totalitarianization of power in politics, for the
ruling authority may wish to exploit the judicial idea of reformative action as a cover for its primary political goal of punishing dissenters.

But this hidden agenda of ruining the artist's mind again
often paradoxically works to the advantage of the artist: the
experience of psychological and physical violence/violation
rather stimulates tremendous creative energy, even towards
greater resentment of the interpellating state apparatus. Wole
Soyinka's narrative of his experience of incarceration in *The
Man Died*, for instance, shows this unique ability of the imprisoned artist to put the bitter experience of prison life at the
service of creative powers, and to interrogate the claims of incarceration as a process of justice. Soyinka, in that life-writ-
ing, creatively reconstructs imprisonment as a journey into
the dark recesses of brutality, as a seeming fictive and fictivizing
of human actions. And so, as Saro-Wiwa says, we would expect the artist in prison to write in an exceptional way about
his or her prison life; for, as he puts, it "we write best" of what
"we directly experience."

## II

Ken Saro-Wiwa's stay in prison custody was because of his ethnopolitical activities which are already well known, and as such, need not be recounted here.[3] But it needs to be noted that his being remanded to prison custody in 1993, and in 1994/95, were on the charges that, in the first case, that he engaged in seditious act and unlawful assembly, and in the second case, he collaborated with some Ogoni people in murdering some prominent Ogoni leaders in 1994. He was released after "a month and a day" of detention without further court trial in the first case. But in the second case, he was convicted of the charge and was hanged, along with eight other eight Ogoni people, in Port Harcourt on November 10, 1995. In this essay, therefore, we refer specifically to Saro-Wiwa's stay in prison custody in the two cases mentioned above, even though he, as a free man, had extensively played with the image of the prison in his *Prisoners of Jebs* and *Pita Dumbrok's Prison*.

As would be expected, Saro-Wiwa's literary activities in prison were not well received by the security agents that consider the practice of art as a dubious but subversive process. In *A Month and a Day*, his detention diary and product of his creative endeavor in prison, he reports as follows:

> When we were left alone [after the departure of Bishop Poromon] Mr Ogbeifun grabbed all the papers I had on the writing-table and went through them. Among them was a diary of my first week in detention, some papers from the Vienna conference, and poems which I had began to write. He warned *that I did not have the right to write*, and that if I was not on good behavior, he would have no option but to treat me according to the book. (196; emphasis added)

The "right" to "write" is a major issue which, in a repressive context (even outside the prison walls), brings about conflict between a writer (who wields the pen) and a military officer (who wields the gun). "Right" and "rights" already always predicate oppositionality as homophonous signifiers. Playfully, we might say that "write" challenges "right," not only in phonological space, but also socio-semantically, for while "right" (in a directorial for context especially) is constrained, "write" or writing, as an artistic engagement, appears yet resistant to the Law. A writer is often torn between subjectivity to the ruling power (which is signified as the Law) and subjectivity to art as a liberal practice. For engaged writers like Ken Saro-Wiwa the subjectivity is even triple, for they are again subject to ideology. As Louis Althusser (1986) has shown, ideology interpellates individuals as subjects, and

> It is ... a peculiarity of ideology that it imposes (without appearing to do so, since these are obviousness) obviousness as obviousness, which we cannot *fail to recognize* and before which we have the inevitable and natural reaction of crying out (aloud or in the still, small voice of conscience): 'That's obvious! That's right! That's true!' (936)

Thus denying the imprisoned/detained committed writer the right to write is an attempt by the state apparatus at hailing the hailer (the literary ideology) and preventing the latter from interfering with its own control of (or attempt at controlling) the reader-citizen as subject. Since writing is a signifying practice that is capable of influencing social behavior (just as Saro-Wiwa's writing has done, at least for the Ogoni Nation), it is located away from the site of right, in the prison context which is already always controlled by the monologic state apparatus.

Writing in detention or in prison custody may also be forbidden because of the fear that the political writer-prisoner may reveal or misrepresent his or her condition in prison and thus make the state/jailer lose face, precisely "positive face," that is, the desire to be a desirable or acceptable part of the community, according to Brown and Levinson. Certainly, the ruling military in Nigeria would not want to be (further) distanced from the Ogoni, the minority ethnic group in Nigeria, Nigerian citizens generally, human rights groups, and the international community, through the ideas that flowed from Ken Saro-Wiwa's pen. But, paradoxically, the deprivation of the writer-prisoner's right to write confirms the writer-prisoner's fears and claims of ill-treatment in prison, and of repressiveness in the society. Such deprivation is particularly punishing since, for most writers, the art of writing is an indispensable part of daily living and an essential means of achieving a purgation of emotion (*karthasis*) which builds up especially in the context of the prison. It would therefore be, for the writer-prisoner like Ken Saro-Wiwa, a double imprisonment—the second level of imprisonment being a "mental" imprisonment as Soyinka refers to it in *The Man Died.*

But Saro-Wiwa, like many writer-prisoners, had to become a smuggler in prison custody in order to survive this mental imprisonment. He became a smuggler of his own mental commodities. According to one of his lawyers, Sam Amadi,

> He (Saro-Wiwa) devised a plot.
> He went to the bathroom as if to clean
> up and wrote his pieces. He asked
> his wife to bring up his toiletries and smuggled out his
> notes. (14)

Thus we see the context of the production of human waste becoming the context of the production of subversive knowledge, just like restroom graffiti, linking and relocating the *anal* to *analysis* of the human condition. That is, the production and transmission of (artistic) knowledge he ex-cre(a)ted, challenging the hegemonic discourse of the military.

The kind of art produced by Saro-Wiwa in prison, nonetheless, offers us a special insight into the impact of the two levels of imprisonment on creative writing. His prison poems/songs, for instance, carry very strong emotional force. Naturally, poems are emotional forms of art. No wonder William Wordsworth, in "Preface to Lyrical Ballads," says that

> ... Poetry is the spontaneous *overflow* of *powerful feelings*: it takes its origin from emotion recollected in tranquility: the emotion is contemplated till, by a species of reaction, the tranquility gradually disappears, and an emotion kindred to that which was before the subject of contemplation, is gradually produced, and does itself

actually exist in the mind. (Lines 694–700; Enright and
de Chickera 180; *emphasis added*)

As an emotional art form, poetry appears to suit prison life
which itself, as we have noted, could be psychologically tor-
turing. Poetry-writing (or song-writing) in prison is, therefore, a response to suffering which, as in the case of the blues
composed and sung by African slaves in American plantations,
is psychotherapeutic. Moved by his condition while in prison
("Alabama city") in Port Harcourt in 1983, Ken Saro-Wiwa
wrote the following song (which is also a poem) titled, "The
True prison":

> It is not the leaking roof
> Nor the singing mosquitoes
> In the damp, wretched cell.
> It is not the clank of the key
> As the warder locks you in.
> It is not the measly rations
> Unfit for man or beast
> Nor yet the emptiness of day
> Dipping into the blankness of night
> It is not
> It is not
> It is not
> It is the lies that have been drummed
> Into your ears for one generation
> It is the security agent running amok
> Executing callous calamitous orders
> In exchange for a wretched meal a day
> The magistrate writing in her book
> Punishment she knows is undeserved
> The moral decrepitude
> Mental ineptitude
> Lending dictatorship spurious legitimacy
> Cowardice asked as obedience.
> Lurking in our denigrated souls
> It is fear damping trousers
> We dare not wash off our urine
> It is this
> It is this

It is this
Dear friend, turns our free world
Into a dreary prison. (*A Month and a Day* 220 - 221)

"What is nearer a cry than a song?" we might join the poet Techicaya U'Tasi in asking. A cry is a song is a cry. And, for an artist/political activist who was picked up by security forces while he was on his way to attend a meeting, who was denied food for almost 48 hours, who was driven in an uncomfortable bus (which he refers to in *A Month and a Day* as a "coffin") by night for a distance of over 1000 kilometers to Lagos, then driven in the same "coffin" for about the same distance to Awka, from Awka to Owerri and then back to Port Harcourt to be tried in a kangaroo court and then remanded to a prison custody that allegories Hell, the song is a cry from the depths of being, a psalm. While in detention at Owerri, as Saro-Wiwa tells us in *A Month and a Day*, he had felt highly inconvenienced by the singing of religious choruses (another variety of psalms) by other detainees. Obviously, he was a stranger to the type of context, and so felt that the "prison artists" were disturbing him with their choral performances. The difference between the "prison artist" and the "artist-prisoner" is in terms of professionalism. The "prison artists" were oral performers (of a kind) whose arts were most relevant to their condition in prison, who performed to encourage themselves and hope for (God's) intervention. Saro-Wiwa eventually overcame the alienation (occasioned by his being an artist-prisoner) to become a (secular) "prison artist."[4] In other words, his status as an artist who had been put in prison custody had reconciled with the status of an artist made by prison condition. This transformation, this adjustment to popular prison culture, is the objective of what is referred to as an initiation or "welcoming" ritual in Nigerian prison language, as represented in Wole Soyinka's play, *From Zia With Love*, which is set in prison.

Saro-Wiwa's (prison) song is an instance of emergent dialogue between his profession as an artist and the prison - two means of interpellation, as we pointed out earlier. His being in prison enables him to deconstruct the prison as an ideological state apparatus (Althusser), to rupture its meaning as a sign so that other interpretations of the sign would be available. In the song, this deconstruction is marked by his negation of the usual interpretation of the sign, "prison." This usual (Nigerian) interpretation is superficial as it only focuses on the visible experiences of being locked in, being malnourished and dehumanized. But for a perspicacious writer-prisoner, who is able to perceive extended configurations and underlying meanings of experiences, the "true" imprisonment is subjection to the reign of injustice and fear. The reign of injustice and fear therefore makes the "conventional" prison a mere symbol of the macro-prison (the society under such rulership).

V.N. Volosinor has called our attention to "multiaccentuality of the ideological sign," which makes the sign "an arena of the class struggle" (67). The accent given to the prison as an ideological sign by Ken Saro-Wiwa is an interrogation of the dominant accent provided by the state apparatus. His use of the modifier "true" in "*The True Prison*" clearly indicates this desire to alter the semiotics of the prison as we have been made to *know* it.

Generally, truth is a metaphysical problem which post-modernist philosophy is very skeptical about. The idea of "the truth" favors monologism which any form of dictatorship values much. In post-modernism, norms such as truth, goodness, beauty, rationality, as Lawrence Cahoone states, "are no longer regarded as independent of the processes they serve to govern or judge, but are rather products of and immanent in these processes" (15). Since "prison" is an ideological sign, its interpretation (in terms of "the true" and "the untrue") is also ideological and subjective. In the context of Saro-Wiwa's counter-discourse, the meaning of "prison" emerges from the reading subject (whose oppositional status is already a given); the meaning that is fixed in advance by the state apparatus (the prison as a place of correction) is not acceptable to the post-modern thinker.

It is not only the meaning provided by the state apparatus that Saro-Wiwa rejects. He also rejects the emergent connotations of the sign, which appear to become stable and delinked from wider social experience. Such connotations (that is the prison as the undesirable place, the place of emptiness, of be-

9

ing locked "in", etc.) delimit the meaning of prison also, making its political functions obscure.

Saro-Wiwa's detention diary, *A Month and a Day*, is also a narrative in which he generally subverts the dominant state narrative of the prison as a place of correction. His own narrative, though not as poetically charged as Wole Soyinka's *The Man Died*, is indeed a testimony of his relentless literary dialogue with brutal human experience. His description of prison environment in Port Harcourt is not striking for anybody who is familiar with other oral narratives produced by ex-prisoners in Nigeria—"a very depressing place . . . its exterior is solid, grey and forbidding, . . ., its interior is grimy, squalid and dilapidated" (224). Even the infirmary, where he was later allowed to stay due to the state of his health, is also presented in a way that we cannot help but feel pathos for him.

> I got to the infirmary late that afternoon, the admission formalities having lasted for five hours. A look at the infirmary and your heart fell. It was leaking like a sieve; there was no ceiling; the entire place was damp; there was only a bucket latrine; the narrow beds had rotten mattresses; and heavens, what else was there not, in that place? (226)

The above excerpt shows a paradox: the infirmary is supposed to be a place of recovery and should therefore be more properly maintained; but it is instead an environment in which the sick would only get worse and die.

Saro-Wiwa's perception of the prison environment thus relates once more to his signification of the nation as a macro-prison, a perception similar to that of Wole Soyinka in *From Zia With Love* (Oha, forthcoming). For Saro-Wiwa, the prison environment is an indexical sign of a nation in ruins:

> You can tell the state of a nation by the way it keeps its prisons, prisoners being mostly out of sight. Going by this criterion, Nigeria was in a parlous state indeed. (*A Month and a Day*, 224)

What we find in the prison, and by extension the prison itself, is a symptom of "illness" in society. Generally, the prison and the society have been viewed as being intersubjective, even though the society would, hypocritically, alienate the prison and treat the prisoner as being an outsider or a very undesirable type of outside. Tunji Lardner Jnr, writing on the prison situation in Nigeria, has, in this regard, drawn our attention to the fact that "The conscience of prisoners might seem degenerate by self-righteous societal standards, but criminals do not exist outside society." He makes the valid point that "The prison is ... a useful metaphor for society: the state and circumstances of a prisoner is a ready index of society's conscience"(7). This same argument appears to underline Ken Saro-Wiwa's prison narrative also, for, as he tells us in *A Month and a Day,* he was disturbed that the prisoner's *otherness* was being symbolized through various forms of dehumanization. Thus, as a committed writer, he tries to bring the Nigerian prison into the discourse of discontent in and about Nigeria. Noting the state of the prison, he writes:

> Oh, the wretchedness of it all is scandalous. And there are Nigerians who have been held under these conditions and have come out and done nothing about it.
> I hadn't been in the prison for more than a day when I knew that the condition of Nigerian prisons and prisoners would be added to the long list of campaigns I had already accumulated. (225)

Thus interestingly, he becomes the corrector of those who put him in prison custody as a way of hailing (correcting) him. Saro-Wiwa shows, through his, posture in the narrative, that the Nigerian prison is part of the story of the injustice he opposes. He shows that it is the same paradigm of differentiation, marginalization, and destruction that applies to the relationships of nation/prison and nation/ethnic group. Just as the prisoner is humiliated, Ogoni is also humiliated in the multiethnic nation. Analogically, Ogoni becomes the nations's prison(er) living in despoiled territory.[5] On the other hand, if the entire nation under dictatorship is a macro-prison as we had examined earlier in the paper, then the ethnic group (Ogoni) is just one of the "prison" locations.

Obviously, the web of significations in Saro-Wiwa's narrativizaion of the prison is amazing. His being remanded in prison custody thus paradoxically appears to have served a useful purpose to us in the narration of the Nigerian nation—something like the Achebean nation of being the "eyes" and the "ears" of an interested but cautious witness to cultural change. Narrations of the Nigerian nation, indeed, cannot overlook the ideological meanings that have been made possible by Saro-Wiwa's literary dialogue with the prison.

It is also obvious that the prison experience was an additional and special training for him as a thinker, a writer, a political activist, and a Nigerian, and we would have been opportuned to encounter the impact in his post-prison career, but for his execution by the government he opposed. An evidence of the impressive advance in the aesthetic and dialogic relation between his art and his politics is the apocalyptic narrative of his death (and burial) at the hands of his "captors." The unpublished work titled *The Death of Ken Saro-Wiwa*, first published by The Masses, humorously tells how he was killed by his captors, put in a coffin which the maker, to insult his dead self, has made shorter than the normal length (obviously a way of making us laugh at a serious matter, especially as we already know that Saro-Wiwa was a short man). Then his body is carried through the streets of Port Harcourt (as a display), and is later taken to be buried. At the burial, instead of the normal grave, he is put into a small hole to be buried upright (again an insult on his dead self). His corpse then moves in vexation and the fellow detailed to bury him runs for dear life.

Could this narrative be a way of signifying the "laughable" process of political victimization in Nigeria, the *littleness* of using various means to symbolize the deprivation and the annihilation of the other? To kill the opponent is a crime on its own; to deprive the dead body certain *normal* rituals suggests some laughable psychology of tyranny, for to extend the deprivation of rights to the dead body is to suggest oneself as being irredeemably paranoid.

The narrative also indirectly evokes the emotion on the relationship of the pen and the pain in the prison situation. The pain or travail causes the pen to produce profound psycho-spiritual narratives through which the prisoner (as an "outsider") interpellates the self-righteous "non-prisoner" (and "insider" of society), particularly the rulers of the nation for whom the prison is purportedly a site of interpellation and reformation.

### III

In the essay, therefore, we have tried to show, among other things that Ken Saro-Wiwa's prison experiences enlarge his vision of the condition of the Nigerian nation in the context of repressive state apparatus. Instead of crippling his creative imagination (as indeed it tried to), the prison created another opportunity for him to further interrogate the meanings produced by the state to control the thought and behavior of the subject. As a site for ideological struggle, the prison, for him, is a semistic for state criminality and subversion of proper judicial process, rather than the conventional denstations available to society.

We have further argued that the re-semistization of the prison by Saro-Wiwa has other crucial mappings onto the macro-discourse of ethnic discontent in the pluriethnic society. The nation under military rule, in which a "grievance identity" like Ogoni aspires to a sovereignty that "competes with the sovereignties of the nation itself" (Steele 1992:2), appears to fit into the paradigm of the "prison"; that is the ethnic minority as the prisoner of the nation and/or of the center controlled by majority ethnic forces. Also, if the "true" imprison/ment is the reign of injustice, then the conventional prison is a merely a sign of the political condition.

In sum, Saro-Wiwa's literary dialogue with the prison points towards the ambivalence of the nation as a humanistic construct, especially as its roles of "reformer" and "deformer" (of the interpellated citizen) cancel themselves out. Yet, Nigeria's future governments have a chance of learning to avoid the national suicide suggested by these paradoxes, in order to build a strong cohesive plural society.

# Notes

1. Saro-Wiwa's view here is very similar to that of Ngugi wa Thiong'o in *Writers in Politics*, who argues that every writer is political, and that the important question rather is: Whose politics is the writer doing service to?

2. Generally, literature has education of the individual as one of its goals, as Chinua Achebe defends in one of his essays, "The Novelist as a Teacher." Such teaching or reforming function is a process of hailing the reader ideologically. The prison, also, is signified by the state apparatus, as a site for the reformation of transgressors. These two forms of interpellation, therefore, could interact or influence each other in the political life of the society.

3. It appears, however, that what Ken Saro-Wiwa wrote or said (about the Ogoni case) got him into trouble, as many sources in Nigeria and at the international level have suspected.

4. One could advance an argument that both Saro-Wiwa and other prisoners were all "prison artist" that the distinctions we are making are unnecessary. Conceived as a slice of the drama of life, the imprisonment, which involves both the jailers and the jailed (agents and sufferers), becomes one special artistic performance. In this case, all the prisoners are artists. However, the differentiation is necessary, especially as we are interested in the ways the imprisonment affects Saro-Wiwa's career as a professional writer.

5. Alternatively, the "oppressed" ethnic minority could be conceived in a similar paradigm as the "prisoner" of the ruling ethnic majority—the image of "prisoner" taken from some implied "conquest" in the form of the process of post-colonial colonialism. In many of his life writings, Saro-Wiwa emphasized the threat of this form of colonialism on the Ogoni. In some other cases, too, he substitutes the image of the minority as a vassal (or "prisoner-of-war") with the more familiar master-slave relation which is also used as a trope in some other liberation rhetorics in Nigeria and elsewhere. See, for instance, Saro-Wiwa's *Second Letter to Ogoni Youth* and *Genocide in Nigeria*.

# Works Cited

Achebe, Chinua. *Arrow of God.* London: Heinemann, 1974.
___, "The Novelist as a Teacher." *Morning Yet on Creation Day.* London: Heimann, 1975.
Althusser, Louis. "Ideology and ideological State Apparatuses." *Art in Theory, 1900-1990: An Anthology of Changing Ideas.* Eds. Charles Harrison and Paul Wood. Oxford: Blackwell, 1986. (Rep.) 928-936.
Amadi, Sam. "Encounter with Ken Saro-Wiwa." *The News* (18 November 1996): 13-14
Brown, Penelope and Stephen Levinson. "Universals in Language Usage: Politeness Phenomena." Ed. E.N. Goody. *Questions and Politeness: Strategies in Social Interaction.* Cambridge: Cambridge Up, 1978.
Cahoone, Lawrence. "Introduction." *For Modernism to Postmodernism: An Anthology.* Ed. Lawrence Cahoone. Oxford: Blackwell, 1996. 1-23.
Lardner Jnr, Tunji. "The Insiders." *This Week* 8.2 (March 21, 1988):7.
Ngugi wa Thiong'o. "Preface to Lyrical Ballades." *English Critical Texts.* Eds. D.J. Enright and Ernst de Chickera. Oxford: Up, 1983. 162-189.
Oha, Obododima. "From Their Acts You Shall Know Them: The Role of Face Wole Soyinka's *From Zia With Love: A View From Literary Pragmatics.*" *Ase* (forthcoming).
Saro-Wiwa, Ken. *Prisoners of Jebs.* Port Harcourt: Saros International, 1988.
_____ *Pita Dumbrok's Prison.* London: Saros International, 1991.
_____ *Second Letter to Ogoni Youth.* Port Harcourt: Saros International, 1993.
_____ *Genocide in Nigeria; The Ogoni Tragedy.* Port Harcourt: Saros International, 1993.
_____ *A Month and a Day: A Detention Diary.* London: Penguin, 1995.
Soyinka, Wole. *The Man Died: Prison Notes of Wole Soyinka.* Harmonsworth/New York: Penguin, 1977.
_____ *For Zia With Love.* Ibadan: Fountain publications, 1992.
Steele, Shelby. "The New Segregation." *Imprimis* 21,8 (August 1992):1-4.
Tehicay U. Tam'si, Gerald Felix. *Poems.* Trans, Gerald Moore. London: Heimann, 1970.

Volosinor, V. N. "Concerning the Relationship of Basis and Super-structures." *Marxist Literary Theory.* Ed. Terry Eagleton and Drew Millne. Oxford: blackwell, 1996. 60-68.

# 2

▼▼

# The Socio-Political Dimensions of Ken Saro-Wiwa's Activism

## Solomon Odiri Ejeke

On the surface, it may appear that I have been making an argument for the Ogoni people. But in essence, I have been questioning the entire Nigerian system—the political structuring, ethnic relations, resource allocation, morality and social justice in Nigeria. I was able to mobilize the Ogoni people to identify with this questioning and to lay themselves open to Babangida's obvious fascism in co-operation with the brutality of international capitalism in the Third World. (Saro-Wiwa 1993:12)

The President of the Association of Nigerian Authors from 1991 to 1993, Ken Saro-Wiwa was born in 1941. He attended the prestigious Government College, Umuahia, a school that has produced famous writers such as Chinua Achebe, Christopher Okigbo, Elechi Amadi. It is on record that at Government College, Umuahia, Ken Saro-Wiwa "conceived a profound admiration for British education and a love of the English language" (Daniel 1993:6). He also attended the University College, Ibadan. During the Nigerian Civil War, he administered the island of Bonny for the Federal Government of Nigeria, for he did not believe in the Biafran cause.

But above all, Ken Saro-Wiwa was a constructive social critic and activist. It is this aspect of him that forms the focus of this essay.

In his lifetime, Ken Saro-Wiwa was an administrator, a writer, and a minority rights activist. His major achievements on earth pendulate between these three lines of vocation.

It is a truism that if you know the truth and speak the truth, it shall set you free. Ironically, the opposite is the case in Nigeria. For many fearless, truthful, and honest men in Nigeria do not, in most cases, survive the contemporary socio-political situation by speaking the truth. The truth is a slippery matter in Nigeria. It does appear that truth and honesty are frowned on in our country. Unfortunately, one of the victims of such circumstances in our time was Ken Saro-Wiwa, who was hanged by the Nigerian ruling military junta on the 10th November 1995, after a military tribunal found him guilty of murder and other charges.

As a writer, Ken Saro-Wiwa was in the forefront in condemning what he considered abnormal or wrong in Nigerian society. Thus, in his writings, he assigns himself the onerous task of keeping the conscience of the nation and custodian of its culture. He asserts that as

> keepers of the conscience of the nation and custodians of its culture, we owe ourselves and the nation the responsibility not only to protect the rot and shame but also to immerse ourselves actively in stopping it and restoring sanity to the land. (1993:1)

He goes on to state clearly that should writers fail to carry out this function effectively, "we may well find that we become irrelevant to our society and that we no longer can protect ourselves and our kind." Hence, for Ken Saro-Wiwa, "the writer has also to be an activist." His notion of literature is such that its production and consumption are of practical necessity for the healing that such effort and knowledge could bring to society. This is how he expressed this belief:

... literature works its way through society and time slowly. Its eventual victory is not in doubt. But since our society demands much more urgency, the writer cannot be a mere story-teller, he cannot be a mere teacher; he cannot merely x-ray society's weakness, its ills, its perils, he or she must be actively involved in shaping its present and its future. (1993:1)

Little wonder then that he did not restrict himself merely to writing vitriolic criticisms of the Nigerian socio-political and economic situation but actively became involved in the attempt to rectify some of these ills. This aspect of his activism is epitomized in his mobilization of the Ogoni people to resist the injustice inflicted on them and all the oil-producing communities of the Niger Delta. He violently protested the economic, social, political, and environmental degradation encouraged and perpetuated by the Federal Government of Nigeria and the oil prospecting and exploring companies. This point will be further elucidated in the progress of our discourse.

In his novel, *The Prisoners of Jebs*, he lampoons virtually every aspect of the Nigerian socio-political and economic development. His criticisms are sharp. For, like fertilizers— though they smell, yet they make plants grow—so also are criticisms and satires. Though sharp and biting on human actions, they tend to correct societal ills. Saro-Wiwa emphasizes that

In the Nigerian context, the writer must see the truth and see it whole. He must make the critical connection between the theft of the oil resources belonging to a weak group and the theft of an election, of a popular mandate. He must condemn a faulty constitution or a faulty constitutional process and the monsters they breed. Or even see that the one is father to the other. And he must not only condemn, he has to work assiduously to destroy a system which breeds aberrations. (Saro-Wiwa, 1993:1)

This is the theory that guides his literary, critical, essays and dramatic texts. It also provides the philosophy with which he reacts to contemporary socio-political events. *The Prisoners of Jebs* supremely illustrates this theory. With a sweeping statement, Ken Saro-Wiwa asserts that the ruling elites in Nigeria—military or civilian—divert the people's attention from their contemporary problems by launching unnecessary debates and discourses. Hence, he asserts that "To keep the people unmindful of their hunger and distress, keep them debating" (1988:27), is the gospel truth in the Nigerian situation. In *The Prisoners of Jebs,* Saro-Wiwa submits that both the civilian and military rulers masterminded, patterned, and orchestrated the ruin of Nigeria's socio-political and economic life. In fact, this is the pivot around which the thematic concepts of the novel revolve.

As president of the Association of Nigerian Authors, he did not relent in his efforts to sensitize the cream of Nigerian writers on the need to muster all the resources available to them to fight and destroy the evils perpetrated in his country by the rulers and some influential and privileged individuals and government. He succinctly declares that the major task before Nigerians is the eradication of "the politics of evil, of force and violence, deceit, of corruption and greed, of banditry masking as patriotism which has reduced our people to penury and beggardom, and institutionalized theft and brazen incompetence."

In *The Prisoners of Jebs*, Ken Saro-Wiwa speaks of and condemns a situation where meritocracy and honesty are frowned at. In *The Prisoners of Jebs*, he writes:

> . . . you see the truth cannot be hidden and good ideas have legs. They walk, and some-times run. That is what the prisoner lecturer said. However, what had surprised him was the regularity with which Africa bred monsters . . .The emergence of these men on the African political scene was an *aliquid stupid'* . . .The fact that African rulers held on to power even when they knew the problems were beyond their ability, was an *"aliquid stupid."*(10).

His crusade against corruption and victimization of people by government turned him into an enemy of the state and a section of the people were adversely affected by his critical and satiric plays, novels, essays/articles, and poems.

He was most bitter about how successive regimes/administrations in Nigeria had used the huge revenue derived from oil exploration in Nigeria to enrich individual members of such administrations and to develop the non-oil producing regions of the country at the expense of the oil producing areas. He decried the neglect of the oil producing areas in terms of developmental projects, employment and government appointments. He was bitter about the environment degradation in these areas which are constantly exposed to pollution, and steady degradation. Nigeria's abject failure in the socio-political and economic spheres, Saro-Wiwa submits, is anchored on the fact that

> Of all the countries who had black gold, Nigeria was the only one that has succeeded in doing absolutely nothing with it. The Arabs used their oil very well indeed; not only had they given their people education and a lot else that conduced to good living, they also had invested their money in Europe and America. But the Nigerians had invested nothing. They had spent their money in buying foreign food which they consumed or even threw away; in paying for ships waiting on the high seas to deliver food. (*Prisoners of Jebs*, p. 10)

The huge revenue derived from the oil-mineral exploration in the country since oil discovery was made had been spent recklessly. The people charged with the administration of these resources often appear confused, according to Ken Saro-Wiwa. In his opinion, "when a people are confused and lack confidence in themselves and each other they are likely to undertake foolish adventures". (*Prisoners of Jebs*, p. 10). His judicial execution on 10 November was one such adventure. The neglect of the oil-producing areas is yet another.

The hard core of Ken Saro-Wiwa's fracas with the ruling military junta was his call for "just compensation and develop-

21

ment for the Delta minorities from whose territory the 'black gold' which accounts for most of the country's foreign exchange earner is obtained. As Ogaga Ifowodo makes clear, other minor oil-producing states of the South also joined in raising the cry for justice and equity in oil wealth distribution. According to Ogaga Ifowodo (1993:329), the Ogoni people and, to a lesser degree, the other Delta oil-producing minorities demonstrated the seriousness of minority rights violations during the year 1993.

The rumblings and travails of the Ogoni people is a practical manifestation of the socio-political dimensions of Ken Saro-Wiwa's socio-political activism. Through his efforts, the Ogoni people became the best organized and articulated minority group pressing for their environmental, social, economic and political rights, thus becoming the foremost crusaders in the politics of the rights of minority groups in Nigeria and perhaps in all of Africa.

The Ogoni people's struggle for justice metamorphosed into a body called the Movement for the Survival of the Ogoni People (MOSOP) with Dr. G. B. Leton as its president. Ken Saro-Wiwa was its chief spokesman. In the addendum to the *Ogoni Bill of Rights* addressed to President Ibrahim Babangida in 1990, to which Ken Saro-Wiwa wrote the forward, it is stated among other things that the Ogonis "abjure violence and would employ every lawful means to press for their legitimate demands" (Ogaga, 1993:329). In his foreword to the *Ogoni Bill of Rights,* Ken Saro-Wiwa declares:

> The Ogoni people will inform the United Nations and the Organization of African Unity that the Nigerian Constitution and the actions of the power elite in Nigeria flagrantly violate the United Nation's Declaration of Human Rights and Peoples' Rights; and that Nigeria in 1992 is no different from Apartheid South Africa. The Ogoni people will ask that Nigeria be duly chastised by both organizations for its inhuman actions and behaviour. And if Nigeria persists in its perversity, then it should be expelled from both organizations. (Ogaga 1993:330)

It is against the background of the foregoing discussion that Ken Saro-Wiwa began to ask very salient questions about "the entire Nigerian system—the political structuring, ethnic relations, resource allocation, morality, and social justice." In fact, the opening epigraph of this essay constitutes the basic premises on which Ken Saro-Wiwa's argument rests. His liberal mind could not let him fold his hands and watch while dubious politicians and the military elite trampled upon a people marginalised, cheated, and/or victimized for no just cause.

Ken Saro-Wiwa joyed in writing humorously. A. M. Daniels (1993) notes that "Saro-Wiwa is a small man, but is unafraid and his laugh is big. When he laughs the whole room seems to laugh with him"(16). Hence, in his first novel, *Sozaboy*, he "beautifully captures the tragedy and pointless waste of the civil war." This is a story he tells through the eyes of a village boy in what he describes as "rotten English."

In his literary career, Ken Saro-Wiwa is notorious for tackling highly serious issues humorously. In short, all his dramatic pieces, including the fifty episodes he wrote for the television series *Basi and Company*, use this technique to communicate their thematic concerns in a very effective manner.

Ken Saro-Wiwa fought and died for his convictions—unjustly. He had the interest of the oil-producing communities and particularly that of the Ogoni people at heart in his struggle against an unjust, illegitimate, and highly repressive politically dictatorial system.

In his short lifetime, he influenced the lives of many Nigerians and awakened their consciousness and ideals. There is no gainsaying that his execution "convulsed our nation and reverberated far beyond its boundaries," just like the death of Steve Biko in apartheid South Africa. All his reasoning amounted to or could be summed up in the opening epigraphy of this essay. Though he is dead today, Ken Saro-Wiwa's questions still loom large over the nation. They still haunt the conscience of Nigeria. How else can one explain the immediate suspension of Nigeria from the Commonwealth of Nations immediately after his execution?

On the whole, Ken Saro-Wiwa was morally sensitive and intellectually alert to socio-political issues on a national and international scale. In fact, on the foreign scene, his image/ status compares favorably with that of Martin Luther-King. He appears even more popular abroad than at home. For the fear of the ruling military junta could not let Nigerians express their outrageous feelings over Ken Saro-Wiwa's execution.

# Works Cited

Daniel, A. M. "The Arrest of Ken Saro-Wiwa". *Association of Nigeria Writers Review 8*, 10 (1993):6.

Ifowodo, Ogoga. *Annual Report on Human Rights*. Lagos: Civil Liberties Organisation, 1994:226-330.

Saro-Wiwa, Ken. *The Prisoners of Jeb*. Port Harcourt: Saro International Publisher, 1988: 27.

Saro-Wiwa, Ken. "Trying Times." *Association of Nigerian Authors Review* 8, 10, (1993):12

# 3

# Ken Saro-Wiwa's *Sozaboy* and the Logic of Minority Discourse

## Harry Garuba

In the last page of Ken Saro-Wiwa's posthumously published detention diary, *A Month and a Day,* the author briefly mentions an interesting but harrowing news story about "132 Ogoni men, women and children, returning from their abode in the Cameroons, [who] had been waylaid on the Andoni River by an armed gang and cruelly murdered, leaving but two women to make a report." He ends the book with this chilling but prophetic statement:

> The genocide of the Ogoni had taken on a new dimension. The manner of it I will narrate in my next book, if I live to tell the tale. (238)

Ken Saro-Wiwa did not live to narrate "the manner of it." On the 10th of November 1995, Ken Saro-Wiwa along with eight of his Ogoni kinsmen were hanged at the Port Harcourt Prisons on the orders of the Nigerian military authorities. Their execution has become the principal site of discursive contestation between the hegemonic powers of the multinational oil industry and Nigeria's military despots on the one hand, and minority and environmental rights activists on the other. The murder of 132 people may be a more horrifying event than the killing of nine others but it is the power of representation which Saro-Wiwa so effectively harnessed that has made his hanging the converging point of the struggle for minority rights in the face of their ruthless suppression by a kleptocratic regime backed by oil interests.

In his various speeches, writings, and other activities, Ken Saro-Wiwa had sought to draw discursive attention to the realities of the slow genocide of the Ogoni people and the degradation of their environment because he recognized the fact that the inability of the Ogoni people to represent themselves had made their situation more tragic and their circumstances more despondent. His mission, therefore, was to give voice to a silenced, marginalized minority who were not only being physically decimated as a people but who had also been representationally erased from national and international consciousness. This is why in the last sentence of the detention diary, he appears so concerned about narrating the "manner of it," placing the emphasis on the manner of telling, of narrative and representation, because he realized that in the post-modern world of multinational corporations, communications, and commodities, *reality* is often processed for us through the images and narratives which we receive. Facts, in a sense, are always discursively packaged, like commodities, for the consumption of markets/audiences.

The phenomenal shifts in critical theory within the last two or three decades have led to the opening up of a new, uncharted space in the area of minority discourses and the power and problems of representation. Minorities of all shades have tried to chart this territory in various ways, inscribing their own unique forms of difference on its blank spaces as maps of their individual identities. Women, ethnic minorities, diasporic blacks and Africans, orientals, post-colonial nations, gays and lesbians, etc. have all tried to stake a claim within this territory by rediscovering their difference and deploying these as badges of identity.

Alongside these developments has grown a regrettable amnesia about the concrete, historical struggles of these minorities in their unending battle against the tyrannies of dominant groups and ideologies. The post-Saussaurean separation of signs from their signifiers and referents has led to the valorization of language over reality, the privileging of culture over and above the material practices which create those cultures. The advent of post-structuralism and post-modernism, with their emphasis on undecideability, self-reflexivity, relativity and contingency has further pushed a potentially liberating discourse into a sclerosized culturalism, arresting other developments in the direction of the material and historical.

The question of post-structuralism, post-modernism, and history is a vexing one. Minorities seemingly offered by critical theory the voice to break their imposed *silence* find themselves unwittingly *decentered* from their own real, historical experiences. This, at least, has been one unfortunate development of certain strands of contemporary critical theory. The primary significance of Ken Saro-Wiwa's writings and his various activities on behalf of the Ogoni people, in this regard, has been to re-inscribe the concrete and historical into the linguistic world of floating signifiers and the culturalist mire into which minority discourses appear to be sinking. For Ken believed so much in the materiality of discourse that he seemed to have lived his life, in his last days, just to prove that point. He believed that his ability to take literature into the streets or, put differently, to take the streets into literature, was his ultimate triumph against those who sought to silence him.

In this brief essay, therefore, I intend first to examine Ken Saro-Wiwa's *Sozaboy* as a novel that enacts the logic of minority discourse and then comment on how in the twists and turns of his life he appears to have fulfilled the dictates of that logic. The intention is not to prove how life imitated literature or how literature imitated life, but to show how both were so intimately interwoven that they became two *events* mediated by the same logic.

Virtually every article on *Sozaboy*, either as a first move or as its dominating maneuver, fastens upon the issue of language in the text. This may well be due to the fact that the author uses a variety of English which he describes as "rotten English" and makes a point of drawing our attention to it both in the title of the novel and the author's note which precedes the narrative. The author's over-investment in the language issue is borne out in this statement.

> Sozaboy's language is what I call 'rotten English', a mixture of Nigerian pidgin English, broken English and occasional flashes of good, even idiomatic English. This language is disordered and disorderly. Born of a mediocre education and severely limited opportunities, it borrows words, patterns, and images freely from the mother-tongue and finds expression in a very limited English vocabulary. To its speakers, it has the advantages of having no rule and no syntax. *It thrives on* lawlessness, and is part of the dislocated and discordant society in which Sozaboy *must live, move and have not his being.* (Author's Note, *Sozaboy; Emphasis added*).

This, of course, is an exaggeration for it is certainly neither correct nor true to affirm that the language of *Sozaboy* has no rules and no syntax. But every author's note performs the function of foregrounding certain kinds of questions and foreclosing others. Critics are then led to accord primacy to the authorized question. And, in this instance, there can be no doubting the importance of the language question. Part of the de-canonizing and counter-canonizing gesture of post-colonial literature has been to question the hegemonic self-representation of the dominant discourse as encoded in a standard, formalized language handed down to the colonies from the metropolis. Bill Ashcroft et al. in *The Empire Writes Back* say that "post-colonial writing abrogates the privileged centrality of 'English' by using language to signify difference while employing a sameness which allows to be understood" (51).

In employing "rotten English" in this novel, Ken Saro-Wiwa is saying that "standard" English is incapable of representing the landscape and the reality that he seeks to portray. A different variety of English has to be invented to do the job. Even the favored linguistic alternatives such as pidgin are also inadequate in conveying the full experience of Sozaboy, whose education ended with a distinction at the level of the Primary School Leaving Certificate. In emphasizing the social and experiential determination of language, he thereby focuses on the material character of linguistic usage. As Bill Ashcroft et al. also say, "language is a material practice and as such is determined by a complex weave of social conditions and experience" (41).

Glossing is usually one of the strategies of inscribing difference in minority texts. Often the indigenous or pidginized word is followed by a parenthetical translation which, as Ashcroft et al. again assert, "may lead to a considerably stilted movement of plot as the story is forced to drag an explanatory machinery behind it" (62). In *Sozaboy*, the author partially saves us from this by appending a full-blown glossary at the end of the novel.

The struggle for linguistic control within the text extends to the very act of writing itself. Even though the novel is a written text, Sozaboy, the narrator, consistently employs *speakerly* strategies to point at the oral nature of his narrative. Apart from his copious use of direct reportage and direct addresses to his readers/listeners, the novel begins by evoking a traditional African story telling scene—"knacking tory under the moon" (1)—and ends with "Believe me yours sincerely" (181). Between the beginning and the end of the novel, there is a constant tussle between the structures of the scribal narrative and the demands of orality.

Having disposed of the language issue, let us now turn our attention to the other questions which the text raises, the subordinate questions which, I believe, deserve equal scrutiny. Perhaps the most profitable way to read *Sozaboy* is to see it as an attempt to give appropriate form to the minority experience in a post-colonial state. The questions we need to ask of the novel therefore are those which lead us to see how the minority experience is narrativized.

*Sozaboy* tells the story of a young, naive primary school leaver who becomes an apprentice-driver in the bid to learn a profession and to become a man of his own. As the only child of his mother and a fatherless child at that, he has modest ambitions of obtaining a driving license, becoming a successful driver, and buying his own vehicle so that he can be of some help to his mother who both "mothered" and "fathered" him. Unfortunately, a military *coup d'etat* changes the normal run of events in the society and the course of his life. The entire community had initially welcomed the *coup* hoping that it would rid the society of corruption and check the venality of policemen and vehicle inspection officers who incessantly harass drivers by continually demanding bribes. However, the expectation that the new dispensation will usher in the millennium is quickly shattered as the soldiers prove to be more oppressive than the civilians who had been booted out of power unceremoniously. Unresolved conflicts and antagonisms in the society lead to a civil war and Mene, the narrator, finds himself joining the army. The rest of the novel is devoted to Mene's experiences as a soldier in the war.

Around this basic scaffold is built a rich, compelling story of the construction of human subjectivity, the ideological interpellation of individuals by dominant discourses, the transformation of reality into carefully processed and packaged images, the confrontation between real life experience and the expectations inscribed in the ideological text and its well-touted images, and finally the sobering realization of marginality and its consequences. In exploring these issues, Ken Saro-Wiwa unmasks the workings of hegemonic discourses and the logic of minority discourse.

We first encounter Mene soon after his formal education at school, during the next stage of his life which is his apprenticeship to a master driver who is supposed to give him the training he requires to become a commercial driver. The socialization process, begun at the family level with his mother through the period of formal schooling in which he acquires some English, continues as he learns the trade at the hands of the master driver, who takes him beyond the confines of Dukana to Pitakwa. His encounter with the world is "processed" through the eyes of his mother, then his teachers, and at this stage the master-driver. In all of these he remains a voiceless but curious young man trying to grapple with the world on terms other than his own.

Helen Chukwuma in "Characterization and Meaning in *Sozaboy*," draws attention to the author's technique of pairing Mene with more experienced characters at every stage of the novel until he acquires a voice and begins to take his own decisions and acts on his own.

> We first encounter Mene as a 'young man and apprentice driver' (p. 1). This low status makes it impossible for him to exert any influence whatsoever on his other or on members of the society at large. Mene is therefore paired off with his master-driver who gives him a sense of directions, with a promise of stability, professionalism and financial independence. (40)

His apprenticeship is brought to an abrupt end by the *coup*, and the beginning of the civil war starts him off in a new direction. As Helen Chukwuma puts it:

> In this part, Saro-Wiwa rests the professional aspect of his protagonist's development by grounding his vehicle and prolonging the process of its repair. This allows the author time to advance his character unto yet another dimension, still using his technique of pairing. Mene, in the absence of the lorry-driver, is paired off with the young girl, Agnes, whom he meets in the African Upwine Bar. (41)

Therefore, he is paired off with San Mazor, and then finally with Bullet. At every stage he is dominated by his environment and the images passed on to him by these more experienced characters.

Agnes, the rather brash young woman from Lagos, insists that he must enlist in the army before she can marry him because she needs a strong man who will be able to protect her. Agnes has completely internalized this image of soldiers as brave men with codes of honor and dignity, duty and selfless service, and Mene is made to accept this image. His acceptance is aided by the fact that he is also in love with the uniforms of the soldiers, their smart salutes and parades, their weapons and show of power. Even though his mother fears for his life, this conflict between his mother's aspirations for him and Agnes' wishes is resolved in favor of the latter, and Mene joins the army after offering a substantial bribe. After being

31

recruited, the Sergeant Major (referred to as San Mazor by the narrator) takes Mene in and educates him in the ways of the army. Apart from being a professional drill master he takes special interest in Mene because he realizes that he is only an inexperienced young boy swept into the army by circumstances he does not fully understand. Mene's disorientation is further compounded by the General's speech to the recruits at the end of their training.

Luckily for him, he has another mentor/father-figure in Bullet, who smooths his way into regular service and the war. Bullet tries to explain to him why he is engaged in the various activities he finds himself performing. He doesn't understand why they have to dig trenches, who the enemy is, and why one of them should come to them waving a white handkerchief. His bafflement is not helped by subsequent events such as the sharing of drinks and cigarettes, their Captain's behavior in hoarding the supplies meant for them, Bullet's humiliation by the Captain after the theft, and Bullet's final shooting of the Captain. By the time Bullet gets killed in an air raid, he is no closer to understanding.

Life after Bullet continues in the same manner. He is taken prisoner of war and only gains consciousness in the hospital where the soldier with the white handkerchief has now materialized as some kind of nurse treating the wounded. After Mene's discharge from the hospital, he goes through a series of bizarre incidents, some fortunate and others tragic. His ability to drive saves him in the first instance and he is given a gun, military uniforms, and made a driver on the enemy side: a job he does conscientiously before he decides to quit the army for good after having served on both sides of the conflict.

Then he begins his own quest for his mother and his wife, the two oases of love left in that terrain of war. He wanders through the war-ravaged country visiting refugee camps in search of mother and wife. At the last refugee camp where he finds a lot of people from his home town Dukana, he is betrayed by his own people and again taken prisoner. But fortunately again, the war ends just as he faces the firing squad. The executioner is the soldier with the white handkerchief who had treated him the last time at the hospital. This continually metamorphosizing soldier turns out to be Manmuswak, the amoral man he had met before the war at the African Upwine Bar.

After escaping from the firing squad, he sets off for home only to find himself rejected even in his home town. All the doors are barred against him and he has to take refuge in the Church. After sleeping for some nights in the Church, Duzia, the village cripple, seeks him out only to tell him that his mother and wife were killed in an air raid and that he, Mene, is also believed by the villagers to have died in the war. The villagers also believe that he did not die properly, so his ghost has been haunting them wherever they go, causing diseases and death. After consulting a medicine man, they were advised that they could only kill his ghost and bury him properly after certain sacrifices involving "money and seven white goats and seven white monkey *blokkus* and seven alligator pepper and seven bundles of plantain and seven young girls" (180). Duzia therefore advises him to leave the village or risk being buried alive. Mene, who had survived the war, finds himself facing the prospect of being buried alive in the peace and he has to leave his own home town in despair. He sums up his experiences in this manner:

> And I was thinking how I was prouding before to go to Soza and call myself Sozaboy. But now if anybody say anything about war or even fight, I will just run and run and run and run and run. Believe me yours sincerely. (181)

At this point, his old ideas about the army now appear antiquated in the light of the new restructuring of consciousness occasioned by the facts of experience flying in the face of the images he had imbibed, therefore leading to corrections in his knowledge of the world.

Michel Pecheux in *Language, Semantics and Ideology* argues that there are three ways in which subjects are constituted, and these are by "Identification," "Counter-identification," and "Disidentification." Identification involves willingly consenting to the images offered by the dominant discourse while counter-identification involves rejecting those images, and disidentification involves "working on and against" the dominant ideologies (157-169). Sozaboy passes through these three stages but finds himself finally thrown into exile at the third stage. These three stages may be said to constitute the inexorable logic of minority discourse. After being framed by the images of the dominant ideology which then passes itself off as the natural order of things, counter-identification and disidentification become so difficult to achieve or are only achieved at great cost. Richard Terdiman in *Discourse/Counter-Discourse* gives us an insight into the power and tenacity of hegemonic discourses:

> Not only are they unable to admit difference, in a sense they are incapable of imagining it. This is so for a simple reason. Once imagined, even so that it might be proscribed, difference acquires a phantom but fundamental existence. If it is countenanced at all, its legitimation, its inclusion within the canons of the orthodox, proscribing it must be proscribed. (14)

In spite of this power of proscription and exile demonstrated in *Sozaboy*, Mene is able to deconstruct the binarisms of the war by fighting on both sides and ironizing the procedures governing the discourse. In this regard, Manmuswak is the ultimate absurd symbol of this deconstruction. Acting without respect for boundaries and divisions, he traverses and transgresses them all with an indeterminate character that privileges the contingent and—well—the amoral. Even knowledge comes to Mene, in the end, through the village "idiot."

In thus depicting the logic of minority discourse, Ken Saro-Wiwa's great feat in this novel is that *Sozaboy* can both be read within the ambience of the representational protocols of mimetic realism and also be seen as an allegorization of the minority experience in a post-colonial state.

The construction of a representational relation of coincidence between Sozaboy's story and the structure of the story of suppressed minorities can in fact be extended to the life of Ken Saro-Wiwa himself. Ken Saro-Wiwa always cut the figure of a small embattled man confronting a material and discursive power far in excess of his ability to overcome. But Ken was born into an awareness of *difference.* Even though the carceral approach which dominating discourses adopt to subordinated ones which the Nigerian government was later to adopt had not become the practice at the time of the author's birth in Ogoniland, something close to a caste-like system of discrimination operated between them and their neighbors. So Ken Saro-Wiwa knew what he was talking about when he spoke of marginality and marginalization. He was, so to speak, fashioned in the very crucible of minority discourse; and thus scarred by history.

It is no surprise, therefore, that after having passed through the first two stages, suffering incarceration along the way, he refused the choice of exile at the third stage and was thus "buried alive." The gory details of his death need no recounting here. What is left is for other marginalised peoples to recognize the logic of minority discourse and continue to narrativize it while picking up the mantle of his material and discursive struggle.

## Works Cited

Ashcroft, Bill, Gareth Griffiths, and Helen Tiffin. *The Empire Writes Back: Theory and Practice in Post-colonial Literatures.* London and New York: Routledge, 1989.

Chukwuma, Helen. "Characterization and Meaning in *Sozaboy.*" *Critical Essays on Ken Saro-Wiwa's Sozaboy: A Novel in Rotten English.* Ed. Charles Nnolim. London, Lagos, Port Harcourt: Saros International Publishers, 1992.

Pecheux, Michel. *Language Semantics and Ideology.* [1975] Trans Harbans Nagpal. New York: St. Martins, 1982.

Saro-Wiwa, Ken. *A Month and A Day: A Detention Diary.* London: Penguin, 1995.

_____. *Sozaboy, A Novel in Rotten English.* London Lagos Port Harcourt: Saros International Publishers, 1985.

Terdimam, Richard. *Discourse/Counter-Discourse: The Theory and Practice of Symbolic Resistance in Nineteenth Century France.* Ithaca, N.Y.: Cornel University Press, 1985.

# 4

# Ken Saro-Wiwa and the Trajectory of Minority Predicament in Nigeria

Oshita O. Oshita

The exploitation of the past almost always lives the victim backward, famished, and sometimes finished. The minorities in Nigeria have had a chequered experience within the nation state of Nigeria. When the Union Jack was lowered and the Green-White-Green flag of Nigeria hoisted, British colonialism had ravaged the traditional institutions of the various nationalities and erected in their place new configurations of ready-made garment. Peculiar as the current problems of different minorities may be, they betray something of the temperament and spirit of the dominant interests in Nigeria which were instituted during colonial rule and perpetuated after if. In this paper, we shall appropriate Ken Saro-Wiwa's ideas in *On A Darkling Plain* (1989) and *A Month and A Day: A Detention Diary* (1995) in burrowing through the trajectory of minority travails in Nigeria.

Ken Saro-Wiwa's conceptualization of Nigeria is that of a polity whose independence was the result of dialogue between the colonized majority and minority groups on the one hand and the British on the other. From this premise Saro-Wiwa's ideas on equity of equal joiners and justice are historically derived. He maintains that benefits from natural resources be allocated on the basis of contribution to the nation's common wealth, taking into account the input element in the process of wealth generation.

*On A Darkling Plain* refers to personalities like late Dr. Nnamdi Azikiwe, Chief Obafemi Awolowo, Sir Ahmadu Bello, Chief Joseph Tarka, and Chief Anthony Enahoro as those who, through dialogue, midwifed an independent Nigerian nation sooner than later. Saro-Wiwa uses the granting of peaceful independence by Britain to demonstrate the predicament which minorities faced in a post-colonial Nigeria. He views this against the backdrop of institutionalized hostility towards minorities' agitations for equity and rational self-determination. Saro-Wiwa reasons that the nation-state of Nigeria owes its components (both minorities and majorities) the duty of care, protection, and fairness. As a minority he found the payoffs were either non-existent or disappointingly meager.

The Willink Commission of Inquiry into Minority Fears of 1958 confirmed that the small ethnic groups of the South East and Middle Belt were the most vulnerable in the "East" and "North," respectively. But the Willink Commission failed to accede to the request for a Rivers State by the Ogoni, Ijaw and Ikwerre of Niger Delta. With Rivers about to be excised out of the Calabar-Ogoja-Rivers (COR) State Movement, the South Eastern units lost their teeth. The setting up of the Willink Commission owing to the cry of the minority groups of domination translated into the recognition that they existed. From the epistemological standpoint that "to be is to be known" the minorities thus recorded some achievements. But this was how far that moment in the history of minority agitation could go.

Saro-Wiwa's *On a Darkling Plain* is full of disgust, disenchantment, and lament for the post-independence condition of the minorities of Nigeria, especially the micro-minorities of the East (to use Bob Nixon's words). As a minority, Saro-Wiwa's tone in his two books is unmistakably about minorities exploitation. Like Martin Luther King's aphorism, "injustice anywhere is a threat to justice everywhere," Saro-Wiwa appealed to the feelings of his readers throughout the world. In his writing, Saro-Wiwa does not discriminate among minorities. His position in *On A Darkling Plain* that the minorities of the North also faced a difficult task fighting for self-determination owing to historical and cultural factors is obvious on this score (OADP 52). He alludes to the struggle waged by the Tivs of present Benue State under the Middle Belt State Movement. Regarded as the most vocal and politically conscious of the minorities of the "North," the Tivs led by Chief Joseph Tarka fought against the Northern Regional Government in a rebellion that lasted about two years and which took the Army and Police to quell just before the January, 1966 *coup* (OADP 52).

In the Niger Delta, Ken Saro-wiwa's Ogoni Movement for self-determination was not unprecedented. By February 1966 a brilliant officer Major Isaac Adaka Boro had proclaimed the Niger Delta Republic inspired by the fears of a stolen future of minorities in a post-independence capitalist Nigeria. Writing in his *The Twelve Day Revolution*, Boro considers his action to be "all the more compelling when the area (Niger Delta Region) is so viable, yet the people are blatantly denied development and the common necessities of life." In anticipation of the future, he warns, "if Nigerian governments refuse to do something to drastically improve the lot of the people, inevitably, a point of no return will be reached; then evil is afoot" (OADP:30). The Boro declaration was crushed by the moribund Ironsi regime which tried and sentenced him to death for treason (OADP:30-31). However, Boro was to die under circumstances other than those dictated by the Eastern Nigeria High Court which condemned him. Considering the charges against him Major Boro could not have justifiably expected a favorable judgement from those he attempted to rob of the oil wells and resources of the minorities which were at this time of the fractured nation's history under the newly declared Biafran country under Col. Odumegwu Ojukwu.

The minorities struggle in Nigeria, like the minority problem elsewhere, borders on a certain perception of unwarranted display of exclusivity of insights by the majority groups in national matters. Since the discoveries of oil and its exploitation, life in independent Nigeria became a sort of self-abnegation for the minorities, a bargain for a new and more painful kind of indigenous enslavement. Thus, post-independence Nigeria and the geographical "East" (which included the oil

39

rich Niger Delta Region and the fertile rainforest of the South East) evoked a thick cloud of topophobia in the minorities. For minorities like Saro-Wiwa and Boro, colonial and post-colonial Nigeria has feasted on the minorities and paid back with inequities, injustices, exploitation, deprivation, and intolerance. They perceived indigenous colonialism to be a function of a conspiracy of the major groups against the small ones. For them, beyond the geographical "East," is the real "East" which is synonymous with Ibo as the "West" with Yoruba and the "North" with Hausa-Fulani. These deliberate constructs of the regions as monolithic entities denies existence to pockets of minorities who are traditional *bete noires* of the larger and dominant ethnic groupings. Saro-Wiwa regards this thinking as misleading while imagining it to be a deliberate ploy to mentally deconstruct the geographical space as well as the social space inhabited by minorities. Saro-Wiwa writes of his aversion to being called an "Easterner" because the "East" of Nigeria is synonymous with the majority Ibo. Quite early in life at Government College Umuahia, Saro-Wiwa formed his impressions of the Ibos whose aggressive exploitation he detested. During his days at Umuahia College, he had been reproached for the action of Ogoni in voting Action Group (A.G.) rather than the National Council for Nigeria and Cameroon (N.C.N.C.), an "Eastern" party.

In prosecuting the Ogoni struggle, Saro-Wiwa demonstrated a curious blend of profoundities and profanities. His pragmatism derived from this blend of ideals and practice. He took the struggle to anywhere he found an opportunity. Once he appealed to the "Babangida administration to extend its human rights dispensation, its social justice claims to the minorities throughout Nigeria, and particularly, to the minorities of the delta region and its environs" (AMAD:64). He applied himself to the struggle in different ways. As one time President of the Association of Nigerian Authors (ANA), Saro-Wiwa enjoined writers to contribute to the struggle, noting, "we write best of the things we directly experience, better of what we hear, and well of what we imagine" (AMAD:81) His experiences at Government College Umuahia issued in his resolve in 1961, soon after completion of his course, to mobilize the Ogoni people for progress against indigenous colonialism. He perceived this self-appointed responsibility to be arduous and was to confess that "uniting Ogoni masses proved an easier task than associating a handful of graduates with my vision for the Ogoni" (AMAD:52). The mentality of the educated Ogoni was always to keep close to the government of the day and pick up crumbs from the master's table. He condemned the few educated Ogoni found pickings by grovelling at the feet of Ojukwu's rebel Biafran government. Yet, this would not deter him from risking his today for his people's tomorrow, thereby preventing them from "sleepwalking their way towards extinction" (AMAD:18). His "worry about the Ogoni has been an article of faith, conceived in primary school, nurtured through secondary school, actualized (during) the Nigerian civil war in 1967-70 and as a member of the Rivers State Executive Council, 1968-73" (AMAD:49).

In April 1968, in the throes of the civil war, Saro-Wiwa circulated some of his thoughts on the minorities predicament captioned "The Ogoni Nationality, Today and Tomorrow" (AMAD:49). It focused on the future of a people and an environment which belches forth petroldollars for Nigeria and yet has only mass poverty and environmental degradation as a trademark. Even more painful, he confessed, was the criminal timidity and ignorance which characterize the response of the minorities to the official injustice perpetrated against them. That the minorities had been in a state of collective amnesia, preventing them from demanding reparation based on equity, pained Saro-Wiwa. It was unmistakable that those who chose to fight the battle might need to pay the supreme price. He was not under any illusion as to what he was ready to pay. In *A Month and A Day*, he makes this obvious when he writes:

> The genocide of the Ogoni people had taken on a new dimension. The manner of it I will narrate in my next book, if I live to tell the tale. (238)

The minorities position clearly demonstrates the futility of the exploited, who believe that the exploiter would willingly relinquish his hold on power. This informed Saro-Wiwa's con-

41

templation of a struggle. He advocated non-violent ways of struggling. He believed that their contribution to the national economy is the basis of the moral claim which the Ogoni have on the Nigerian nation-state and hence their request for a fair deal (AMAD:76-77). The struggle was to be rough but it was to be non-violent and non-stop until the desired results were achieved. Speaking prophetically, he says,

> as I see it, the generation to which I belong is about to leave the scene. There is a need for the next genera- tion to prepare itself to continue where we shall have left off. (AMAD:77)

The phenomenon of denigration of the minorities as tools to be used by majority groups understandably irked Saro-Wiwa. The NCNC regime of Okpara displayed this in the East and the Shagari regime of 1979 in the South East. They both dem- onstrate this instrumental significance of the minorities of the East in particular and the country in general. Okpara's gov- ernment had a policy of turning eastern minorities lands to farms to feed the urban commercial "east." These "farms" did not need tarred roads and the people there did not require basic amenities. The Shagari regime needed the eastern mi- norities votes to square up and defeat the "eastern" and "west- ern" presidential candidates of the NPP and UPN respectively. But that was how and when the minorities become significant, just as dry figures to add to the real numbers, the majority. Thus, the minorities were always what the dominant ethnic groups make of them by commission or omission. For instance, the Ahiara declaration meant so much for the Ojukwu's East- ern government turned Biafra but the minorities were not guaranteed any place. In places outside Ibo areas, like Ogoja, Okuku, Ikom, etc., native minorities had their properties al- ready enumerated as spoils of war to be appropriated by the new Ibo colonial masters in a Biafran country. The Nigerian minorities have been victims of different strokes, a fact that remained prominent in the personhood of Saro-Wiwa, a man who fought for Nigeria but got killed by Nigeria. On one oc- casion of his several arrests by the security agents his rumina-

tions went deep into the life of the Ogoni people and the travails they had been fooled to endure for over a century, "which
travail I was as determined as iron to mitigate in my lifetime"
(AMAD:17). Only an iron resolve would give one the tremendous courage and determination to pursue a course that runs
counter to an ironcast ruling class whose temperament had
been nurtured by the most brutal of colonial and post-colonial
forces for centuries. Only with such resolve could anyone ask
the unwanted questions, questions that many knew but no one
seemed willing to confront (AMAD:17).

Saro-Wiwa often visualized the golden age of the minorities which had to be reached through intense struggles and
sacrifices in his moments of quiet. Like Saint-Simon, Saro-
Wiwa located the golden age which blind history placed in the
past to be in the great future. To attain that robust future the
minorities would need to turn away from their somnambulism
to become active agents willing to be transformed even if from
life to death. As he once put it, dying in the course of

> fighting to right the wrong would be the greatest gift
> of life! Yes the gift of life .... May it be worse. The
> designers of the iniquitous system must be shamed. My
> spirit would not be broken. (AMAD:19)

It would appear that the short, strong Ogoni man with a black
pipe never got a broken spirit. He only had a gift, the greatest
gifts of all, death. Surely, a man's spirit is not broken when he
stirs a monumental struggle that is bound to change the lives
of many generations to come. Minority struggles have moved
a step further and Saro-Wiwa may just be another passover
lamp for not just the Ogoni nation but all minorities of Nigeria. As the nation-state of Nigeria is strewn with the danger
of unjust official policies towards the minority groups, the future must be faced today. State policies must be altered, without which the real genesis of minority agitation for equity is
not at the beginning, which is past, but at the end, which is yet
to come. In the midst of it all, Saro-Wiwa shall continue to
live and speak with the present and future generations of Ogoni
and the other minorities long after his transition. This is part

of the message which he and his Ogoni countrymen have taken to Isaac Boro, J. S. Tarka, and the other compatriots who have been transformed by the immutable gift of death the struggle for equity, self-determination, and restoration of human worth.

## Works Cited

Nixon, Bob. "Pipe Dreams: Ken Saro-Wiwa, Environmental Justice, and Micro-minority Rights". *Black Renaissance* (Fall 1996)39-55.

Saro-Wiwa, Ken. *On A Darkling Plain.* Port Harcourt: Saros International Publishers, 1989:52.

Saro-Wiwa, Ken *A Month and A Day.* London: Pengium Books, 1995: 64.

# 5

# Social Conscience, Aesthetic Purpose, and the Dissenting Temper in the Farcical Plays of Ken Saro-Wiwa

## Imo Ben Eshiet

Few people in the enlightened world today, perhaps are unaware of Kenule Saro-Wiwa—influential environmentalist, provocative politician, prolific essayist and critic, accomplished creative writer, and mordant controversialist. Although two years have elapsed since his judicial murder, yet in death he has become even more colossal and irrefragable in stature. On the contrary and in a profoundly ironic way, the country he loved, yet which snuffed out his life, has since become an international pariah for the signal outrage. Thus, even in death his influence is still so palpable and emphatic that he remains the invisible spokesman against degeneracy and sustainable development, a decrepitude against which he pitched a fearless and unyielding opposition.

Allen Tate, erudite American literary theoretician, in his essay, "The Man of Letters in the Modern World," remarks that "the function of the writer is to render the image of man as he is in his time" (1957: VII). In a formula that strikingly anchors Tate's insight, his compatriot and controversial playwright, Edward Albee, commenting on the crucial issues which should exercise contemporary dramatists, writes that:

> A playwright has two obligations: first to make some statement about the condition of "man" (as it is put) and second to make some statement about the nature of the form . . .. (1969:9)

Equally remarking the kind of vision the modern writer should project, Erwin Piscator, famous for his principles of agitation and propaganda theater, argues that "vision has always created reality" and adds that "drama can" as indeed "did the Greek theatre" . . . be a place of fascination through exemplification of truth'. (1969:473)

Saro-Wiwa, who in his meteoric trajectory across the Nigerian literary scene has to his credit a corpus of serious works in all the literary genres, epitomizes in his subtleties of styles, theatrical inventiveness, and socially resonant subject-matter, this vision of virile social conscience and aesthetic purpose. Dan Izerbaye, University of Ibadan professor and Saro-Wiwa's classmate in the same University from 1962 to 1965, candidly testifies to this when he declares that Saro-Wiwa "engaged himself in writing social satire which links his literature with politics" (1996:8). Grounding his writings in the disordered contemporaneous with post-colonial experience and giving this a compelling visionary interpretation, Saro-Wiwa is fiercely dedicated to stripping the haunting social ills that so frustrate and stunt the balanced development of a country he ceaselessly seeks to detoxify.

In his authorial notes, appearing in a collection of his plays titled *Four Farcical Plays*, the dramatist explains that:

> The plays represent my early concern as much with the social problems of our time as with an adequate language of communication of a Nigerian theatre aimed at the broadest possible public. (Saro-Wiwa 1989:7)

Thus, a relentless engagement with the public questions of social and political morality and the sharp precariousness of the whole larger setting within which his agents of action exist, are the constants in Saro-Wiwa's art. Remorselessly, he challenges with sustained aesthetic grip, the unabating threat of chaos in which his plays are situated.

In *The Transistor Radio,* for example, he paints a panorama of anchorless men and women locked away in the trackless maze of a common squalor and the confinement of a social vacuum. Bereft of all supportive structures, the best impulses of the human race among the wretched of the earth, are completely stifled. The puzzling and spiritually famished world of Lagos, a city famous for its magnificence as it is notorious for its dark, dingy chasms of vice and multifarious disorders, is the playwright's wry choice for his point of moral reference for his dramatic action and characters.

This choice of setting and the fertility of his dramatic device are enabling as they facilitate his consistently satiric purpose of unearthing the increasingly manifold socio-political aberrations that have cornered the Nigerian nation. Setting, for instance, enables the playwright to counter-point in a profoundly ironic and disturbing manner the gilded lives of the idle but obscencely *nouveau riche* in the city "who make millions each year for doing nothing' and those of the alienated masses (13). In a powerful elocution, Basi, a con-man, tutoring his friend and pupil on the harrowing quality and grinding framework of destitution that have taken them hostage, asks:

> Have you slept under Carter Bridge? Or in the rubbish dumps of Isolo where men who have lost their sense of smell live and scavenge right in the dump, waiting for the lorries bearing the waste of rich and poor alike? Have you been thrown out by land lady for non-payment of rent? Have you taken refuge in the back of a truck and woken up to find yourself one hundred kilometres away without money for the return journey? (13)

These rhetorical plaints are aimed at leading the audience beneath the glittering surface to a deeper perception of the underlying, appalling, but central questions of poverty, inequality, and all sorts of deprivations arising from a yawning social polarization in the sprawling city. With the poetizing instincts of a painter, the playwright right at the beginning of the play theatrically intuits and conjures with riveting details a composite image of the frightening social strains and paucity of space, including unemployment afflicting the vagrant city drifters whose exodus into exploding cities is rewarded by the denial of the austerest right of existence. In a panoptic presentation, the first stage direction compresses and projects with mimetic accuracy an unbroken view of the staggering poverty of the under-privileged and later through the valency of his dialogic and visual powers, the playwright demonstrates how desperation impels the hard-bitten to little schemes, ingenious knavery, and all sorts of negations:

> Basi's hovel in Lagos. It is a single room with a bed, a clothes-hanger, a good cup-board on top of which is a kerosene stove, two single cushioned seats and a low narrow centre-table. Alali enters, he pretends to be snoring. Alali looks at him stealthily and rummages for food in the cupboard.

In this masterly enactment, the dramatist, through a broad visual humor, synthesizes the artistic design of his dramaturgy with extensive social concerns. Through the illusion of theater, the playwright deftly fuses setting and character to the effect that the physical details of the scene convincingly provide an image of the shape and quality of lives led by the characters. With the skills and precision of the painter, the playwright astutely foregrounds the whole dramatic situation through the articulation of parts imbued, however, with wider, associative, reverberating patterns. Izevbaye, who identifies "writing and political struggle for the improved life for Nigerians" as two of Saro-Wiwa's "obsessions," recalls that the talented writer was constantly concerned that proceeds from oil money should be used for the collective prosperity of all Nigerians and adds that "Ken always marveled at the way a few privileged people misappropriated and misused the oil money" (1996:6).

Despite his temper against misrule and the use of his plays as a platform for airing other firm political views, Saro-Wiwa's sensibilities sublimate politics to the rigors of art. Hence although the underlying constant in all his works is a deep repudiation of misrule and its spiraling negations, politics is, however, assimilated into his aesthetic unobtrusively, obliquely, naturally. For instance, in the play-within-a-play scenes, Saro-Wiwa skillfully wields the accessories of buffoonery, slapstick, indeed, the entire comic gear, for purposes other than the stirring of laughter. Beyond comic evocation, the embellishments exemplify aggrandizing powers through the bloated assumptions of the swanky Basi and how such unrestrained powers brutalize and cower the populace as demonstrated through the docility and indifferent servitude of Alali. A good grasp of the machinery of comic theatre thus enables the dramatist to make pungent political points without a trace of preachment against the *carpe diem* mentality and other noxious characteristics of the Nigerian glitterati.

Thus disposed, the heart of the action of *The Transistor Radio* seems designed to suggest that squalor and its sinister influences, foul economic conditions accented by political malaise and social injustice, are fecund seedbeds for the endless swing and heritage of evil in society. An eloquent testament to the human garbage in Nigeria's premier city, Lagos, the first stage direction in *The Transistor Radio* early takes on associations of a sinister nature. Alali, a pupil con-man "stealthily . . . rummages for food in the cupboard" (11). The idiom heavily endows him with parasitic, insect-like and animal-like qualities. His stealth, act of rummaging and gnawing under which he complains of so often that it gains the intensity of a motif, provide a stark spectacle and metaphor for the numbing social and political deprivations which castrate the enormous potentials of the sprawling slum and minority elements in Nigeria and their consequent reduction to forlorn beggary.

Again, the callous indifference of Basi, the master con-man, to Alali's hunger-harassed condition, the viciousness of the bullish landlady, and the counterfeiting activities of almost all the characters are not merely accurate reflections of cornered lives, but also aesthetically pleasing presentations of the ugly.

George Lukacs, who has pondered on "the displacement in the relations among men" in contemporary life, argues that the main characteristics of traditional societies "was the way men's dependencies and relations were brought into unity" which he contrasts with the modern "tendency to depersonalize and to induce dissonances." (432)

Saro-Wiwa typifies and protests these dislocations and through a thematic imagery of hardness and metallic grit, castigates the drought and aridity of fellow-feelings in the city. From the banter between Alali and Basi one gets the impression that the city's "toughness" makes people "as hard as stone." Warning his acolyte against filching his effects, Basi tells Alali "next time you lay your hands on anything of mine, I'll show you what metal I'm made of" (11). In all this, we find in the author an impassioned imagination deeply stirred with compassion and empathy subtly communicated through satirizing the damming-up of improved rights and opportunities for all.

An avid human rights avatar, Saro-Wiwa is concerned to create and objectify the irrefragable view that the denial of basic rights such as the right to shelter, food, and other essential social amenities is the motivating energy for discord and stymied development. This is the awareness that dawns on a disenchanted Alali at the end of the play when he confesses "the wretchedness of our life. The hunger, the joblessness, but above all the meaninglessness of our situation" (30).

As the crushing weight of the social patterns of the society it caricatures comes into sharper focus as the action progresses, the play's social and political significance become even more palpable. The irrepressible con-man Basi, priming the neophyte Alali on the art of surviving in a society held hostage by its own skewered values, urges him to:

> Learn the lesson, then. You've got to be clever and smart if you must live. I learnt the lesson trudging the streets of Lagos. You must have your wits about you all the time or you're ruined. You need brains to bargain in the markets, brains to avoid the Policeman on the prowl for bribes; brains to outwit the con man on the trail for a fast deal. Yes, you need brains all the time. (19-20)

The amusing spectacle, the dexterous maneuvers and art-
ful dodgings evoked here do not only balk our expectations of
a society that makes even a forlorn attempt at decency but
their entire disagreeableness staggers our belief in reason and
necessity. The order of events depicted here is of a society that
has lost its bearings and accordingly has surrendered to social
deformity and its crippling forces. With these, the playwright
affords us amusement and lures us into show of life as farce.

Saro-Wiwa has an intimate and firm foothold in the various degrees of the laughable and the comic. Thus, he subtilizes
his disapprobation and dissension of vice abhorrent to him
through a panoply of the species of militant wit including irony,
satire, caricature, and the entire gamut of the ridiculous, defined by William Hazlitt as:

> the highest degree of the laughable . . .which is con-
> trary not only to custom, but to sense and reason, or is
> a voluntary departure from what we expect from those
> who are conscious of absurdity and propriety in words,
> looks and action. (1974:603)

Laughter, however, is merely a subterfuge for the playwright's
assault on social feelings. While laughter is a mask disguising
his indignation at and lampoon of the bewildering state of affairs all round him, the real essence of his method and subject
of dramatic orchestration is to force us to brood over the ex-
travagance of contradictions so very prevalent in our society.
This accords with George Meredith's insights in this connection that "the test of true comedy is that it shall awaken
thoughtful laughter" (1974:622).

Saro-Wiwa directs his satirical barbs to lance the abscess
and drain the pus and excess of society through an enactment
of society's aberrant ways. Frank examination may lead to con-
sternation or perhaps restoration. Soren Kierkegaard antici-
pated this when he observed that "satire also entails pain, but
this pain has a dialectic which gives it a teleology in the direction of a cure." (1974: 556) Thus, teleologically, Saro-Wiwa's
farces are shaped by a purpose: to re-orientate society and make

it conform to the image of its true potentials or, at least, what is accepted by civilized standards.

This explains why his social concerns are very embracing. Given the depth of treatment he affords to the manifold forms of degeneracy in his plays, Saro-Wiwa should perhaps compel more critical response than he presently does. In demonstrating the periods of accelerated and unchecked urban drift, he seems to suggest that cut away from the inner controls of the folk world, the drifters are trapped in a dislocated, dissociated and impersonal moral framework, a world whose bright lights can only lure them into facelessness, joblessness, duping, fakery, and all such fraudulence. This reality confronts Basi when he introduces himself and Alali to Dandy: "We are jobless and nameless" (22), he says blandly.

With a keen sense of psychology, Saro-Wiwa delves into chambers where the selves of the slum-dwellers are locked away. Surrounded by scant medical care, dysfunctional amenities, and voided institutions, the vagrants are routinely assailed by guilt, cross-cultural shock, and nostalgia. After an "exhausting, unrewarding search for a job in the offices" to earn a decent living, "hiding under the bed" and "feigning sickness" to dodge paying arrears of rent to a ferocious landlady, a hungry Alali regresses into nerve-wracking helplessness, directs guilt to himself and threatens suicide: "I'll kill myself one of these days!" (15). At other times, dizzy with frustration, he regrets his loss of rural innocence and desires to flee from the disruptive forces of the city: "I'll be back in the village, away from the frustrations of living here" he tells "a completely stumped" Basi (30).

As the stream of social sanctions which gives life cohesion dries up in the city, life for the rejects of society becomes a bundle of caprices and so the dramatist mixes their suffering and sorrows, their despairs and fantasies into the soul of his farce. At times putting aside their frustration, they lean on parasitic fences and get embroiled in wanton webs of get-rich-quick schemes. It is significant that the transistor radio which becomes a source of contention for the two friends, Basi and Alali, and from which the play takes its title, is a windfall from gambling and opportunistic stakings.

Interestingly, the play ends with pools-staking. Urging Alali to bring the radio so they could have it hazarded, Basi says, "We'll sell it for staking money" (31). The playwright's resolve to effect dreams of unattainable rewards and to depict gambling as a discreditable means of livelihood need no comment. However, with deft strokes, he lampoons opportunism, traces the mechanisms by which the poor are checkmated in their penury and with genial satire points the deadly significance of the absence of discernment in private and public lives.

Artistically, Saro-Wiwa animates and impacts positively on his audience through his bold innovation and experimentation with the linguistic abundance and varieties of the English language spoken in Nigeria. Playfully juxtaposing standard usage with local pidgin, he spontaneously reflects the cultural wealth of his literary and linguistic background, buoys the farcical thrust of his play, and achieves ingenious aesthetic variations and effects. Apart from being fluent exemplifications of a battery of the devices and intensities of farce, the scenes involving Madam, Alali, and Basi are exquisite comic creations in their complex admixture of pidgin and standard English expressions.

Witness, for instance, the endless, uproarious amusement arising from the grostequeries, the histrionic over-statement of emotions, mistaken identity, surprise, physical action, and Madam's bullish obsession with recovering the arrears of rent owed her by Basi, and Basi's tricksterish efforts at out-foxing her in the scene where she descends on their ramshackle hovel. Saro-Wiwa's concern with an adequate language of communication aimed at, as he puts it, "the broadest possible public," comes to the fore in the scene as he ably puts on stage the lively and piquant pidgin inventively fashioned by the common man to project and articulate his fractured universe:

Madam: *Wuruwuru* man! You think say I no get sense?

Basi: Not at all, Madam. You are a beautiful, intelligent, proud landlady.

Madam: You tink you fit deceive me?

Basi: Of course not, Madam.

Madam: Why you bin hide under de bed wen I enter?

Basi: Hide under a bed? I am a millionaire-on-the-make, Madam. I don't hide under beds. I was looking for my pen.

Madam: And your friend him belly ache, wetin happen to am? 'E stop automatic like watch, not so?

Alali: I beg, Madam, make you no vex.

Madam: Lagos life don enter una head finish. Una de lie, make cunny, play *wayo*. [*To* Basi] wen you get money, you gi'am to woman . . .

Basi: Which woman?

Madam: [*Ignoring him.*] But to pay house rent, na him be palaver. Anyway, you go see dis time. If you no pay me, I show you pepper, proper pepper.

Basi: I promise, Madam.

Madam: Promise yourself! Armed robbers! [*Leaves the room* with a final glare at Alali and Basi. Slams door *behind her.*](19).

This nimble blending of pathos and standard expression is a credit to the playwright's acuity and power of dramatic imagination, especially as this heightens the farcical conception and purpose of the play: poking fun at the incongruities and fiasco in an aberrant society. Dramatic spontaneity apart, the fusion has manifold intensities. As a linguistic and dramatic experiment, the device enables the dramatist to enrich the language resources available to dramatists of his time and place. Also, it enables the playwright to depthfully resonate with an anatomy of textual allusions, including hints at the historical contact of Nigerian life with cultures other than the British.

The word "palaver," meaning long windy talk, may have come into usage following the early European, perhaps Portuguese traders' parley with natives living on the coast of the Atlantic. 'Wayo" and "wuruwuru," (no doubt with similar etymological connections) are permeations of local dialects into the English idioms spoken in Nigeria. This mode of dialogic texturing fabricates and suggests the ambivalent gains and inchoate values accruing from colonial history and contact. Thus, through the idiom, Saro-Wiwa dramatically counterpoints the wealth of linguistic possibilities consequent upon the contact with a satire on the corruptions and deviations equally attending the cultural rendezvous.

If *The Transistor Radio* is an analogue of the social and economic evil that frustrates the sustainable development of society at all levels, *The Wheel* with its laconic but suggestive techniques exemplifies the unending *faux pas* that deterioratingly enwreathes the nation in an avoidable and thus ironic sociopolitical dystrophy. Though farcically conceived, *The Wheel* is pervaded by a foreboding atmosphere in which State matters are roundly trivialized. In it, situations and characters augur despondingly and cynically in a world perennially without bearings or moral center. "Full of dirt and putrefaction" (59), as Director (one of the key helmsmen of this scatological universe) remarks, the creed of the leaders is "Manage or Damage" (68, 69), a guiding philosophy which trenchantly echoes the moral emptiness of the world represented. The General Manager, another character, misanthropically chants the obscenity thus: "That's the way it was in the beginning. That's the way it is now. And that's the way it shall be for evermore" (69).

As the playwright arranges the outward deeds of his characters to exemplify their convictions, irrationality outruns reason and denudes common sense so much so that it becomes the common denominator of action. As the play opens, an election has just been won and the Chief Minister is seen pacing his new office. He is flushed "with a sense of wonder and excitement" (58) at the articles of furniture which lavishly adorn his expansive office. A "pile of congratulatory telegrams on the desk-tray" announces the transformation of traditional

groitic praise-singing into a modern art. Satisfied by the telegrams and by his vantage, the Chief Minister is ardently trans-
ported far and above the ponderous state matters imposed on
his shoulders. Completely taken in by dreams of self-aggran-
dizement, the Chief Minister, in a strange contrast, repudiates
in his reverie his custodial duties. In unrestrained delight, he
muses:

> Comfortable, eh? They do lay the carpet here thick,
> don't they? And pictures of me at airports, in office
> across the land, in our embassies throughout the world.
> I say, the flashing bulbs of cameras almost blinded me
> the other day. Ha! Ha! And did the telephones ring! Oh,
> you should have heard them. Some cacophony. Well,
> well, well, if the wheel turns this way continuously and
> continually, there should not be much to worry about,
> eh? Ha! Ha! To think you matter so much to so many!
> To think they look up to you to solve their problems.
> Their problems! But listen. Our elders have a saying:
> In taking care of others, do not forget yourself. Words
> of wisdom. Oh, no ancestors. I do not mean to forget
> myself. By no means. Not after spending that much time
> and money electioneering. Oh, treasury, look to your-
> self. I will take care of myself and the future. (58)

The myopic obsessions with material satisfaction, pleasure, and
power for private graft rather than for national interests may
be regarded as intimate perceptions and clues to the quality
and absurdity of the Nigerian political machinery Saro-Wiwa
knew well. He was at one time an administrator and politician. In this political arena, nimbly and even brazenly filching
the treasury is an avid national passion. Based on a succession
of episodes of theatrical vitality, each founded on analogous
farcical patterns, each presenting in its narrative strategy characters determined to make a career out of fraud, the plot-scheme
of *The Wheel* revolves around actors and agents who are sav-
agely embarrassing clichés of the Nigerian political milieu.

The play in several ways seems to be the playwright's response to Soyinka's "The Writer in a Modern African State,"

wherein the Nobel Laureate warns that considering the miasmic despondency spread in the continent by failed leadership,

> the time has now come when the African writer must
> have the courage to determine what alone can be sal-
> vaged from the recurrent cycle of human stupidity.
> (1968:20)

It is to this essence that Saro-Wiwa answers when he presents in action images of those who zealously orchestrate the movement of society towards the precipice of chaos. *The Wheel,* for instance, scornfully presents with impactful irony scoundrel politicians and con artists who have usurped power only to contribute their Judas kiss to nation-building.

Warming up to monetary gratifications at the beginning of the play, the Chief Minister snares political appointees who in turn inveigh and capture by guile their own victims. In his sarcastic and scoffing portrayal, the playwright pillories the sad results of graftage and highlights these as robbery, nebulous duplications, and all manner of excrescences, primarily designed for the satisfaction of political opportunists. Witness, for instance, the grandly ludicrous situation of having in a single cabinet, "The Minister in the Ministry of Commerce, the Minister of Industry, the Minister of Industry and the Minister by ..." (65), all of them armed with *carte blanche* powers!

In a keenly critical attitude, the dramatist shows the spongy Ministers in their racketeering for filthy lucre, demanding outrageous bribes which they variously and euphemistically refer to as "soldiers," "cigarettes," "biscuits," and "kola." For a parliamentarian to get the plum job of the Minister of Commerce and Industry, he hands out two hundred thousand "soldiers" to the Chief Minister. In turn, he too demands and collects a "considerable" hundred thousand "cigarettes" from another official. As the wheel rotates phenomenally, "the magic of the padded envelope" (72) bakes "biscuits" voluminous enough to fill a seven-ton truck of an official whose victim in turn obtains from another victim enough "kola" to comfortably sustain his life. In this spinning, vicious wheel, bribery ebulliently supplants qualifications and experience and thus becomes the necessary requisite for employment of any kind. The euphemisms given to these sharp and despicable practices are of immense social and artistic value. Artistically, they provide a cover for the playwright to launch his searing onslaught against political obscenities, especially those perpetrated by sensitive targets. His oblique reference to the military is thus socially and aesthetically potent. In Nigeria, the military has distinguished itself as the career not only for those manically enthused with instant wealth but also for those in quest of opportunistic political offices and lurid pleasure. The predatory associations often identified with the Nigerian military apart, soldiery here also incarnates absolute powers and the *carpe diem* principle and is accordingly an apt imagery for shady dealings in a grossly disreputable and faithless world.

"Cigarette," with its dangerous toxic elements, is also used metaphorically for lack of monetary transparency in Nigerian establishments. In the darkling canvass of the play, "cigarette" as a trope would possibly suggest evanesce, dissipation, or squandermania. The Director-turned-Chairman of the National Supply Company, luxuriating in his elevation through bribery, exclaims, "Oh, the smoke from my cigarettes should burn the vaults of the Central Bank!" (66). After receiving mouth-watering "biscuits" as his own cut from the racket, he very ironically apostrophizes, "This is progress! Yes makers of Mercedes, Leyland and Styr trucks, keep your assembly lines open . . ." (69).

The key to the figurative usage of biscuits as a euphemism for *kickbacks* lies in the baleful, gormandizing appetites of government officials who voraciously gouge the treasury and fellow citizens with the result that the fraudsters get so gorged that the nation is impoverished. In his clinical exploration of the labyrinthine pathways of political corruption and moral turpitude instituted at various levels of the Nigerian polity, Saro-Wiwa seems to suggest that the bewildering vertigo castrating the nation is officially orchestrated and sanctioned, especially given the ravenous, Epicurean gluttony of the country's leadership. That the playwright works to arouse condemnation for the intricate but discreditable passageways of fraud and its sinister operations is evident throughout and even more forcefully at the end of the play when the rotten wheel turns full cycle. The battleground for the forces of disorientation and disintegration, the playwright demonstrates, is laid out by the ironic betrayal of trust by impostors who wrest power only to champion narrow and primordial interests.

The security guard, the last in the chain to bribe and to be bribed, indicts the vulgarization, enfeeblement, and imperiling of national ethics and destiny thus:

> Stoopid teeves. Stoopid teeves. All of dem na teeves . . .
> Stoopid teeves. Look dem foto everywhere. If I just
> break dis foto now dem go talk say I don do bad. Stoopid
> teeves. Dem fit tief anything self. Look dis one. Jus take
> two hundred Naira for common gateman job. And if I
> no pay am e' no go give me work. If I no get the work,
> wetin I for do after all said and done? My wife . . . six
> children. Dem go chop, dem go wear cloth, dem go go
> school and when dem sick, I must to buy medicine. Hm,
> E hard o!

The visual scheme which exemplifies the menacing insanity of a society standing on its head at the end of the play by showing the guard refusing the Chief Minister entry into an establishment until the latter "dips his hand into his pocket and places a naira on the Security Guard's outstretched palm" and further mollifying him with "another naira on the left palm" as well as the guard's attitude of "Grabbing the note" (78) dramatizes how society loses its bearings, gets dwarfed and hindered from normal growth. This grim tableau and astute summary of the play's main action are succinct portrayals of social degeneracy, a stunt against conventionally accepted behavior, and a demonstration of how ignominious leadership could scuttle the ship of state into the perilous sea of misrule, mistrust, and nightmarish paralysis.

According to George and Portia Kernodle et al., "The nature of theatre art is to give shape to the bewildering complexities of human action and experience" and to "search for new paths through the disorder." (1985:245) The farcical analogy of *The Wheel* suggests the need to steer a course other than that charted by dubious politicians bent on grounding the nation in the abyss of irrational darkness. Germane to this conclusion is the gripping ironic humor mouthed by the blue devil of a Chief Minister as he responds with deviousness and hypocrisy to the guard's audacity: "You convince me of the need of an Ethical Revolution to change the morals of this country. How debased can you get" (78). This wind-up scene with its serrated humor simultaneously iterates the moral view point and dialectic of the entire action, the social conscience and aesthetic purpose of the playwright, as well as his dissenting temper against the conversing, super-irrational forces of perturbation furiously gnawing away the very sinews of society.

## Works Cited

Albee, Edward. *Program of Buffalo*. New York: Studio Arena Theatre Production of Box-Mao-Box. Cited in Roby Cohn, Currents in Contemporary Drama. Bloomington: Indiana University Press, 1969: 9.

Hazlitt, William. "On Wit and Humour." In Bernard Dukore, ed., *Dramatic Theory and Criticism: Greeks To Growtoski*. New York: Holt Reinhart and Winston, Inc., 1974: 603.

Izevbaye, Dan. "Saro-Wiwa Was An Awoist." *The Punch Newspaper* November 10, 1996, p. 8.

Kierkegaard, Soren. "*The Comic*." In Bernard Dukore, ed. *Dramatic Theory and Criticism: Greek to Growtosky*. New York: Holt Reinhard and Winston, 1974: 556.

Kernodle, George and Portia et al., *Invitation To The Theatre*. New York: Harcourt Brace Jovanovich Publishers, 1985:245.

Luckacs, George. "*The Sociology of Modern Drama*." Trans. Lee Bazandell. In Eric Bentley, *The Theory of Modern State: An Introduction to Modern Theatre and Drama*. Hammondsworth: Penguin Books, 1969: 432.

Meredith, George. "*An Essay on Comedy*." In George Dukore ed., *Dramatic Theory and Criticism: Greeks To Grotowski*. New York: Holt Reinhart and Winston, Inc., 1974: 622.

Piscator, Erwin. "The Theatre Can Belong To Our Century." In Eric Bentley, ed., *The Theory of Modern Stage: An Introduction to Modern Theatre and Drama*. Hammondsworth: Penguin Books, 1969:473.

Ken Saro-Wiwa. *Four Farcical Plays*. London: Saros International Publishers, 1987: 7

# 6
▼▼

# The Gift of Voice:
## Ken Saro-Wiwa's *Prisoners of Jebs* as a Political Discourse

*An artist differs from the rest of us mainly because he reacts
sharply and in an uncommon manner to phenomena which
leave the rest of us unmoved, or, at most, merely annoy us
vaguely*
—H. L. Menchken.

Apart from being "the totality of communication devices
deployed in literary communication," languages, according to Chidi Amuta is "the totality of the means available for
communicating a cultural form to the greatest majority in a
manner that will achieve a clearly defined cognitive ideological effect in the consciousness of the audience" (113). Let us
begin by admitting from the outset that this essay is about the
language of literature and how it provides rich pleasures for
the readers. In fact, one of our contemporary critics, Robert
Alter, defines literary language as "an intricate, inventively
designed vehicle for setting the mind in restless pleasing mo-
tion, which in the best of cases may give us a kind of experiential knowledge relevant to our lives outside reading" (10).

Although the rise and fall of nations and empires are mysteries that have perennially fascinated scholars, the striking fact is, when it begins to rise, each nation gathers its energies—military, political, and economic—to make a decisive entry onto the stage of history. In the same way, each nation defines itself in terms of its uniqueness. In Nigeria, there has always been what Chinua Achebe sagaciously referred to as "squarely a failure of leadership." This refers to the "unwillingness or inability of its leaders to rise to the responsibility, to the challenge of personal example which are the hallmarks of true leadership" (1).

Very little research has been done in the area of political discourse as it affects the great scholar and critic, Kenule Saro-Wiwa, who was executed by the Nigerian state on November 10, 1995. The main issues that this piece deals with are: the different attitudes the author assumes in *Prisoners of Jebs;* why certain words, which are known to the majority of the population, represent concrete descriptions of facts; and what it is about certain words which makes them important, objectionable, and the description of the Nigerian attitude as veritable accounts of disdain through adequate parody.

Van Dijk and Walter Kintsch have delimited the processes of text production or understanding as "strategies" which are often flexible and goal-oriented and extrapolate effective guesses about the underlying structures, meanings, or functions of discourse fragments. In another study, "Discourse Analysis: Its Development and Application to the Structure of News," Van Dijk reinforces this approach with a thrust by declaring unambiguously that readers must make use of many different kinds of previous knowledge, including knowledge stored in memory. As we enter into *Prisoners of Jebs* with effusive enthusiasm, we are eager to dialogue with the author and soon we discover that the author's views are in line with those of other established writers (Okot P'Bitek, Grabriel Okara, Mongo Beti, Festus Iyayi, and Niyi Osundare) who have employed similar commitment in denouncing our apparent complacency. There is a battery of evidence from post-independence African novels as Neil Lazarus has articulated in *Resistance in Post-Colonial African Fiction* that what is offered is a:

64

> Scalding critique of the irresponsibility of post-colo-
> nial leadership in Africa . . . All portray this elite as a
> murderously hypocritical social fraction, living not only
> beyond their own means but beyond the means of their
> societies as a whole. They show us the elite, thus, as a
> kleptocracy, with the continuing poverty and power-
> lessness of the peasants, proletarians, and marginals
> toiling below them. (21)

The overriding principle in this essay will be a pragmatic theory
dealing with an aspect of evidentiality provided by the rela-
tion-ship between forms of utterances and the conditions under which they are used in texts which, according to Akio
Kamio, have defined "the territory of information." This focus
is a creative rehash of Van Dijk's studies in which the idea that
texts have "content" or thematic structure account for the so-
called semantic macrostructures. This hierarchical structure
consists of propositions that define the most important or relevant information in the text.

Saro-Wiwa assumes a variegated attitude, drawing from
many disciplines—history, sociology, linguistics, theology, literature, politics—in order to penetrate the special character
of the Nigerian state through an enduring persiflage. In demonstrating a people's complacency, he gives the Nigerian attitude in its morbid indolence:

> [The] Nigerians do not normally ask questions about
> anything. Things just happen. It is taken for granted
> that things will happen. So a bloke just strolls to the
> radio station and says, 'Hello, brothers, I'm now your
> new Head of State'. And the Nigerians take to the street,
> dancing. They love excitement. They hate to question.
> (*Prisoners of Jebs*, 2)

To complete this image, we are given a weird historical trajectory as we are taken to the 70s when the country was rich and
one of its leaders boasted that his problem was not money, but
how to spend the billions. But soon, the billions performed
the disappearing trick because in Nigeria, money "has a way of
disappearing quickly."

Employing the pathological image of a prison, the society
soon acquired the status of a veritable prison where

> individual homes were as good as a prison as any. Did
> not citizens in the cities barricade their houses to pro-
> tect themselves from robbers and assassins? Did not
> citizens put gates on streets and lock them at night?
> Nigeria was a veritable prison, although the prisoners,
> sorry, citizens did not know it, and did not indeed care.
> (1)

From the text above, we can poke at the declarative "Nigeria
was a veritable prison" and adduce that this mood comes out as
a signal or act whose interpretation leaves us in no doubt. In
using this "free direct speech" (Leech and Short), we are encouraged to have the feeling somebody is speaking to us more
immediately with the narrator as an intermediary.

The analogy is that what is true of individuals is also true
of sympathies. We are persuaded to say this because the role
of propositions in a discourse can become conventional in a
given culture and for given discourse types in such a way that
they be regarded as structural categories (Van Dijk, 1983a).

This engagingly written text of fifty-three related chap-
ters, which first appeared in the author's column in national
newspapers, is replete with jokes, anecdotes, quotations, and
readily intelligible examples, all of which offer an accessible
entreè to the full range of linguistic knowledge. With this
author, one is led to believe, the evidence suggests that it is
possible to write many cogent critical accounts in a variety of
styles embracing a number of doctrines and a host of principles. The language is the expression of the inherence of nihilism in metaphysics as the Yale gang of five—Harold Bloom,
Paul de Man, Jacques Derrida, Geoffrey Hartman, and Hillis
Miller—had done with deconstruction (Barfoot 1981). You
cannot miss the abundant nihilism in "What the Director Discovered" in relation to the Nigerian concept of heroism:

> In Nigeria, theft of public property was no crime. The
> Nigerians praised their thieves and showered them with

praise songs and huge advertisements in their newspapers. Once when the Nigerians made the mistake of locking up the bosses of the thieves, the men who had made the mistake of locking them up were then locked up, just so they could see how nice it was in prison. All this made it clear to the world that in Nigeria honest men were prisoners and the thieves, free men. (18-19)

Readers who are not Nigerians will probably think that in this country, the illiteracy rate must be suffocating; but they only have to note the *ad valorem* of the text below to grasp the full range of meaning:

In Nigeria, certificates are either stolen or forged, and when they are not, they are invalidated by one fact: its holders do not think, cannot think (58).

This is because, in the author's view,

The worst sin on earth is the failure to think. It is thoughtlessness that has reduced Africa to beggardom, to famine, poverty and disease. The failure to use the creative imagination has reduced Africans to the status of mimic men and consumers of the product of other imagination. (58-59)

In Michael Billig, we are informed that plainly targeted discourse bears an obvious danger for royalty or other forms of authority, for it is clearly partisan and signals that a side is being taken in a matter of controversy. This makes the argumentative sense plainly visible and splits the potential audience with which the speaker might identify and thereby threaten the state's claim to represent the whole realm. In fact, the state comes out as the monster sprung up to swallow its subjects. This protean monster with various levels, degrees, and complexions "refused the challenge to work hard night and day to improve themselves" (77). The military adventurists are also denounced for contributing negatively to the development of Africa. Thus in "The Military Factor," we are told that:

Amin was not the only military man to be feared. All
African soldiers, it appeared, abhorring the chores of
soldiering, longed for the delights of civil administration. (89)

This parallel structure comes from the realization that soldiers are supposed to cherish soldiering, but our contemporary African soldiers dread this but relish the chores of civil
administration, thereby validating their role as a group that
has lost its collective bearing.

The author's classification of Nigerian politicians is all-
knowing and boundless. To complete the lampoon, the author presents the Nigerian politician in his true colors:

A Nigerian politician is venomous. A Nigerian politician of the Second Republic is a curse. The Nigerian
politicians of the Second Republic in one body add up
to an epidemic. (99)

Although the use of targeted discourse involves some kind of
distancing, situations may be present where the preceding or
following context may move towards directness. In the next
text he opens anaphorically:

Once upon a time, ten out of twelve military governors
of Nigeria had been found to have committed fouls during a game of tribunals. The governors had been banned
from holding public office for ten years. In at least one
famous case, University professors had said that corruption of a Governor was no big deal. Indeed, they
considered a Governor who had misused public funds a
very clever man who had made obvious contributions
to knowledge. And they had awarded the gentleman a
doctorate degree *honoris causa*. The man who had not
acquired even meaningful high school education had
gone berserk with joy: he had not known that looting
of public treasury was such a great service to his countrymen. And he was determined to repeat the feat. (101)

This is a concrete example of the problem that nimbles the soul of the nation. The sidekicks of this debased leadership continue to dog the nation's every step. It is this strategy of targeted discourse that informs his summary of the Nigerian politicians as "eminent men who had supervised the ruin of their country" (107). This epicurean note is alluring and didactic at once.

Another rewarding strategy which runs in the middle of this text is the employment of what Van Dijk in "Story Comprehension: An Introduction" calls "action sentences." It may be about any sequence of actions, under the only condition that the discourse itself is coherent. This means, roughly speaking, that the respective propositions of the discourse, expressed by the sequence of sentences, are interpreted as a related set of facts, e.g., events and action in some possible world. The relation will often be conditional: one fact will make another fact possible, probable, or necessary (Halliday and Hassan 1976). Let us illustrate this with the role of women in Nigeria's story of disrepute as represented by the story of Madame Kokane and her daughter, both arrested for drug trafficking. When interrogated, Madame remains defiant:

'Why did you do it?'
'For money' piped she sweetly.
'Foreign exchange'.
'Really, asked the Director.'
'Yes, now' Madam answered.
'And you really needed the money?'
'Yes, now', answered Madame.
'I have to train my children'.
'How many children?' asked the Director.
'Ten', answered Madam proudly.
'You did not have the money before you produced the children?
'Oga Director', said Madame, 'children are the gift of God. I have to look for the money myself. To feed, clothe the children and send them to school and university'.
'Did your daughter here go to University?'
'Yes, now', answered Madame.
'She is a graduate'. (83)

What comes up in the above dialogue is crime conditioned by societal decay and moral depravity. Crime has become a veritable industry as national leadership continues to embrace greed, avarice and sophisticated short-cuts to personal satisfaction. In a similar interview with Miss Smuggle Kokane, she defeats our expectations:

> 'Why did you do this thing?'
> 'My mother asked me to do it.'
> 'You do whatever your mother asks you to do?'
> 'The Bible enjoins us so to do' answered Miss Smuggle Kokane.
> 'How come that an educated girl like you couldn't find a decent job to do?'
> 'How much is a good monthly salary? A year's salary is far less than I get on one trip to the United States of America,' answered the young Miss. (85)

Ken Saro-Wiwa's grouse in this witty exposition of one of the evils of the society today aptly tallies with the question and answer tactic Charles Murray carefully presents in his "In pursuit of Happiness":

> How are we to construct society so that anyone, no matter what his gifts, can look back on his life and say it has been happy, filled with deep and justified satisfaction? The answer is that he will in a properly run society be able to say such things as, "I was a good parent, a good neighbour."(44)

Gifted as it is, this author's scalding voice is directed at our leaders, who should know, as the timeless words of Adam Smith remind us that:

> When the happiness or misery of others depends in any respect upon our conduct, we dare not, as self-love might suggest to us, prefer the interest of one to that of many. The man within immediately calls to us, that we value ourselves too much and other people too little, and that, by doing so, we render ourselves the proper

object of the contempt and indignation of our breth-
ren. (*The Theory of Moral Sentiments*, 1759)

Since literature is inconceivable outside the context of language (Owomoyela), the effectiveness of the strategies that
writers adopt in their efforts to create involvement and to co-
operate in the joint development of specific themes depends
on their control over a range of "communicative options and
on their knowledge of the signaling potential that these options have in alluding to shared history, values and mutual
obligations" (Gumperz, 1982:206). Through Ken Saro-Wiwa's
panoramic lens, we are made to see the Nigerians as:

> . . . the most contentious, the most troublesome, the
> most greedy, the most venal, the most vicious group of
> people God ever put together in any corner of the world.
> (35).

Apart from the effect of the pre-modifying superlative (most),
the words carefully selected to describe the Nigerian attitude
represent the extreme form of villainy. The same cord is retained when we are told humorously that

> The Nigerians tell too many lies. If a Nigerian tells you
> "Good morning", watch the clock. If he shakes hands
> with you, count your fingers. (36)

The Nigerian customs officers also come under scrutiny in a
parallel structure designed to show the monumental disrepute
into which the country has fallen:

> The Nigerian Customs officials existed to please them-
> selves, not the country. On the borders of any country,
> the task of customs officials is to stop smuggling and
> smugglers. Nigerian customs officials know their jobs
> better and were said to possess magical powers which
> enabled them to obtain from their meagre monthly sala-
> ries such expensive items as palatial homes, industries,
> large farms, opulent cars, fat wives and slim, elegant
> girlfriends. (39)

71

On Abuja, the new capital city, the author's biting sarcasm remains unabated. He calls it "the whitest elephant any nation on earth had ever created" (90). In a euphemistic tone, he employs the metonymic image of the cemetery proposed by government at the unbelievable sum of twelve billion Naira. The Director of Jebs Prison and his uncrowned deputy, Chief Popa, are shown in an important dialogue whose subject is Abuja:

> 'What about the cemetery in Abuja?'
> 'Twelve billion Naira' Twelve billion Naira for a cemetery? What the hell! Are the Nigerians going to bury every citizen in Abuja?'
> 'I believe so,' answered Chief Popa and smacked his lips. The place is the burial ground of Nigeria'. (94)

The distorted image of this capital city as the burial ground of Nigeria's resources, vision, and progress have been validated by current events.

Any conclusion to the analysis of a book as rich and relevant as *Prisoners of Jebs* whose subject remains topical is bound to be necessarily indecisive and certainly not the place for idle speculation. This is because, as Osundare concludes, all theories we apply in our critical enterprise indeed leak. But to glimpse at the vision of Ken Saro-Wiwa and understand what he means to people when he wrote his numerous books and scholarly articles, let us consider one of his last letters before he was executed by the state:

> I am a man of peace, of ideas. Appalled by the denigrating poverty of my people who live on a richly-endowed land, distressed by their political marginalisation and economic strangulation, angered by the devastation of their land, their ultimate heritage, anxious to preserve their right to life and to a decent living, and determined to usher to this country as a whole a fair and just democratic system which protects everyone and every ethnic group and gives us all a valid claim to human civilization; I have devoted all my intellectual and material resource, my very life, to a cause in which I have total belief and from which I can not to be blackmailed or

72

intimidated. I have no doubt at all about the ultimate success of my cause, no matter the trials and tribulations which I and those who believe with me may encounter on our journey. Neither imprisonment nor death can stop our ultimate victory. ("Before I am Hanged," *ANA Review*, 1995)

Ken Saro-Wiwa's was the voice of an educated and sophisticated African truly in search of progress. His deft criticism of the ruling class, jaundiced view of the ineptitude of the political class, and the gifts of wit and language enabled him describe our continent as a "prison"—all this will make this great fighter a hero to a generation of Africans and lovers of freedom everywhere. His demand for a return to civil society is a legitimate one which will season an appreciable degree of independence where national economy will not be embedded in an international frame of conspiracy. His execution was the final demonstration of state cruelty and idiocy. It is one of the harsh and meaningless fiats of destiny that this maestro of language was to end his days through agents of his first enemy: the Nigerian State.

As his voice suggests in *Prisoners of Jebs*, man is still utterly dependent on the natural world, but now has for the first time the ability to alter it, rapidly and on a national scale. But the Nigerian has yet to do this conscientiously. Until this grand inertia is jolted to a reawakening, Albert Einstein's verdict on the impending holocaust of the discovery of atomic energy, "that we shall require a substantially new manner of thinking if mankind is to survive," still seems apt.

# Works Cited

Achebe, Chinua. *The Trouble with Nigeria*. Enugu: Fourth Dimension, 1983.
Alter, Robert. *The Pleasures of Reading in an Ideological Age*. New York: Simon and Schuster, 1990.
Barfoot, C. D. "Current Literature, 1990." *English Studies* 62, 6 (December 1981).

Bell, Daniel. "American Exceptionalism Revisited: The Role of a Civil Society." *Dialogue* 87,1 (1990):9-14.

Billig, Michael. "Common-places of the British Royal Family: A Rhetorical Analysis of Plan and Argumentative Sense." *Text: An Interdisciplinary Journal for the Study of Discourse* 8,3 (1988):191-217.

Gumperz, J. J. *Discourse Strategies*. Cambridge: Cambridge University Press, 1982.

Halliday, M. A. K. and Hasan, R. *Cohesion in English*. London: Longman, 1976.

Kamio, Akio. "The Territory of Information in English and Japanese and Psychological Utterances." *Journal of Pragmatics* 24,3 (September 1995):235-265.

Lazarus, Niel. *Resistance in Post-colonial African Fiction*. New Haven: Yale University Press, 1990.

Leech, Geoffrey and Michael Short. *Style in Fiction: Linguistic Introduction to English Fictional Prose*. London: Longman, 1981.

Murrary, Charles. "In Pursuit of Happiness" *Dialogue* 87,1 (1990):41-47.

Osundare, Niyi. *African Literature and the Crises of Post-structuralist Theorizing*. Dialogue in African Philosophy Monograph Series 2. Ibadan: Options Book and Information Services, 1993.

Owomoyela, Oyekan. "Language, Identity, and Social Construction in African Literatures." *Research in African Literatures* 23,1 (Spring 1992):83-93.

Saro-Wiwa, Ken. *Prisoners of Jebs*. Port Harcourt: Saros International Publishers, 1988.

Van Dijk, T. A. "Story Comprehension: An Introduction." *Poetics* 9 (1980):1-20.

_____ "Discourse Analysis: Its Development and Application to the Structure of News." *Journal of Communication* 33.2 (1883): 20-43)

_____ "New Developments in Discourse Analysis 1978-1988" *Journal of Interdisciplinary Literary Studies* (1,1 (1989):119-145.

_____ and Walter Kintsch. *Strategies of Discourse Comprehension*. New York: Academic Press, 1983b.

74

7

# Aspects of Language in Ken Saro-Wiwa's *Sozaboy*: *A Novel in Rotten English*

David Eka

1

*Sozaboy* is apparently an uncommon example of a novel written in a subvariety of English that is beyond the limits of regular acceptability and intelligibility—local, national, or international. The author has demonstrated a unique ability: consider his management of what, at first, sounds like utterances from a demented mind. Then imagine his control of general communicative lawlessness and commotion and his eventual arrival at what can pass for an innovative communicative patterning. Reflect on the part he plays consistently mangling the language and then channeling the pieces into an irresistible variegation! Or, let us consider the author's suggestively unusual acquaintance with low level communication in English and the frivolous behavior exhibited by the characters he recreates. There are not many authors who, confronted with this kind of task, could have done better than Ken Saro-Wiwa has done in this novel.[1]

Being a Nigerian and, more importantly, one highly connected with communication matters, Ken Saro-Wiwa was, without doubt, aware of the vast possibilities within the English process of nativization of nonnative varieties of English and that the English language (like any other natural language in contact) adjusts itself to the milieu of the environment (the users) within which it finds itself. Perhaps the author's aim was not just to experiment with nonstandard English usage but also to get to the bottom of it. It would appear he did so and got to the abyss. . . leaving in its wake unclassified usages; structures without modifiers; bold and unusual swapping of grammatical elements; unique verbal groups and phonographological instructions, among others. This article deals with the above matters collectively and individually as being appropriate.

## II

The first intriguing issue about language use in *Sozaboy* is probably the use of the "word" *Lomber*. From the viewpoint of English phonotactics,[2] "lomber" is a potential word. I recall vividly that I came by this "word" for the first time during my reading of *Sozaboy*. No dictionary could help; the glossary did. Then I asked myself: why did the author resort to this? The answer possibly is: the characters he recreated used it, perhaps as a way of demonstrating that they had "mastered" the English language and so could show off with it in a "big way," using the liquid laterals /I/ instead of the familiar and "common" alveolar nasal /n/. Then, one more point would remain: from my experience with learners of the English language in Nigeria, the central vowel /D/ is problematic and so the nearest equivalent to it, the back vowel /D/ is often used as a replacement since the majority of Nigerian languages do not have the sound and all of them have /D/. So I could account for the use of /"O"/ realizable as /D/. However, this "word" *lomber* must remain an important addition to the vast experiments which are possible with English.

## III

The first utterance in the novel is clearly an adverbial clause of concession introduced by the word *although*. Yet it is written as though it is a lot more important than a clause: from the punctuation and the arrangement of words, it is highly suggestive of a sentence which has the status of a paragraph: "Although, everybody in Dukana was happy at first (p.1)."[3]  In formal writing, and even in spoken prose or published conversation, one would have expected a main (independent or major) clause to follow, to complement the idea expressed.  But that has not been the case!  Then the next paragraph begins:

> All the nine villages were dancing and we were eating
> plenty maize with pear and knacking tory under the
> moon. (p.1)

At this point, the reader begins to wonder whether the language of this novel is the normal one—English—that he knows. He probably wonders, first, whether the word *we* refers to membership of the nine villages; why there is no grammatical word *of* between *plenty* and maize: and whether this *maize* is a special one that has *pear* to go with it!  He also probably wonders what shape the moon now has as people can dance, eat, tell stories under it!  These two initial utterances demonstrate instances of unclassified usages.  But there are many others. Witness the following:

(i)  He was crying *with water from his eye* (p.2)
(ii)  Then he told Okonkwo *to not to worry* (p.2)
(iii)  My master say it is *very bad at all*  (p.2)
(iv)  So we must *to believe you* (p.7)
(v)  I must *to do* (p.8)
(vi)  I am *prouding plenty* (p.12)
(vii)  *Policeman's stick's blow* (p.46)
(viii)  ... if two people *are loving themselves* they will
be talking *small small things.*
(ix)  ... when *the come comes to become* ... (p.62)
(x)  ... which time will they *learn us* how to shoot the gun?
(p.73)
(xi)  You *are ghost* (p.131).
(xii)  ... if *that Sozaman have pregnanted my young darling*
(p.138).
(xiii)  ... that is *the exactly thing* that happened (p.140)
(xiv)  ... did we not think that *he have already dead?* (p.152)

77

(xv)  *Pastor Barika is the in-charger of the church and he* is very
wicked man (p.173)

(xvi)  After he have dig for some time and *made hole in the
ground* they put the bundle inside in the ground *and
covered the hole that they have dig with soil* (p.173)

(xvii)  Somebody must kill any person who *have dead before
he can die.* (p.181).

(xviii)  I was just thinking how the war have... uselessed
many people... (p.181).

I invite the reader to believe that I originally intended to list
only ten of the numerous unclassified expressions in this novel
but I could not end at ten, for each time I wanted to stop, there
was another one more appalling. To put the matter very mildly,
there is none of the 181 pages of this edition that does not
have at least five shocking (unclassified) expressions!

Even though this sequential listing is enough to explain
one aspect of language use in this novel, we shall still do a
brief (un?) necessary discussion.

We can reclassify this listing into five main groups:
(a) Those which introduce unnecessary words e.g. *to not to
worry; must to do;*
(b) Those which show unacceptable agreement between subject and verb, e.g., *he have* already dead;
(c) Those which have introduced strange words, e.g., *prouding
plenty; in-charger; pregnanted; uselessed;*
(d) Those which will for a long time continue to defy e x p l i -
cation e.g. *when the come comes to become; it is very bad at all;*
(e) Others, e.g., *policeman's stick's blow;* the *exactly thing.*

In the first group we see that the word *to* is regularly introduced to obstruct the meaning which the verbal group would
otherwise have signaled. This is so because "not to worry",
for instance, is meaningful; "to not to worry" is something
else. In the same way, "must go," "must believe," and "must be
careful" are examples of English utterances; but "must to go,"
"must to believe," "must to be careful" are not.

In the second group, the characters have demonstrated that
they have not managed to observe the commonest rules of

concord: singular nouns or pronouns and singular verbs; plural nouns or pronouns and plural verbs. However, it is interesting that the apparent violation has tended to be one sided: singular nouns or pronouns with plural verbs:

*He have* never done this (p.98);

*Sozaboy have* already dead (p.130);

I will see everyone *who have* fit able to return (p.171).[4]

In the third group we encounter what we have described here as "a bold swapping of grammatical classes" e.g., from adjectives *proud* and *useless* to verbal *prouding*, and *uselessed*. But we shall return to this shortly.

We also encounter uncommon coinages, e.g., *in-charger, pregnanted, surprisation* (pp. 51; 103), *surprised* (pp.172; 172).

We have already indicated that those in group four have defied explication. However, in group five the tortuous comparison is worthy of note: instead of what is often heard ("The blow from the policeman's baton"), the character has talked about "policeman's stick's blow." This may be compared to another oddity: where the possessive raker is not indicated at all:

"The Soza captain body" (p.108);

"The Soza captain tent" (p.109);

## IV

Reduplication is a feature of Nigerian, indeed African languages. It is not a known feature of English, particularly the educated variety. When, therefore, we observe that there are numerous instances of reduplication in *Sozaboy*, we can say that the English used in this novel has a strong basis in the mother tongue of the characters who use it.[5] Because of the numerical strength and diversity of this phenomenon we have divided it into two parts: simple reduplication and complex reduplication. Reduplication that has two items is referred to (in this article) as *simple* reduplication. One that has more than two items is classified as *complex* reduplication. This separation is not only for convenience of analysis and discussion, it is also intended to prove that reduplication is not used and applied here in the usual sense in language description. It is used as feature of

79

language use in *Sozaboy: A Novel in Rotten English*! At the beginning of the novel, we have simple reduplication (pp.1-6), thus:

> ...yams were growing *well well*.
> They were all chopping bribe from the *small small* people.
> *big big* grammar.
> *long long*, words.
> *Before before*, the grammar was not plenty...
> ... the sun will shine *proper proper*...

In other *Lombers*, there are also many instances of simple reduplication. Witness the following:

> The thing pained me *bad bad*. (p.11)
> Army is for *tall tall* men. (p.26)
> Because I am now Soza *true true*.
> Nothing was worrying him *at all at all*. (p.163)

As can be seen from the above, some instances of reduplication occur at the beginning and some occur at the end of each utterance shown above. At the end of each utterance, they tend to function as adverbial—

> "growing well well;
> ... shining proper proper;
> ... now Soza true true.

At the beginning and immediately before nouns or nominals reduplications tend to function as adjectivals—

> Big big grammar;
> Long long words;
> Tall tall men;
> Small small people.

In other environments, each tends to constitute an adverbial group: Before before, the grammar...

In general, some simple reduplications serve to emphasize the issue hinted at by the word that is reduplicated. For instance, in:

Growing well well
Tall tall men

The characters uttering the words may be understood to mean:

... growing very well;
... very tall men

In that situation, the first item in a simple reduplication serves a function very similar to that of the intensifier/emphasizer in educated English.[6]

However, there are other situations in which reduplication are not productive at all. For example, in:

Before before;
True true;
Bad bad;
At all at all.

One of the words (or set of words) is simply wasted, as it would have been adequate to have, for instance:

Before now, the grammar . . .;
... I am now Soza truly.,
It pained me seriously ,
Nothing worried him.

Instead of:

Before before, the grammar...;
... I am now soza true true.;
It pained me bad bad;
Nothing was worrying him at all at all.

But there is something consoling, perhaps surprising: the same character that, at the beginning, said:

My master say it is very bad at all (p.2) is also the one
who now (towards the end), says "But he is not worrying about anything at all" (p.163).

With regard to complex reduplication, we have the following
illustrations:

. . . some of them were just shaking
their head small small, small small. (p.158)

The man just begin to move the landrover
small small, small small. (p.159)

I begin cry small small, small small. (p.160)

They were all walking, walking, walking very very slow
because you can see that they are tired and have no
power again. (p.170)

One point that can be noticed readily is that each complex
reduplication has a comma separating the first pair from the
last one (where there are four items), as in:

... small small, small small.

Alternatively, there is a comma separating each item where
there is an additional dimension of complexity as in:

They were all walking, walking,
walking very very slow . . .

This could be compared to the simple reduplications, which
were, in all cases, entirely contiguous.[7]

Another point: in addition to suggesting some kind of emphasis or intensification, the complex reduplications have, in
some cases, tended to be onomatopoeic. For instance the cluster /s m/, which begins each item in the pairs, suggests extreme inaudibility arising from tiredness or a near-total exhaustion in the camp. They had to shake their heads "small
small, small small" to show that they were not yet dead! The

same can be said of Sozaboy, who, after being tied to a landrover and being dragged along rough roads, became exhausted. So, the exhaustion, the pains, and the afloat voice could be seen in onomatopoeic terms:

Crying small small, small small.

In the case of the landrover, however, the complex reduplication is apparently more suggestive of progression (the vehicle beginning slowly and going fast eventually), than onomatopoeia.

## V

We have used the term phono-graphological intrusions in this article to refer to the use of lexical items in a manner that suggests the user's inadequate acquaintance with the pronunciation of such items. As the term suggests, the items (words) are written following the character's pronunciation—usually unacceptable pronunciation—and not the usual spelling of the word. They are also said to be *intrusions* because they feature suddenly among other well formed words—words spelled following the usual conventions. Examples of such intrusions include:

(i)      sarzent (p.2p)
(ii)     gratulate (p.2)
(iii)    porson (pp.7,61, 135, etc.)
(iv)     whasmatter (p.7)
(v)      odah odah (p.8)
(vi)     awright (p.7,8)
(vii)    praps (pp.25,43)
(viii)   terprita (p.41)
(ix)     ammo (p.123)
(x)      Soza(s) (pp.27, 102, etc.)[8]

We shall briefly explain each entry, beginning from the top.

(i) The entry *sarzent* (sergeant) apparently stems from two main problems: the attempt to write the first syllable *ser* to reflect the usual pronunciation /sa:/ and the inability to realize the voice palato—alveolar affricate /dy/ hence a replacement of this by both /z/ and the clear vowel /e/—/sa:dyent/ as against [sa:zent-].

(ii) *Gratulate* (congratulate) has a simpler explanation: the character uttering this is likely to be one who has heard the appropriate pronunciation of this word very often and has noted that the first syllable *con-* in the full word *congratulation* in generally made unclear, being one that realizes an unclear vowel /e/ as in /ken/. Shortening the word therefore to "gratulate" implies rendering the first syllable so unclearly that it practically fails to exist!

(iii) The form *porson* (person) is a very close imitation of the pronunciation of the word *person*. As shown here, the first syllable constitutes the problem: instead of the central vowel /3:/ in that first syllable, the speaker apparently chooses the back rounded vowel / :/, resulting in /p :s n / as against the general acceptable realization / p3:sn/.

(iv) The next item *whasmatter* is clearly a contraction of four words into one—what is the matter—generally *what's the matter*. There is also a suggestion here of what could pass for an unsatisfactory rendering of the cluster /ts/ in *what's*, quite apart from the total elision of the specific modifier *the*. It is a good example of simplification in nonstandard English speech.

(v) *Odah Odah* (order) is indicative of two problems, the first with the realization of *or* and the second with *---er.* / :/ and /a/ is replaced with /a:/. / :/, as shown, is replaced with [o] and /a/ is replaced with /a:/. In this way, the two syllables are irreconcilable from the standpoint of accentuation.

(vi) The next entry *awright* is a contraction from two words: *all* and *right*. With the contraction, the liquid lateral /1/ is eluded, giving prominence to the back rounded vowel / :/.

(vii) The utterance *praps* is an example that is suggestive of an attempt to elude the schwa /e/ and to give prominence to the linking /r/ in the writing system. It is actually a very faithful imitation of the educated pronunciation of the word *perhaps* when it occurs in the company of other words. This utterance therefore is all right as an attempt to imitate the pronunciation on p.25. But on p.43, where the entry receives full prominence, *praps* features in a wrong context; in that situation the usual pronunciation (from the speech of edu-cated speakers) is /pa'haeps/ not [praeps].

(viii) The entry *terprita* (interpreter) appears to stem from the lack of prominence which is usually known to mark the realization of the first syllable in the word *interpreter*. How-ever, the last vowel in the word suggested a lower variety—indeed a very low variety—of /a/ generally shown as [ä] in place of the educated pronunciation, which regularly features /a/. Put differently, the entry *terprita* suggests two phono-graphological problems—an initial elision and a vowel alter-ation, the latter in particular being a marker of nonstandard pronunciation.

(ix) The item *ammo* (a short rendering for the word ammu-nition) represents also an attempt at simplification. The diffi-cult part of the word is where we normally notice the glide / mju:/; so, to avoid that environment, the speakers substitute the letter o which also has the sound suggested by it [o]. From the way it features in the novel the word is used by the charac-ters to refer to bullets, not general military wares. So, we can say the word suggests double simplification: pronunciation and reference.

(x) The item *Soza(s)* refers to soldier(s). Phonological prob-lem here is the replacement of the voiced palator-alveolar sound /d/ by the voiced alveolar fricative /z/, medially. From the general level of mediocre expressions in the novel, it is almost certain that the /a~/ in *sol-* is also replaced, this time by [o], thus leaving the word [soza: (s)] as against the educated pro-nunciation generally heard: /s od (z)/.

The above are only a few of the phono-graphological rep-resentations in the novel, representations which give very help-ful insights into the pronunciation problems of the characters portrayed. These representations also serve to complement the syntactic and general construction problems which con-stitute a major feature of *Sozaboy*.

# VI

Verbs are among the most interesting aspects of language use in *Sozaboy*. We can isolate at least four features. First, there is an attested inclination towards the use of many verbs in a single utterance. Put differently, the great majority of sentences in this novel are of various levels of complexity. Here are a few examples:

> (i) And if we see him, we should fight him and if he is too strong, we should return to tell the soza captain. (P.105)

> (ii) Like everything I want to do I must do it well well. (p.33)

> (iii) Then she will tell me that I am very fine man with plenty of hair for my chest and I am smiling very well all the time. (p.20)

> (iv) So Terr know my way and road to Dukana.

In the first illustration, we can isolate two main clauses and two subordinate clauses. The main clauses are:

> (i) We should fight him;
> (ii) We should return to tell the soza captain.

The subordinate clauses are:

> (i) (AND) if we *see* him,
> (ii) (and) if he is too strong.

Notice the implication here, that having four clauses presupposes that there must be four verbal groups too, implying that the sentence is a compound/complex one. Also, notice that each subordinate clause begins with a dumy conjunction—one that has little or no function, except perhaps to add to the verbosity of the expression! The second illustration is a complex sentence, having one main clause and one subordinate clause. The main clause is:

> I must do it well well.

The subordinate clause is

Like everything I want to do.

The third illustration is an example of a compound complex sentence, having two main clauses and one subordinate clause. The main clauses are

(i) (that) I a very fine man with plenty of hair for my chest;
(ii) (and) I am smiling very well all the time.

The subordinate clause is:

Then she will tell me.

The fourth illustration is the most complex, having three main clauses and two subordinate clauses. So, from the viewpoint of sentence structure, we can refer to this as an example of a multiple sentence. The main clauses are:

(i) (That) he will tell me...;
(ii) (As) i am good young man;
(iii) (and I) can know my way and road to Dukana.

The subordinate clauses are:

(i) So Terr Kole told me;
(ii) Because he likes me.

Since the great majority of sentences in this novel are of the complex type, we can agree with the views in Kachru (1982) and Labov (1973) that speakers of nonstandard English have usually tended to be verbose and to have an inclination towards complex sentences. From the above analysis into clauses, and from the structure of the verbal groups below, we will agree also with the latter (Labov) that in spite of the verbosity in the utterances and complexity of sentences, there is an appreciable system and logic in nonstandard English. After all, nonstandard, even rotten expressions in English, also serve certain communication purposes!

A second feature worthy of note is that there is an attested tendency to covert nouns or adjectives to verbs. The following are striking examples:

(i)        Prouding (from the adjective proud).

The following are attested.

(a)        Zaza and his *prouding* stupidity (p.38).
(b)        Myself I was *prouding* plenty (P.65)
(c)        And I was *prouding* plenty too (p.71)
(d)        And I was prouding of myself... (p.125).

(ii)        Confuse (d) (from the adjective confused).

Notice the following:

(a) Chief Birabee is *confusing* before this man... (p.39)
(b) And I *come confuse* proper (p.38)
(c) If not to say I am very old man in Pitakwa self I should *have confused* completely (p.52).
(d)I *begin to confuse* (p.34).

(iii) Shaming (from the noun shame).

Here are a few illustrations:

(a) ... because to talk true I was *shaming bad bad* (p.62).
(b) I was beginning *to shame,* (p.14).
(c) I must not show that I *shame pass woman* (p.14).

(iv) To glad (from the adjective glad).

Here is an instance:
Even, when I think that I will see Agnes again I begin *to glad* more than (p.35).

(v) Pregnanting from (pregnant).

Here is an example:

If that Sozaman have *pregnanted* my young darling (p.138).

As everyone knows, classes of grammatical elements in English cannot be determined until they (the elements) are actually used in sentences. Thus, we can have the word *back*, for instance as a noun, a verb, an adjective, or an adverb. What we have shown above is clearly different from this, however. Indeed the use of words like *prouding* and *to glad* and *pregnanting* shows that the characters involved are virtually illiterate ones as far as English is concerned.

A third feature of verbs in *Sozaboy* is the occurrence of either outright verbless constructions or those without main verbs. The following are a few of them:

> In the afternoon (p.44).
> In the night (p. 44).
> Even in dream (p.44).
> God in Heaven (p.33).
> e too (p.1).
> You stupid people of Dukana (p.39).
> Plenty blood and plenty shout (p.167).
> God, no more amo (p. 167).
> Now, my son, and you, my daughter (p.67).
> No trouble at all (.125).
> Making plenty of noise in the house (p.15)
> For work or anything at all (p. 38).

It should be remembered that verbless constructions can be quite elegant, stylistically, but when they occur in doubtful contexts as many of the ones above do, they tend to serve the negative function of obstructing communication.

Finally, notwithstanding the problems indicated here, the structure of the verbal groups in *Sozaboy* is hardly different from the structure of verbal groups in any educated variety of English. For instance, we can single out simple verbal groups (those with only one entry), each serving as head (h). Examples of this include:

(a) She *paid* the money (h) (p.68)
(b) The Soza captain body *was* in the bottom of the boat (h) (p.108).

We can also isolate complex verbal groups—those (each) with an auxiliary and a main verb. Here "x" represents the auxiliary while "h" represents the head or the main verb. Examples:

(a) ... they *have followed* the sozas ... (xh)(pp.140-141).
(b) They *were laughing* ... (xh) (p.46).

Again, we have seen instances of compound verbal groups, groups with two or more heads functioning contiguously or conjunctival. Examples:

(a) ... in their house *eating* and *drinking* and *sleeping* and *fucking* ... (h + h + h + h)—conjunctive compound verbal group (p.140).
(b) I just ... *stand* (still), *chop, piss, shit* (h h h h)—contiguous compound verbal group (p.114).

There are also instances of compound complex verbal groups, those with a *minimum* of an auxiliary and two heads. Examples:

(a) The sozas were *walking, prouding, asking* for the chief (xh h h)—contiguous compound complex verbal group (p.38).
(b) I *will* (just) *run* and *run* and *run* and *run* and *run* (xh + h + h + h + h)—conjunctive compound complex verbal group (p.181).
(c) "... this Chief Birabee *will be shouting* and *prouding* and *bullying* on him". (x h + h + h)—conjunctive compound complex verbal group (p.39).

# VII

We have shown in this article that language use in *Sozaboy* belongs to a peculiar class, one that appears to have drawn beneficial influences from the non-standard variety of Nigerian English, English-based pidgin, and the mother tongue of the characters involved. In particular we have drawn attention to expressions which defy classification, those which introduce unusual dimensions such as reduplication, and those which demonstrate pronunciation not acceptable to the native speaker or the nonnative speaker properly educated in the language. Also, we have shown that in spite of the apparent disharmony in the operations, underlying structural patterns (such as the structure of the verbal group), share consoling similarities with the educated and even the sophisticated varieties. What remains to add is that studies on this novel are only just starting: a novel with a specific character which says:

> "I am prouding plenty"
> "So I kept quiet with several people shouting little shouts inside my head from the policeman's stick's blow"

and on other occasions asserts:

> "Oh, I was very happy and very proud." After that, "I said goodbye to them and went away"

certainly deserves many rounds of investigation.

## Notes

1. Readers interested in finding out more about nonstandard Nigerian English and indeed the other varieties (sophisticated, educated, basic etc.) can consult any of the following sources: Brosnahan 1958; Banjo 1971; Jibril 1979; Adesanoye 1980; Eka 1987.
2. Phonotactics deals with the combinatorial possibilities and restrictions in English. For instance, *was* is an actual English word: "wood" is a potential English word because the rules of sound combination do not stop the word from existing; but "wpoob" is an impossible one, for English does not have the initial consonant combination "wp."
3. All page references are to 1986 (reprinted) edition of Saro-Wiwa's *Sozaboy*.
4. In the general context of the novel, this cannot be seen in the same light as "everyone are wanted outside," for instance.

5. We should not be understood to be saying that reduplication occurs only in the English used in *Sozaboy*. Indeed, I have heard it on many occasions among people who are barely educated in English. I have actually heard expressions like:
"The car moved softly softly"
"We should know that one day one day we all must die"
"The center forward player came closer closer"
6. More information on intensifiers/emphasizes may be read in Eka 1994:131-139.
7. We have used the word "entirely" to draw attention to the fact that even with the case of complex reduplication, the patterning is still technically contiguous.
8. For further information on phono-graphological problems, see Folarin 1975.

# Works Cited

Adesanoye, F. "Patterns of Deviation in Written English in Nigeria." *Journal of Language Arts and Communication* 1, 1; (1980):53-65.

Banjo, A. "Towards a Definition of Standard Nigerian Spoken English." *Annales de University d'Abidjan* (1971):24-28.

Brosnahan, L. "English in Southern Nigeria." *English Studies* 3; (1958):97-110.

Eka, D. "The Phonology of Nigerian English." In: A. E. Odumuch ed., *Nigerian English: Selected Essays.* Zaria: Ahmadu Bello University Press, 1987: 37-57.

Eka, D. "The phonological Study of Standard Nigerian English." Unpublished Ph.D. dissertation, Ahmadu Bello University, Zaria, 1985.

Eka, D. *Elements of Grammar and Mechanics of English Language.* Uyo: Sammuf Educational Publishers, 1994.

Folarin, B. "Phono-graphological Problems in Student English." *Journal of the Nigeria English Studies Association* 7,1/2 (1975):51-60.

Jibril, M. "Regional Variation in Nigerian English." In: Ebo Ubanhakwe, ed., *Varieties and Functions of English in Nigeria.* Ibadan: University Press, 1979:43-53.

Kachru, B. B. "Models for Nonnative Englishes." *In:* B. B. Kachru ed., *The Other Tongue: English Across Culture.* Chicago: University of Illinois Press, 1992: 31-37.

Labov, Willia. "The Logic of Nonstandard English." *In:* Richard W. Bailey and Jay L. Robinson eds., *Varieties of Present Day English.* London: Macmillan Publishers, 1973:319-355.

Platt, John, Heidi Weber, and Ho Lian. *The New English;* London: Routledge and Kegan Paul, 1984.

Saro-Wiwa, Ken. *Sozaboy: A Novel in Rotten English.* Port Harcourt: Saro's International Publishers, 1986

Strevens, Peter. "The Localized Forms of English. *In:* B. B. Kachru, ed., *The Other Tongue: English Across Cultures.* Chicago: University of Illinois Press 1982: 23-30.

# 8

# A Metaphor of the Nigerian Situation:
## A Socio-Political Situation: A Reading of Ken Saro-Wiwa's *Prisoner of Jebs*

### Francis Unimna Angrey

I

Martyred on November 10, 1995, Ken Saro-Wiwa has been described in various ways by various people. To some he was an environmentalist who sacrificed his time and energy for the preservation of his native Ogoni land, devastated and ravaged by the activities of oil companies that have been operating there over the years. He always complained about the fact that his people did not benefit much from the rich resources with which their land is endowed.

He saw the injustices his people suffer. He saw that while his people got impoverished and waded through misery and disenchantment, the rich endowments of his native land went to other lands; they went to the insatiable people from other parts of the country and of the world who connived at getting the native Ogonis polarized and benighted even in their own steads.

To many other people, Ken Saro-Wiwa was a writer, a social critic, a commentator on national issues, a satirist, a humorist, a dramatist who made his long pipe and his often sardonic laughter his trademarks. The fecundity of his pen and the themes of his writings that traverse prose, drama, poetry, and journalism are not in doubt. His books, which include *On a Darkling Plain, Sozaboy: A Novel in Rotten English, A Forest of Flowers, Basi and Company: A Modern African Folk-tale,* among others, can attest to that.

*Prisoners of Jebs* is one book which can be said to belong to the Voltairian or to the Diderotesque genre of the French eighteenth century known as the Age of Enlightenment. The main feature of this era is the love for ideas, the quest for truth and liberty. More than this, the writers of this period are guided by an ideal of humanism. Writers do not concern themselves with the beauty of the language in which they write. L. Gazamian posits:

> The new period bears the distinctive mark of a national tendency, so outstanding that few ages of literature can be so safely classified under one label. With most writers of the time beauty was not the primary object, it became as it were the by-product of an energy that spent itself in the eager pursuit of truth. (1953:126)

Writers of this period in France had the ambition of reaching out to the majority of the French populace through their writings. But the French people were not yet as enlightened as they are now. It was thought they would not be able to read complicated and long novels. It was, therefore, proper that to reach out to such an illiterate populace, a language that they might understand and a style that they might comprehend had to be used.

Most of these memorable works that have created everlasting impact on the French people and indeed on mankind are letters, collections of essays, and newspaper articles that are steeped in irony, satire, and allegory. Such collections of letters and essays as *Voltaire's Lettres Philosophiques, Dictionnaire Philosophique, Montesquieu's Lettres Persanes, Diderot's Oeuvres Philosophiques* and other masterpieces of the period were written with a view to reforming the French society, which suffered from the excesses of the "ancient regime," and the nobility, from religious intolerance whose trumpcard was inquisition, and from the despotism and highhandedness of the king. In their writings, they use a style that does not tell them from the people in power who might misjudge them and their intentions. It is this kind of style that Ken Saro-Wiwa has employed in *Prisoners of Jebs*, a collection of newspaper articles that he wrote in 1986 for the *Vanguard* Newspapers. The tone is not only satirical and sardonic, it is also humanistic, trenchant, and caustic. This paper aims at looking, with a critical eye, at the way Saro-Wiwa succeeds in delivering his message without stepping on the toes of those in power in his country, Nigeria.

## II

The setting for the fifty-three stories in Ken Saro-Wiwa's book, which forms the basis for our short study, is Jebs. The activities described therein are those of the people who make up the Jebsian society. Jebs is, in the eyes of the author, one huge prison yard where all the inhabitants are prisoners.

Jebs, the fictional prison yard of the author, was born after heads of state of the African continent met at one of their OAU summits and decided to create a common place where all African prisoners could be lumped together and made to study African problems with a view to finding solutions to them. It is reasoned that it is only through this rather obnoxious way that progress and development could be achieved on the African continent.

Although many African nations welcome this proposal to set up a common prison yard for their citizens, they are not ready to provide a place where this all-important dream could be actualized; they all seem to abdicate their responsibility to their fellow countries. Thus, Nigeria accepts to offer a solution to this problem. To the author, it is not surprising that Nigeria decides to play host to the Jebs experiment. Nigeria is a ready place for that because it can boast a large number of prisoners of different descriptions. Ken Saro-Wiwa gives reasons:

A location for the prison was not difficult to find. Nigeria, the continent's most populous nation, was overflowing with prisoners from the "ancient regime".(POJ1)

Ken Saro-Wiwa's book is relevant both in time and space. The "ancien regime" he talks about here is the Second Republic government headed by Shehu Shagari, the first ever elected executive president of the federation of Nigeria. In 1983, that government was overthrown by the military under the guise that it was corrupt. Most of the major actors on the political scene at the time were jailed for various terms of imprisonment. Some of the trials were quite genuine, while others were mundane, burlesque, and childish; hence the country was "overflowing with prisoners."

Besides all this, Nigerians themselves have opted to live like prisoners, even in their personal homes. They tend to live in fear, a fear that is harbored in the inner recesses of their mind. Their houses are always under lock and key. Owners of these houses always build tall fences round them to protect them from lurking armed robbers, and from enemies both real and imagined. Nigeria, like Jebs, the fictional prison yard of Ken Saro-Wiwa, is one large prison. By extension, every Nigerian living under the conditions described above is a prisoner, hence the Nigerian does not care whether Jebs prison is established in his territory or not. The author explains further:

> Did not citizens in the cities barricade their houses to protect themselves from robbers and assassins? Did not citizens put gates on streets and lock them at night? Nigeria was a veritable prison, although the prisoners, sorry, citizens did not know it, and did not indeed care. So, the addition of an elite African prison would not make a difference to the Nigerians. (POJ 1).

The author goes a step further to talk about the docility that characterizes the national ethos of the Nigerian people. To him, Nigerians have been suffering all types of indignities at the hands of the adventurers in power because they hardly fight for even what they consider their inalienable rights. He portrays Nigerians as people who fold their arms and wait for divine intervention. It is this invisible force that they tend to await that can change their fortunes for them. Such inexplicable docility has, over the years, been paving a smooth way for all types of rulers who come to power not to serve the society but their own constituencies and to maintain their hegemony. This is how he describes Nigerians:

> The Nigerians do not normally ask questions about anything. Things just happen. It is taken for granted that things will happen. So a bloke just strolls to the radio station and says, "Hello, brothers. I'm now your new Head of State." (POJ 2)

Ken Saro-Wiwa's portrayal of the Nigerian citizens shows that they are in no way different from the slaves from Africa who came back to Africa as recaptive thinkers. Basil Davidson describes them in his book, *The Black Man's Burden*, as people who believed that their problems could only be solved through Christianity and constitution shaped for them by the western lords. These recaptive thinkers did not see themselves as capable of finding solutions their own way. Davidson describes them thus:

> With christianity and constitution as their watchwords, the recaptive thinkers held that Africa needed to be saved, and salvation come from outside the continent. (1993:27)

It is this kind of slavish attitude, which inhibits creativity and dwarfs the mind, that Saro-Wiwa condemns in his fellow Nigerian citizens. Saro-Wiwa would want to see a Nigerian people that do not slavishly accept subjugation of their mind and suppression of their thoughts by a few gangsters who are fond of seizing power and of imposing themselves on the docile and meek-minded populace. He wants Nigerians to assert themselves as a people who know what they want and who know how to go for what they want.

99

# III

In the wake of the tight-fisted Buhari/Idiagbon regime that ousted the largely corrupt civilian government headed by Shehu Shagari on December 31, 1983, hospitals and other medical institutions in Nigeria were described as "mere consulting clinics." The military men, who had just seized political power from a democratically elected government, were irredeemably appalled by the degeneracy which had attended such health institutions.

Drugs were in short supply where they were supplied at all. Pieces of equipment that were to be used by medical personnel were non-existent. Where they existed at all they were just obsolete or they had deteriorated beyond redemption. If the situation in the country's health sector had been so bad it was not necessarily because the country lacked the required resources to adequately cater for the hospitals and other health institutions.

The many problems of the nation came out of sheer neglect of the entire socio-political system in which both the civilian leaders and their military counterparts, more often than not, ran out of ideas as to what they should do with the numerous resources with which the country is endowed. In most cases, as in the past, the country was a rudderless ship whose moors were broken and was allowed to sink in the high seas as no one took care of it. In this state, it sank into a moral miasma. This is the state which the country is today.

In this book, Ken Saro-Wiwa shows Jebs, a representation of Nigeria, as a country whose numerous resources are not being used for the benefit of its citizens. He regrets the fact that the many endowments of the country, in terms of material and human resources, are not adequately exploited and used for the overall development of the beleaguered nation. He draws a parallel between Nigeria and some countries of the Persian Gulf which have achieved a lot in terms of development in the areas of education, health, industry, and the betterment of the citizens' lot. He laments:

> Nigeria had squandered her wealth and made herself the laughing-stock of the world. Of all the countries

who had black gold, Nigeria was the only one that had succeeded in doing absolutely nothing with it. The Arabs used their oil very well indeed; not only had they given their people education and a lot else that conduced to good living, they also had invested their money in Europe and America. (POJ 11)

The author shows that the accomplishments of the Arabs with their petrodollars are not done in Nigeria not because the Nigerian nation lacks the means or ability to do them. The problem is basically embedded in the leaders' inability and inefficiency in the running of the affairs in the socio-political sphere. Budgets mapped out for the country on a yearly basis are hardly adhered to. Public services are neglected and left to rot away as this state of affairs benefited leaders who kept lining their pockets and numerous bank accounts at home and abroad. He extrapolates that Jebs, in this case Nigeria, is a pot of corruption and profligacy. It is a country where, unfortunately, millions of the local currency and foreign currencies disappear into thin air without any one in particular taking responsibility, even remotely, for such disappearances. In Nigeria, government is considered a faceless, nameless, and impersonal individual. T. M. Aluko shares this view in his novel, *Kinsmen and Foremen*:

> . . . He was not very much worried about this because he knew that the society in which his father lived and died did not consider any acts of dishonesty against government wrong. Government was an impersonal organization not endowed with the sense of feeling and was, therefore, incapable of feeling any crimes committed against it and any wrongs done to it. (1966:132)

In *Jebs*, Saro-Wiwa tries to show the manner in which millions disappear. To him, leaders of the Nigerian nation devise various means, some of them unorthodox, to empty the national treasury to the detriment of the country's populace. One of such methods is through the award of bogus and fictitious contracts which are never seen to be executed even when a lot of money has been paid for such. In most cases, nothing whatsoever is done to arrest the ugly trend. It is rather a paradox that those who succeed in milking the cow (Nigeria) are looked upon as honest men and heroes.

> I am afraid there is nothing I can do. Because in their country, assisting the millions to disappear is no crime. The men and women who aid this magical act are regarded as heroes of their revolution. (POJ 22)

More than this, those in power contrive to detract the attention of citizens from the main issue of development. There is the deliberate action of government that citizens should be kept busy debating issues that are of no relevance to the progress and development of the country. By so doing, the citizenry is given that wrong impression that it is participating actively in the running of the affairs of the nation. What actually happens is that while the citizens are kept busy debating irrelevancies, the leaders revel in squandermania and profligacy. This type of governance, which Ken Saro-wiwa decries in *Prisoners of Jebs*, is reminiscent of the Babangida regime known for its seeming serendipity and its apparent inscrutability. In the early days of this regime, there was a nationwide debate on the IMF loan in which experts and non-experts took part. Although a cross section of the Nigerian society opposed an IMF loan at that time, the government went ahead to collect the loan under different guises. This is how Saro-Wiwa reports this debate in *Prisoners of Jebs*:

> .. but you must understand that the times are difficult. Our millions have disappeared, we are tightening our belts. We are looking for money to borrow, so we can give our citizens food. In the meantime, we keep them debating loans, politics, religion and foreign affairs. (POJ 24)

Ken Saro-Wiwa goes further to show that it is only bad governments, of which Nigeria has had its own fair share, that use the means of debate as a stratagem to keep their citizens away from the realities of hunger, starvation, malnutrition, undernourishment, corruption and all its facets, squandermania and profligacy that stare them in the face.

## IV

When one reads Ken Saro-Wiwa's writings one may be tempted to conclude that these are not serious. One might even be led to conclude that the writer engages wholeheartedly in "art for art's sake." But a close look at his writings shows that Ken Saro-Wiwa's penchant is concerned with the denunciation of the ills of his society. He brings out what he perceives as the persistent malaise of Nigerian life: bribery, corruption, graft, inefficiency of public utilities, profligacy, ostentatious living, a harsh intolerable socio-political system, tribal jingoism and nepotistic attitudes of the country's leadership. Saro-Wiwa does not, thus, write for writing sake. He writes with a view to teaching lessons that will help to reshape the destiny of the nation. William Boyd, an English novelist and Ken's friend for many years, is of the opinion that Saro-Wiwa's writings, especially *Prisoners of Jebs*, are funny and wincingly accurate, but this does not stop them being unashamedly pedagogic and didactic.

Saro-Wiwa lived and died as a voice that spoke for the helpless and hapless citizens. He was an indefatigable fighter who was well known for his activism in the Nigerian social milieu. He saw literature as an efficacious weapon which a writer must use to advance the cause of his people. He lived steeped in the belief that literature should not and cannot be divorced from politics because the two of them are inextricably bound to each other. Hence he did not just pontificate or deliver social sermons from his books; he took active part, in the Sartrean sense, in the liberation of his people. He expatiates upon this belief thus:

> . . . it being my credo that literature in a critical situation such as Nigeria's cannot be divorced from politics. Indeed, literature must serve society by steeping itself in politics, by intervention, and writers must not merely write to amuse or to take a bemused, critical look at society. They must play an interventionist role. (1995:81)

In spite of this important role that the writer in underde-
veloped societies such as Nigeria's ought to play in the amelio-
ration of the human condition, he is often looked upon as a
"bush-toad" that is tracked down and often eliminated like a
common criminal by the government. The writer is a target of
all types of attack, especially in a country like Nigeria where
unpopular regimes have been succeeding one another. For
Saro-Wiwa these developments should not daunt the writer,
who should rather learn to be *'l'homme engage*, the intellectual
man of action" (1995: 81).

True to his ideal of ENGAGEMENT, *Prisoners of Jebs* is a
fine book that depicts contemporary Nigeria in all spheres of
social and political life. Although the stories contained therein
are hilarious and rib-cracking, they are embedded in caustic
and acerbic criticism of the social, moral, and political spheres
of the people of Nigeria, especially those who find themselves
in positions of authority. The book spares no one in particular
as it takes a swipe at all those persons and all those events in
the country which have not helped the society to grow and
progress.

In his writings, Ken Saro-Wiwa does not intend to make a
caricature of the Nigerian socio-political system. The caricature, he seems to point out, is already inherent in the corrupt
and corrupting system where everything seems to have
crumbled. Even the educational system, which is supposed to
produce sound men and women that society can rely upon,
produces men and women who cannot think. This, in Ken's
account, is dangerous for a society that thinks of attaining enviable height in the spheres of development and progress at
the dawn of a new millennium. The system produces only mimic
men:

> The worst sin on earth is the failure to think. It is
> thoughtlessness that has reduced Africa to beggardom,
> to famine, poverty and disease. The failure to use the
> creative imagination has reduced Africans to the status
> of mimic men and consumers of the product of others'
> imagination. (POJ 58-59).

Ken's style of writing follows the Molieresque injunction that a writer should not only write to entertain the reader. He should also teach by laying bare the vices of the larger society in his writings. That is what Ken Saro-Wiwa has tried to do in his *Prisoners of Jebs*.

## V

There is no doubt that Ken Saro-Wiwa's fiction, plays, and even poems represent one of Nigeria's most powerful literary critiques of the contemporary Nigerian society. In an effective manner, he employs humor, sarcasm, and irony to lay bare the malfeasances of a corrupt system embedded in injustice, exploitation of the weak by the strong, lack of fair play. These literary devices, as employed by Ken, are not gratuitously used. In a society where everyone is insane, where men of great intelligence and artistic sensibility are condemned by circumstances to live in a more or less foolish and philistine social environment such as Nigeria, great writers are often misunderstood. These writers generally hide behind such literary devices to hide or becloud their intentions. James Reeves defines irony, one of these devices, as

> the weapon of the intelligent obliged to associate with the foolish and the barbarous. It enables him to maintain his own private standards while appearing to conform to those of society. It enables him to criticize without his being apparent to those he does not wish to offend. (1956:42)

The humor so embedded in *Prisoners of Jebs* is not created from nothing by the writer. It docs not spring from any deeply satirical motive on the part of Ken. It springs from the incongruities and absurdities not only of the lives of the ordinary citizens but also of the wrong-doings of those in whose hands the leadership of the country is entrusted.

In this paper we have tried, through a socio-political reading of *Prisoners of Jebs*, to show that Jebs is a metaphor of Nigeria. Ken Saro-Wiwa shows the ills that have plagued the Nigerian society over the years with a view to moralizing, in the

Prevostian tradition, the society to which he belongs. In his book, we have shown how he denounces the prevalent spate of corruption, financial imprudence, and profligacy that keeps bedeviling the Nigerian society and retarding her progress.

Ken Saro-Wiwa lived ahead of his time. Perhaps this explains why he was grossly misunderstood and found fit only for the gallows.

# Works Cited

Cazamian, L. *A History of French Literature*. Ibadan: Oxford University Press, 1953: 126.

Davidson, Basil, T*he Black Man's Burden: Africa and the Curse of the Nation-State*. Ibadan: Spectrum Book, 1993: 2.

Fellows, O. E. and Torrey, N. L., eds., *The Age of Enlightenment: An Anthology of Eighteenth-Century French Literature*. Englewood Cliffs, New Jersey: Prentice Hall, 1971.

Lagarde, A. and Michard, L. *XVIIIe siecle: les grands auteurs francais du programme*. Paris: Bordas, 1985.

Reeves, James, *The Critical Sense*. London: Heinemann, 1956.

Rice, P. and Waugh, P., eds. *Modern Literary Theory*. England: Edward Arnold, 1993.

Saro-Wiwa, Ken. *Prisoners of Jeb*. Port Harcourt: Saros Publisher, 1988.

_____. *A Month and a Day: A Detention Diary*. London: Penguin Books, 1995.

Taylor, R., ed. *Background Lectures in English Literature*. Benin: Ethiope Publishing Corporation, 1977.

Udenta O. Udenta, *Revolutionary Aesthetics and the African Literary Process*. Enugu: FDP, 1993.

Wellek, R. and Warren, A. *La theorie litteraire*. Paris: Editions du Seuil, 1971.

# 9

# On a Darkling Plain:
## The Darksome Lyric of an Outsider

### Azubike Iloeje

*It is a matter of guess work whose fault it is that we do not understand one another; for we do not understand them any more than they do us. By the same reasoning, they may consider us beasts as we also consider them.*

—Michel de Montaigne.
*Apology for Raimond Sebond"*

An enormous volume of writing—fictional, dramatic and non-fictional—has been the literary harvest from the carnage that engulfed Nigeria between 1966 and 1970. No title has captured and symbolized the disorientation and despair of both mind and system of that time as Wole Soyinka's *Season of Anomy* (1973). In it the author interrogates in order to affirm within the humanistic idiom, what Olalere Oladitan (1979:14) has described as the place of "ideology and violence in a revolutionary transformation of society." Yet no text calls attention to itself on account of its use of bold pictorial and adversarial language as does Ken Saro-Wiwa's *On A Darkling Plain: An Account of the Nigerian Civil War (1990)*. Its epigraph, from Matthew Arnold's "Dover Beach," pictures a contingency of chaos, of "confused alarms" as "ignorant armies" engage themselves on "a darkly plain." It images Saro-Wiwa's possible conviction that ignorance was an attribute of both sides in the conflict. Also it figures the desperate fate of a country which, in just six short years, had plummeted from the highest peaks of optimism and radiant hope to the soundest depths of distress, hysteria, mass slaughter, generalized fear, and a bloody fratricidal war. It would appear that nothing yet written on that Nigerian crisis captures and illustrates as vividly—in the programmatic tempo of the narrated events and the capriciousness of the narrative voice—the fury of that treacherous hour as what Saro-Wiwa himself calls "my civil war diary," (*A Month and Day, 50*)

*On A Darkling Plain*, as a contribution to the political discourse on the meaning and de-meaning of Nigeria, promises to be Saro-Wiwa's most remembered work. It followed on the heels of his pamphlet, *The Ogoni Nationality: Today and Tomorrow,* which was written in 1965 but was not issued until 1968, in the heat of the Civil War in Nigeria (*A Month and Day, 49*). As a writer, Saro-Wiwa could truly be described as a product of that war. Fortunes and misfortunes as made determinate by that contest in arms seem to have made him see clearly, act clearly, and record clearly. In addition they induced him to assume the role and functions of a political thinker and functionary, writer and social leader. His profounder imaginative works, *Songs in a Time of War* (1985), *Sozaboy: A Novel in Rotten English* (1985), and *Prisoners of Jebs* (1988)—are a continuation of his own pattern of discourse—remarking on the significance of that era of our turbulence, and the kind of nation it has bequeathed to its survivors and their offspring. But nothing in his whole corpus is as important to the author, perhaps in being a true rendering of the workings of his refractory political/social soul, as *On A Darkling Plain (A Month and Day, 59*).

It is the premise of this essay that the significance of *On A Darkling Plain* can be grasped only if it is understood that he was an outsider constantly in search of an alternative context that would convert him into an insider. It is also the position of this endeavor that this mode of aspiring which defined Saro-

Wiwa and his cause would arrive at little vindication and triumph because, like each of the ignorant armies in Arnold's "Dover Beach," Saro-Wiwa did not fully comprehend the issues and forces in contention within and about Nigeria. His opponents—he would think of them more as antagonists—also did not fully understand the capacity, depth, and orientation of Saro-Wiwa's mind. Whether, with regards to the political discourse on ourselves as a nation, the phenomenon of Ken Saro-Wiwa has done much more than accentuate the discordance in our multivocality is, perhaps, too soon to estimate.

*On A Darkling Plain* was conceived during the Civil War and written within three years of its end (*A Month and Day*, 59). By his own admission Saro-Wiwa "delayed its publication in deference to the process of reconciliation in Eastern Nigeria, it being strong in it views" (*On A Darkling Plain*, 9). It is to be stated that the seventeen-year waiting period did not significantly abate or moderate the vehemence and trenchance of Saro-Wiwa's views and the bitterness that fashioned and fed those views. This is in spite of the spirit of forgiveness which he admits was awakened in him by the visit of Zik to Port Harcourt in 1969 and Zik's soulful apology for the perceived misdeeds of the Igbo with regard to their neighbors in Eastern Nigeria (*On A Darkling Plain*, 219). Nor did any real consideration for reconciliation deter him. Nor indeed did the recognition that since sharply differentiated views were held across the combat divide, his derisive expression of his brusque views about people and events would inevitably elicit from his opponents their own truculent articulation of their own views of Saro-Wiwa and his postures, it being a fact of our lives that "views are like goat skin bags and everybody carries his own." The meaning for the well-being of a fragile polyethnic country if in peace time vulgar views about any component ethnic group(s) are generally and vigorously expressed; if the culture of invective and insult is elevated to the status of etiquette in our national discourse on issues of ethnicity, ideology and religion would not, and did not, press much on Ken Saro-Wiwa. This could be because he was psychologically an outsider in the quest—it has turned out to be a tortuous one for Nigeria—for a functional cohesive, and interactive but still polyethnic state in the sense Elman Service (in Cohen and Service 1978: 28) would mean when he speaks of the state as "the supreme integrative apparatus above the level of kinship [and ethnic] institutions." In many ways *On A Darkling Plain* is a defiant document of protest against the impulsion, in Nigeria, towards an integrative multi-ethnic nation state.

*On A Darkling Plain* is, in a significant way, a political autobiography; it is the texting by the *self* of its own encounter with the defining social circumstances. It narrates the trajectory of the author's own making in the fire and anvil of what would also make post-civil war Nigeria. It probably has also not escaped the narcissistic alignment of the autobiography as a genre, what Sesan Ajayi in his review of Doreen Irvine's *From Witchcraft to Christ* (1991:B5) has described as the drive in the autobiographical narrator to "capture his own doings by setting out the contours of experience in agreeable and revised manners as deemed fit." Fyodor Dostoevsky records this urge very sensitively in his short story "The Peasant Marey":

> These memories rose up of themselves, it was not often that of my own will I summoned them. It could begin from some point, some little thing, at times unnoticed, and then by degrees there would rise up a complete picture, some vivid and complete impression. I used to analyze these impressions, give new features to what had happened long ago, and best of all, I used to correct it, correct it continually, that was my great amusement.

The imaginative re-shaping, revising of experienced event(s) now recollected in keeping with the dictates of the current time provides a tendentious aspect to the autobiography, making the responses as recorded rather suspect as honest renderings of the responses elicited by the experienced event(s) at the moments and places of those experiences. Conscious self-promotion, the drive for contemporary self-relevance could become then a major motivation of the autobiography. We can now only speculate on whether Ken Saro-Wiwa's account, *apropos* himself, of the Nigerian Civil War would be *On A Dar-*

Azubike Iloeje

*kling Plain* if the war ended in victory for secession and the
state of Biafra became a respected member of the international
community.

Like fellow citizens of Nigeria, Saro-Wiwa was an outsider
at the historical point of the conception and inauguration of
Nigeria as a nation-state. Ours was not the result of a self-
initiated movement of the component ethnic and clan units
towards national coalescence, the kind that Kendal (1968:376)
has in mind when, in relation to the ideas of Hobbes, Locke,
and Rousseau, he speaks of "a freely negotiated contract among
men in the act of emerging from the state of nature." Nigeria
was the product of external imperialist conquest and the consequent entrapment and conscription of the component ethnic units and individuals into the provenance of common territorial administration and jurisdiction. The Nigerian Civil War
is the most convulsive moment yet in the still on-going post-
colonial trauma of Nigeria. Nigeria's history since amalgam-
ation in 1914 has been a constant testing of the basis, foundation, and suppositions of that historic British corralling of subject peoples into what was christened Nigeria. It has been a
persistent interrogation of the paradox of an ethnically plu-
ralistic state made and sanctified, for its own purposes, by an
otherwise ideologically repugnant colonial conquest; a seemingly unending sounding out, in Lincoln's phrasing, of "whether
[a] nation so conceived and so dedicated, can long endure."
This interrogation, arguably, was the fundamental of the
Biafran venture and also of Ken Saro-Wiwa's repudiation of
that enterprise.

Ken Saro-Wiwa's relative *outsider-ness* within the framework of the ethnic tapestry in Nigeria derived from his not
belonging to any of the three largest and therefore—(in accordance with the equation of social and political influence and
attendant privilege, patronage, and preferment) the most powerful ethnic groups in Nigeria: the Igbo, the Hausa, and the
Yoruba. The "minority" identity became for him the most ur-
gent, the most cogent identity index. He was convinced that
the operations of what he calls "indigenous colonialism" of the
members of three ethnic groups over the minority groups and
the competition between the majority ethnic groups them-

111

selves, were the bane of the Nigerian state. Within the regional landscape of erstwhile Eastern Nigeria, Saro-Wiwa was non-Igbo in a region in which the Igbo as an ethnic group possessed a commanding numerical strength, non-Igbos accounting by Saro-Wiwa's own reckoning to only "about thirty-five per cent of the total population." Beyond such supercilious comments as the Igbo having "over the years learnt to live symbiotically on their neighbors" (53); beyond Saro-Wiwa's rueful recollection of the taunts he bore in boyhood from unread Igbo cooks and traders as he got educated at an elite Government Secondary School where, Ogoni though he was, he was admitted on merit, there is no evidence provided in *On A Darkling Plain* of blatant pre-1967 cynical use of Igbo massive political power to the detriment of the Ogoni or any other Eastern minority group.

What we have in the memoir is an insistent expression of awe at the sheer number of the Igbo. It was a kind of fear that was so overwhelming, so palpable that it has provided the only looking glass through which Saro-Wiwa saw and has assailed the Igbo and later the Ijaw who within the administrative unit of Rivers State, also came to out-number others among which were counted the Ogoni. Ken Saro-Wiwa was repeatedly hard put to explain the considerable support for the Biafran cause even among many ethnic minorities of the East. He would simply wish to revile those of them who stood firm with Biafra as mere "stooges and quislings" (55). The optimism with which May 1967 the resolution to pull the East out of Nigeria was greeted even in Bori, Ogoniland, is only plaintively conceded (81).

> There was general jubilation when the next day, Saturday, the Assembly voted for secession. Ripples of such jubilation seeped into even sleepy little town of Bori.

Ken Saro-Wiwa was a member of the nascent Rivers State government which had to confront, upon the Federal conquest of Port Harcourt in 1968, a variant of the problem which Ukpabi Asika had on his own earlier arrival at desolate Enugu to assume his duties as Administrator of East Central State: the problem of administering a de-peopled territory. By Saro-Wiwa's own account (227),

> There was a general insecurity [in Port Harcourt] . . .
> Equally distablising was the fact that most people in
> the state were still in the rebel-area. These consisted
> of most of the trained manpower in the state who should
> have assisted in establishing the bureaucracy.

If, one would ask, Biafra was nothing more than an odious move to ensure their own perpetual captivity, why did most of the professionals, intelligentsia, and bureaucrats of the new and alternative Rivers State stick with Biafra to the end? Why was their boycott of Rivers State as thorough and profound as Saro-Wiwa has recorded? His explanation offered on pages 87-89 of *On A Darkling Plain* imputes considerable little-mindedness to his own people. This is stated more brusquely in *A Month and a Day* (51) *apropos* his Ogoni kinsmen:

> The mentality of the educated Ogoni was always to keep
> close to the government in order to pick up crumbs
> from the master's table. Accordingly, although Ojukwu's
> rebel Biafran government was hostile to the Ogoni as a
> people, the educated few yet found pickings by grovel-
> ling at the feet of the administration.

Little concession is made here to cultivated and discerning minds being able to respond rationally to an epoch-making historical event in accordance with reasoned self- and group-interest.

As a member of the Rivers State Cabinet, Saro-Wiwa was repeatedly at the battle front with elements of the federal army operating in that state. In spite of his considerable stature in government, he would acknowledge himself as no more than "an observer" (*Darkling Plain*, 9), an outsider in the formulation of the policies and issues of procedure which governed the activities of the Federal Government during the military pacification of Biafra. Even with regards to the government of Rivers State itself, his relationship with the Secretary to the

Government would be "decidedly sour" and he would be "not entirely at peace with the Military Governor and his style of governance" (*On A Darkling Plain*, 206).

It became inevitable that Saro-Wiwa's positions and attitudes were often at variance, both during and after combat, with those of the Federal Government and its agents in the effort to restore to some wholeness the broken fabrics of Nigeria as a pluralist but interactive nation-state. One incident is particularly indicative. Joseph Tarka, "an experienced politician" and "well-known as champion of minority rights" (212) and the Federal Commissioner (Minister) for Transport, was paying an official visit during the war to Rivers State. Saro-Wiwa sardonically recalls Tarka telling him "matter of factly that once the war ended and there was a return to party politics, politicians of whatever persuasion would rely more on the Ibos than on Rivers people" (*A Darkling Plain:* 211). Predictably, this sorely rankled Saro-Wiwa:—"needless to say, I did not like that" (212).

Joseph Tarka, himself a spokesman for the Northern minority Tiv ethnic group, was conducting, even prior to the cessation of hostilities, a pattern of discourse on post-war Nigeria from which Saro-Wiwa was fundamentally alienated. He was psychologically unequipped to comprehend it. Tarka knew—the way Saro-Wiwa, a fellow minority man, could not— that ultimately the Igbo must be taken into account even by those seekers of political power and office from amongst the minority ethnic groups. Tarka's was a recipe for a post-war democratic Nigeria, for a sustaining kind of cohesive political relationship between the majority and minority ethnic groups. He was looking forward to the Igbo regaining after the war, the stature (and the functions and responsibilities deriving therefrom) to which their size as a group should entitle them.

In 1969, it is recounted in *On A Darkling Plain*, Dr. Nnamdi Azikiwe, Nigeria's foremost national hero and "a man of great presence and charisma" (218) was to pay an official visit to Port Harcourt. Great Zik, himself an Igbo, had abandoned Biafra and defected to Nigeria and was on a goodwill tour of Rivers State to prepare minds for the eventual termination of hostilities and the reconciliation that would follow. Ken Saro-

Wiwa was instinctively irritated by the prospects of that visit until an uncompromising Federal insistence compelled its acceptance on him.

> The announcement of his projected visit to Port Harcourt was received initially with misgivings. I particularly resented it for reasons that I could hardly understand. But the military in Port Harcourt made it absolutely clear that the visit was imperative and in the national interest. (218)

It is apparent that the dimensions of national interest in relation to which the authorities perceived the visit of Zik were not readily obvious, at the time, to Saro-Wiwa. He could hardly hide his displeasure when, during his own visit, the British Prime Minister, Harold Wilson, disdained the frivolity of the carnival spirit in order to address weighty issues regarding humanity, albeit Igbo, as the victim of war.

> He showed some impatience with the dances that were laid out for him and was keenly interested in our rehabilitation efforts spending quite some time in the camp for 'refugees' which were inhabited by the Ibos, and asking questions. (210)

Alienation from the dream that was Biafra, we have already seen, was the key factor in the psychology of Ken Saro-Wiwa as recorded in *On A Darkling Plain*. A great deal of this was tied up with the enormous importance that petroleum had assumed in Nigeria's national economy. The impetus provided by the fact of oil deposits in the Niger Delta, by the fact that "almost 94% of the region's crude oil product before came from the non-Ibo sections of the region" (53) in accentuating, even before the war, sectional self-assertiveness among the Eastern minorities is recognized by Saro-Wiwa on page 46. The claim that minerals and the proceeds from their exploration are the primary possessions of the ethnic group under whose ancestral land the mineral is extracted was not made as stridently in Nigeria prior to the discovery of oil as has become fashionable ever since. It certainly was not much made with regard to tin from the Jos highlands or, more relevantly for our purposes, with regard to coal in the Udi hills.

Saro-Wiwa speaks affectionately (115) of "Ogoni Oil." But he refrains from speaking of coal discovered in Enugu early in the century in such corresponding ethnic possessive terms. If there was Ogoni oil, would there not also be Igbo coal? Yet, Enugu and her coal played a major role in initiating the inter-dependent ethnic socializing in Eastern Nigeria long before oil was struck in Ogoniland or anywhere else in the Niger Delta. It was the discovery of coal in the hills around Enugu in 1909 "which necessitated the building of a railway to the coast in what is today known as Port Harcourt," which had been "originally built as a Coal Port" (115). Port Harcourt in its conception and its subsequent rise as seaport was, there-fore, consequent on the anteceding rise of Enugu as a coal city. A great deal of the relationship in the individual fortunes of both cities in Eastern Nigeria would feed on this historic bond in their respective origins. Port Harcourt was at that time well on its way to becoming the way Enugu, even as the ad-ministrative headquarters did not, a vibrant metropolitan hub, a meeting point between the coastal and hinterland peoples of Eastern Nigeria (234).

Saro-Wiwa would recognize the major point in the socio-ethnic existential reality of the eastern region of Nigeria (11):

> In Eastern Nigeria, the Ibo will continue to predomi-nate, their industry and their numbers have ensured that.

With specific regard to the city of Port Harcourt he would agree, doubtless with trepidation and resignation, with Chief Amachree and the Rivers State study group even in 1969 that "Port Harcourt could not do without the Ibos" (234). Yet little real consideration for post-war restoration of confidence would attend Saro-Wiwa's rather cavalier rationalization of the Aban-doned Property Edict. By that promulgation, Igbo landed prop-erty was, in wholesale manner, expropriated after the war by the government of Rivers State of which Saro-Wiwa was a member. He would on one hand strangely accuse the Igbo, whom he acknowledges were now "leaderless and passing through a most difficult period in their communal history" (234), of bringing about the "imbroglio" by not reciprocating the goodwill ostensibly offered by the minority ethnic groups of the East. Nothing is said to suggest that an enormous duty and responsibility now devolved on the leaders of these groups, fully in place and triumphant, to provide selfless statesmanly leadership in order to bind wounds and lay the foundation for true fraternal reconciliation and restoration of confidence amongst the peoples of Eastern Nigeria.

On another hand, Saro-Wiwa would hint at the opportunity offered by the abandoned property issue for weak-minded people to wreak sheer vengeance on the prostrate Igbo.

> The troublesome edict would not have been passed if there had been no war, and there was no point trying to behave as though the war had not happened. (235)

No questions could be asked regarding the implications of this kind of rationalization for reconciliation even under an official Federal policy of "No Victor and No Vanquished." At any rate, Saro-Wiwa would not wish to cover up his distaste for that policy; he would indeed regret that the Igbo avoided being made to pay "reparations" after the war (237). He certainly would not wish to be privy to a rapid rehabilitation of the Igbo and also of their full rights of Nigerian citizenship. Nor could he anticipate that the one predictable consequence of massive dispossession of the Igbo of their property in Port Harcourt would be their subsequent recoil from further "real estate development" there, "a definite loss to Port Harcourt" (235).

Ken Saro-Wiwa's understanding of the temperament and direction of Nigeria's pre-1966 politics is generally consistent with those of such key players in the January 15, 1966 *coup* as Ademoyega in *Why We Struck* (1981) and Gbulie in *Five Majors* (1981). His account of that military uprising, "a brilliant move" (19), is considerably distanced. Regarding the charge of that military intervention as ethnically inspired he would come to the conclusion (27) that "the Ibos should on no account be calumniated for that coup". His evaluation of General Ironsi is sympathetic: "he was an honest man" (36) from whom "the choice was indeed an impossible one (29). He considers the mass slaughter of Easterners resident in Northern Nigeria as "calculated and dastardly" (*On A Darkling Plain*, 33). That program of ethnic cleansing was in Wole Soyinka's view "on a scale so vast and so thorough, and well organized" (*The Man Died,* 120) that it deserved to be described as genocide. Perhaps Saro-Wiwa was truly touched by what he calls the consequent "pain of the Ibo people" even though he gives an ethnic badge to what in the context was the tragedy of all Eastern Nigerians, regardless of ethnicity. He could not, however, be troubled by what Nnoli (1978: 245) and Wole Soyinka (1972: 180) recognize as a factor which fuelled Biafran resolute and defiant resistance anchored on the fear of possible extermination: the ominous indifference of the Federal Government of the day and the vast majority of non-Eastern Nigerians to the pogrom, the fact that no official apologies were offered, nor condemnation issued, nor protest marches mounted to indicate revulsion. Indeed, there was little done to arrest and try the perpetrators. In effect, Saro-Wiwa would be an outsider to the deep hurt in the souls of those in Eastern Nigeria—many of them his Ogoni kinsmen—who, all things considered, had genuine reason to succumb to the fear of genocide. He was alien to the dream which Biafra became to such people and also to their tenacious clinging to that dream and its promise of security and the pursuit of happiness.

He could therefore not understand the position and dilemma of Colonel Ojukwu, whom he merely accuses of "exploiting Ibo suffering for personal purposes" (110). He would suggest (40) that Ojukwu encouraged mass return to the East; he would pretend not to notice the general operation of the will to life and the impulse to self- protect:

> No responsible leader would have encouraged many Eastern Nigerian to remain in Northern Nigeria . . . But in Ibadan and Lagos, the weak-minded only needed a word of encouragement and they were instantly on the move back home. (40)

He could not perceive that something really must have been very rotten in the state of Nigeria in those dismal days for encouragement to work on the affected people only in the direction of precipitating their prompt abjurement of the rest of Nigeria. But he would himself eventually confront the grim nature of those unjust hours. On a trip to the East from Ibadan he witnessed the gruesome brutalization of hapless Eastern (Igbo and non-Igbo alike)—"Nyamiri" travellers by Nigerian soldiers. He arrived at his own fearful (or is it weak-minded?) estimation, non-Igbo that he was, that he needed no further encouragement to seek his own refuge in that sanctuary which, in the context, only the East could aspire to offer to every Easterner, even to Ken Saro-Wiwa himself:

> It decided me against returning to Ibadan. I would take up a job in Eastern Nigeria while I waited to leave for the University of California at Berkeley where I had been offered a place on the doctoral programme in drama. (58)

The proclivity to abandon embroiled Nigeria and seek academic self-advancement way beyond her shores indexes a self-centered personality. Nonetheless, the plan to proceed to the United States would be later aborted in favor of efforts to advance the cause of nascent Rivers State: the war to keep Nigeria one would offer Saro-Wiwa an opportunity to assume some form of role and function as an insider in Rivers State, and that for a time.

Rivers State would, of course, not be Ken Saro-Wiwa's paragon for too long for the simple reason that it could not, and did not, annul his ethnic minority status and the complexes of the mind which attend it. These complexes would lead him to an early disenchantment with Rivers State:

> My experiences in Rivers State has convinced me that the State should be further split—then creating a Port Harcourt State for the nine non-Ijaw ethnic groups who are together outnumbered by the Ijaws in a very undemocratic situation. (*Darkling Plain,* 247)

The "un-democracy" of Rivers State, as in the case of Eastern Nigeria before it, did not consist in the wilful suppression of the outnumbered by the group which outnumbered them. It derived, paradoxically, as we have stated, from the operation of that aspect of democracy which would allocate and/or allow power and influence commensurate with the numerical strength of constituent groups. Rivers State could not, and so did not, abolish polyethnicism; neither did it, nor indeed could it, equalize in the material aspects of size and power all the ethnic groups within its administrative borders. Within Saro-Wiwa's disillusionment with Rivers State, however, lies a certain kind of vindication of Eastern Nigeria, the acknowledgement, albeit belated, that what was seen as objectionable in that Region had really little to do with the Igbo people and their *Igbo-ness*. It simply had to do with the place of demographic numbers in a polity:

> The Rivers State itself did not prove to be any better than Eastern Region in reconciling the interests of its component ethnic groups. (*A Month and a Day*, 54)

Port Harcourt State was effectively created late in 1996 when the Ijaws were excised into a separate, somewhat mono-ethnic Bayelsa State. What new sectarian cleavages would emerge in that new State is yet to be seen. In rump Rivers State composed of about ten ethnic groups,—the *outsider-ness* of the Ogoni may not have been completely eliminated, for they still are not the single largest ethnic group in that state.

Claude Ake (1973:357), himself a member of the Eastern minorities and also from Rivers State, once explained:

> political instability in the new [nation] states is explicable in terms of the high propensity among political elites to invest in the goal of controlling or capturing the reins of government.

Nnoli (1978:258) agrees and emphasizes the role of segmental allegiance in the way the Nigerian elite organize themselves:

[the] desire of the various regional factions of the privileged classes to carve out their spheres of economic
[and political] influence.

The history of Nigeria's "season of anomy" could be seen, then,
in the light of intra-elite contest. In that wise, Ken Saro-Wiwa
was an insider, waltzing on (like each of his counterparts in
Nigeria) to power, influence, and privilege to the tune of his
own darksome music of sectarian chauvinism. The saddening
consequence may have been that we have all aligned Nigeria
with the idea of the downright unjust state about which Ronald
Cohen (in Cohen and Service 1978:1) has bleakly posited:

> as a sociopolitical system, the state permits greater in-
> equity within its population than any known earlier form
> of association.

# Notes

1. The views expressed in this essay were well known to Ken Saro-
   Wiwa, in his life time, as mine regarding the work under discussion. My very friend, he had given me a free copy of *On A Darkling
   Plain* soon after its release in 1990. This was to enable me do a
   promotional review of the book at its formal launching in Calabar,
   Nigeria. On being acquainted with the contents, I explained to
   him that I could not be involved in any form of public endorsement and celebration of his book, my views on the Nigerian Civil
   War being rather different from his. Obviously, my being Igbo was
   a factor. Ken Saro-Wiwa understood and we remained great friends
   and continued to exchange often heated opinions about Nigeria,
   her history and condition. He was a man of tremendous courage
   and candor.

# Works Cited

Ademoyega, Adewole. *Why We Struck: The Story of the First Nigerian Coup.* Ibadan: Evans Brothers, 1981.

Ajayi, Sesan. "A Time to Live." [Nigerian] *Guardian:* September 15, 1991. B5.

Ake, Claude. "Explaining Political Instability in New State." *Journal of Modern African Studies* 11,2 (1973):343-60

Cohen, Roland and Elman E. Sevice, eds. *Origins of the State: The Anthropology of Political Evolution.* Philadelphia: Institute for the Study of Human Issues, 1978.

Gbulie, Ben. *Nigeria's Five Majors.* Lagos: Africana, 1981.

Kendall, W. "Social Contract" *International Encyclopaedia of Social Science.* 14 1968:376-381.

Magarshack, David, Trans. *The Best Short Stories of Dostoevsky.* New York: Random House, 1955.

Nnoli, Okwudiba. *Ethnic Politics in Nigeria.* Enugu: Fourth Dimension, 1978.

Olalere, Oladitan. 1979. "The Nigerian Crisis in the Nigerian Novel." In: Kola Wole Ogugbesan, ed., *New West African Literature.* London: Heinemann, 1979:10-20.

Saro-Wiwa, Ken. *On A Darkling Plain: An Account of the Nigerian Civil War.* London: Saros International Publishers, 1990.

_____. *A Month and A Day: A Detention Diary.* London: Penguin,1995.

Soyinka, Wole. *The Man Died: Prison Notes.* Hammonsworth: Penguin, 1972.

_____ *Season of Anomy.* London: Rex Collings, 1973.

# 10

# The Female Narrative and Ken Saro-Wiwa's Discourse on Change in *A Forest of Flowers*

## Grace Eche Okereke

Ken Saro-Wiwa has written many books and the versatility of his works makes them relevant and open to discussion in different arenas of discourse, especially the political. This paper limits itself to the aspect of gender discourse with specific attention to the female narrative in his collection of short stories—*A Forest of Flowers*. The paper analyzes Saro-Wiwa's exploitation of the female consciousness as narrator and narrative, and the intersection of these with the male construction of gender (as implicated in the male authorial consciousness). It also reads the absenting of the ideal in gender relationships, especially in marriage, as a subterranean but powerful discourse on change.

The major female narratives in *A Forest of Flowers* that will concern this paper are "Home, Sweet Home" and "The Divorcee" in Part One, "Night Ride," "Love Song of a Housewife," and "A Caring Man" in Part Two. Other narratives will be mentioned as the need arises.

The female narrative in *A Forest of Flowers* is told by two male consciousness. One impersonates the female consciousness and functions as the female narrator, as in "Home, Sweet Home," "Love Song of a Housewife," and "A Caring Man." The other narrates directly as a male consciousness in sympathy with the female experiential consciousness, as in "The Divorcee" and "Night Ride."

It is a split consciousness that employs the female as narrator and narrative. Saro-Wiwa's appropriation of a dual gender consciousness in narrating female experience reflects Mikhail Bakhtin's view of consciousness as different ways of apprehending the world:

> Consciousness knows the world by visualizing it but can see it, as it were, only through the optic of the self or that of the other. Each of these instruments refracts what is perceived in quite different ways, much as do the right and left eyes in the physiology of vision. In my attempts to make sense out of what confronts me, I shape the world in values that are refracted from one or the other lens. (Clark and Holquist 1984:73).

One would expect that the position of narrator (signified by "I") confers subjectivity on the female since she is the teller of her own story. For as Monique Wittig (1986:66) affirms in "The Mark of Gender,"

> It is when starting to speak that one becomes 'I'. This act—the becoming of *the* subject through the exercise of language and through locution—in order to be real, implies that the lucutor be an absolute subject . . .In spite of the harsh law of gender and its enforcement upon women, no woman can say 'I' without being for herself a total subject—that is ungendered, universal, whole (Author's emphasis).

One would also expect that the position of narrative confers objectivity on the female as she becomes the story that is told by an/other (the male). But in both cases the female remains the narrative, the story—as told by the male, whether disguised as female or undisguised as male. Thus the seemingly split consciousness that authors the female narrative in *A For-*

*est of Flowers* ultimately coalesces into one—the male consciousness— showing how difficult it is for a man to convincingly
appropriate *femaleness* as disguise. The male remains male even
in the most deceptive female gender garb. This is because he
continues to see and narrate the female with the optics of his
gender even when he pretends to be female.

Part One of A *Forest of Flowers,* titled "Home, Sweet Home,"
narrates the Nigerian rural context. Saro-Wiwa tells the title
story of part one, "Home, Sweet Home," through an educated
female on her way home to the village after finishing school in
town. The "I" in the story is a female consciousness imbued
with awareness and capable of subtle ironic comments on the
people and the government. This narrator is unnamed but is
an informed and, therefore, analytic mind—she is going to teach
and nurture young minds at her alma mater in Dukana.

By giving voice to a female to narrate the opening story of
the collection with its multiple political inflections, Saro-Wiwa
empowers the woman in articulatory space which tradition-
ally is a male space, as I have established in "African Gender
Myths of Vocality and Gender Dialogue in African Literature"
(Okereke, 1996). However, by keeping the female narrator
unnamed, Saro-Wiwa robs her of identity and dispossesses her
of some of the power that her vocal status confers on her.

The female narrator collectivizes in her story the communal (male/female) narrative of her people (Dukanans) and the
gender narrative of her sex. In the course of the narration,
both the communal and gender narratives intersect, thus
intertextualizing the communal experience with the gender
experience in a common destiny of oppression and domination.

The narrator speaks the pain of her people. As a conscious
mind, she apprehends the deprivation her people suffer as pro-
ducers of oil wealth which others consume. She narrates:

> Now and again we would drive past a gas flare remind-
> ing us that this was oil-bearing country and that from
> the bowels of this land came the much-sought-after liq-
> uid which fueled the wheels of modern civilisation.

I felt then that excruciating pain which knowledge confers on those who can discern the gulf which divides
what is and what could be. And my mind drifted to the
men and women of Dukana acting out their lives against
a backdrop of great forces they would never understand.
(Saro-Wiwa 1986:4)

She carries on a dialogue in her mind in which she empathizes
and sympathizes with her people over their ignorance and poverty, their exploitation by "alien" predatory forces.

Her journey is both literal and symbolic, with positive implications for the communal and gender narratives. At the
literal level, the narrator is undertaking a physical journey
from the town to the village. This journey has taken her
through the entire Dukana country, highlighting its poverty,
ignorance, backwardness, and the natural resources which are
there and yet absent for the people. The journey illuminates
in her mind the positive and negative sides of her homeland.
And so home becomes not only a place of joy and refuge as
configured at the gender level around the mother-image; it is
also a site of anxiety, conflict, and struggle when configured
around one's troubled birth place.

Because the negative outweighs the positive, the narrator
dozes off, thereby shutting out the sights and her pain, as she
analyzes these sights in her mind. She is all too aware of the
weight of her responsibility as an informed mind among an
exploited people, and her own puniness (both in view of her
gender deficiencies and the numerical deficiency of the informed) in fighting the economic predators preying on her
native land. And so she seeks temporary escape in sleep
(oblivion).

Saro-Wiwa in this communal narrative, told by an unnamed
female narrator (who collectivizes the communal voice in herself), intertextualizes the helplessness of the exploited oil-rich
minority Ogoni people in their struggle for survival against
the monstrous economic predators, with the helplessness of
the female in her gender deficiencies in sites of power struggle.

At the symbolic level, the female has journeyed into consciousness through Western education outside the rural set-

ting. Her people (whose collective identification with her is signified in their turning out *en masse* to welcome her) are proud

> that I had gone out to the world to acquire the new knowledge, new treasures; and that I had returned to plant some new seeds in the Dukana earth. (Saro-Wiwa 1986:6)

Like the rickety bus "Progress," Dukana's "only fast link with the modern world of the brick town" (1), the female narrator is a symbol of progress and the good, unattainable life to the illiterate, indigent villagers.

But the men are afraid of the awareness of the female that accrues from education. This is because it will change the female narrative from one of acquiescence and subservience to one of rebellion and self-assertion, especially within the sphere of marriage. Duzia, the wag, articulates the male fear of the rebellious consequences of female awareness thus:

> You're [the narrator] going to change the life of the women in Dukana. But whatever you do don't teach them to disobey their husbands. I'm not going to spend the rest of my life judging cases of wife-beating (6).

Thus, the intersection of the female narrative and the communal narrative generates a dialogic struggle between the genders born of female rebellion, which inflicts fear on the male cultural psyche.

As is the case in society, the gender narrative is subsumed under the larger communal narrative. The gender narrative is initially inscribed in the confrontation between the narrator on her journey home and the male driver of "Progress." This battle is waged within articulatory space. The driver's appropriation of vocality as a weapon of oppression and his failure to subjugate the female angers him—and anger signifies defeat. The female narrator, on the other hand, employs the weapon of silence which, in certain sites of gender struggle, is more powerful and subversive than speech. Her victory in this gender battle with the driver is brought out in her assessment of the situation: "I must have exasperated him [the driver] by my silence and studied indifference to his antics. And he took it out on me by pressing harder on the accelerator" (4).

The narrative of Sira (the narrator's friend) better illustrates the female narrative in rural Dukana, for hers is the fate of many young girls in tradition. It is a narrative of the female as doubly a victim of patriarchal values that deprive her of education by imposing premature motherhood on her, and in the same breath consigns her to silence and exile for bearing twins, while the male partner walks Dukana, a free man. It is a narrative of the female being made a prostitute by the same tradition that demands (virginity and) marriage as the legitimate context of motherhood. Thus the female narrative tells of patriarchal society's tossing of the female on the sea of asphyxiating contradictory male values.

The gender divisiveness that socialization inflicts on the female psyche ensures a perpetuation of male victimization of woman that forms the content of most female narratives. The older women (Sira's mother and the narrator's mother representing the unschooled women in tradition) side with patriarchal dictates to condemn Sira and symbolically the female narrative of pain to shame, silence, and exile. We never meet or hear from Sira, and so her pain is only reported.

It is symbolic that despite her book learning and the vocality this is expected to confer on the narrator, she loses her power of speech when she confronts the weight of injustice that tradition uses to victimize the female. After her mother tells her Sira's painful story (skeletally and in hushed tones), the narrator tells us: "The words I wanted to say came flooding to my lips, but died there" (9-10). She feels helpless as a lone voice crying in the wilderness of painful female narratives, and so she remains silent. While she articulates the communal narrative in her mind, the gender narrative robs her of articulation and so is silenced.

While the people find consolation in their common destiny, their communality, as expressed in their spontaneous song of joy and hope, the female is alone in her gender troubles. Her aloneness is emphasized in her silencing (as signified in the women's secretive attitude towards Sira's fate, and in the narrator's loss of the power of speech), and in the "mournful" nocturnal sounds that echo in the narrator's ears as "she could not sleep and lay staring into the darkness" (10).

Thus, the narrator's education equips her with power to speak and articulate her illiterate friend's pain (that she undoubtedly feels), but she shuts her mouth. In male psyche, the female is normally dumbfounded when in confrontation with male oppression, and so the male author's imposition of silence on the educated female voice, which remains the hope of the female in African culture, is not surprising.

But African women writers within the short story genre, as in other literary genres, have liberated and empowered the voice of the educated female to speak out against male oppression, thus subverting the silencing agenda of the male writer. This is evident in the short stories of Flora Nwapa, Buchi Emecheta, Bessie Head, Ama Ata Aidoo, Grace Ogot, and other women writers.

The female gender narrative outlives the communal narrative, and so concludes the story of "Home, Sweet Home." This is because the government may one day redeem the community from its poverty, ignorance, disease, and undevelopment when it embarks on rural development programs, and so this victim status is only temporary for the community. But it is a different story for the female, whose gender narrative has remained the same across time, space, and governments. It is only the female that will free herself (and her gender) from her position of victimhood, through education and consciousness-raising, as symbolized in the narrator. The narrator's incipient analyses and interrogation of Sira's narrative are indicative of her readiness to assume this redemptive role despite gender obstacles in her path.

The narrator of "The Divorcee" is male, but he narrates the story from the experiential consciousness of the heroine, Lebia, thereby subtly unveiling his sympathy with the female in her gender predicament. Lebia is beautiful and well-bred, but Saro-Wiwa identifies her within her failed relationship with a husband whose cruelty is culturally defined, and so titles the story "The Divorcee." This encases Lebia's destiny in a negative experience which need not define her life. This is reminiscent of Elechi Amadi's negative identification of Ihuoma, the heroine of his novel, *The Concubine* again in negative relation to men. Male writers often author a male-defined destiny for the female in their works, thereby marring her life with patriarchal confinements.

Saro-Wiwa, deliberately and with ironic inflections, x-rays the male cultural psyche in male-serving traditional marriage, thus subtly calling for change. Saro-Wiwa uses the context of Lebia's marriage to the driver to analyze and interrogate various retrogressive cultural norms that spoil the female narrative. These include marriage as a male space constructed around male distance and female silence, high male value and low female value, the commodification of the female, cradle and child marriages, male sexual objectification of the female, childlessness in marriage as a female offense, divorce as punishment of the "failed" female, while the male enjoys the best of all worlds and still collects the bride price. Male violation of the female is ignominiously complete.

In the face of all these, the female is expected to be silent, thereby interiorizing her pain, making it more traumatic and asphyxiating. The narrator tells us that when her husband packs her home like the object that she is in the story, Lebia, "obeyed as expected. Quietly. Without a Word. What pain she bore she carried in her heart" (51). As Sara Ruddick (1980;356) asserts: "Obedience is largely a function of social powerlessness." And so the woman's personal narrative is silenced, while her collective gender narrative is vocalized in the tradition (see Okereke 1996a: 162; 1996b: 6).

In "The Divorcee," Saro-Wiwa also configures the maternal hearth as a place of refuge for the female traumatized in marriage, for indeed as my people (the Ututu Igbo in Abia State of Nigeria) put it in a nuptial song, "the fire of the husband's home scorches" (inflicting pain on the female psyche). A corollary of this female axiom is "the fire of the mother's hearth soothes" (with somnolent effects healing the woman's wounds). The narrator articulates this concept in "The Divorcee" thus:

Her mother's house. She had said goodbye to it three years before. And now she had returned to it, there to seek solace once more ... Her mother's house. She was lucky it was still there, and her mother in it, alive and well. The hut bore the happiest memories of her life; memories which had now dimmed beside the nightmare of those three years whose brutality she would have given the world to forget. (Saro-Wiwa, 1986:47)

Part Two of *A Forest of Flowers* is entitled "High Life and narrates the Nigerian urban context. The title story of Part Two –("High Life") is a male narrative where the female is narrated as a sexual object sought after for conquest by the questing male. The male narrator tells us of the inexhaustible goodies, including women, that can be found in Aba:

And then when you think of fine *babies*, you can't beat Aba. If you want high society, you will get; if you want proper teenager who sells in the chemist shop, you will get. And sometimes, you will get them cheap because everything in Aba is cheap (65; Emphasis added).

Thus, the female is not only infantalized ("babies"), but also commodified ("cheap") in the male-constructed amoral urban environment. She becomes a commodity sought after as a "cheap article." The narrator schools himself in the easy acquisition of "cheap" sex through the Onitsha market books like *How To Make Love Without Spending Money*. And so he ironically sets himself up for a nasty experience with a fellow male disguised as a female.

The narrator and the impersonator (both male) narrate the female prostitute as constructed in the male psyche. She is stereotyped as homeless, moneyless, virtueless, and voiceless; while the male customer undresses her, "she is very very silent like church on Monday" (71). In effect, except for her body (which is a mere object), she is condemned to absence. This is in opposition to the male prostitute who at least has a home, a voice, and is the actor, while the female is the acted-upon.

"Night Ride" concurrently narrates the people's story and the gender story. Each story is constructed around "the war" and its evil destructive consequences. The civil war has robbed the people not only of the oil wealth (which caused it) and their farms, but also their very lives, as they die from disease represented by cholera in the story. The story of the ravages of the war is narrated through the male consciousness as he reminisces on his duty as a government official assigned the task of rehabilitating the people.

The issue of female education is again narrated—girls are circumscribed by their domestic gender roles.

> Only that morning he had stood in the village square at Dukana asking them to send the girls to school. But who will help us tend the farm, the women had asked? Who will baby-sit for us while we plant the yams? (110)

The narrative of the girls replicates that of the old woman who laments the confiscation of her land and the destruction of her farms without compensation by oil-hunting alien exploiters of the people (the government and the foreign imperialists). The girls are going to end up like the old woman— illiterate, poor, sick, and victims, unable to fight for their rights.

The narrative of the war that is filtered through the female consciousness is constructed around her loss of male presence at the death of her husband. We are told that "the world ended" with the death of her husband. This articulates the total dependency of the female on the male in marriage. Her story is only meaningful and fulfilling so long as it is constructed around his story, or hers becomes a truncated narrative at his demise.

The man and woman (who are the protagonists of the narrative) are taking a night ride through war-ravaged villages, and the sights are those of poverty, disease, death, and despair. I have established elsewhere that the journey is often liberating and expanding (Okereke 1997:144), but here it is a "night" ride into a dark past of broken relationships and regrets, a present of disease, death, and separation redeemed only by the male's plea to the female: "You will have to teach me to live with death" (Saro-Wiwa 1986:116). This is a call for help which suggests hope of reconciliation and a future together to transcend the ugliness around them.

The male and female narratives intersect as each of the occupants of the car reminisces on their love, its betrayal, and their alienation from each other. And now loneliness has brought them together, but each refuses to let go the past and initiate the healing of their relationship. This mutual antagonism is constructed on male offensiveness and female defensiveness. And so because of gender egotism, the man and woman reject another chance at happiness together. The ride remains a "night ride"—with no light breaking through except the hideous gas flares that speak of the betrayed hopes of an exploited people.

Saro-Wiwa's discourse on change in this story is subterranean, and seems to urge the man and woman to forgive each other, bury the past, and work out a new future anchored on each other for collective strength. The man takes the woman in his arms portending a new male/female narrative.

The narrator of "Love Song of a Housewife" is an unnamed female. The "I" that tells her own story is a housewife. The first-person viewpoint confers authenticity on the experience, since it is narrated by the subject (housewife) who experienced it. The lack of naming universalizes this experience to all housewives, making it a universal female narrative. It is a narrative of anxiety—female anxiety over the male (without whom, in patriarchal construct, the world ends). The story narrates a confused grill of emotions—love, praise, doubt, jealousy, antagonism—all constructed as issuing from the neurotic female psyche in marriage. She, in her confused state, adopts alternating offensive and defensive positions.

"Love Song of a Housewife" symbolically narrates the conflict and lack of trust that define most male/female marital relationships among the working class in the urban context. The interiority of the domestic space in which the full-time housewife is imprisoned all day, has an incarcerating effect on her psyche. It engenders excessive concern with the self and constructs phantasmagoric images of the other in conflict with the self in woman, leading to a destructive narcissism.

The short sentence structures and the rhetorical questions seem to correspond with the palpitations of her heart, and construct her fear and hysteria. The whole picture of talking to herself brings the housewife to the verge of insanity, as each monster of suspicion against her husband assumes disturbing proportions. By calling it a "love song," Saro-Wiwa ironically comments on this as the negative language of tenderness that the housewife drums into her husband's ear regularly, which eventually creates a monster out of him. This is a subtle call for change in nagging wives.

In "Love Song of a Housewife," the male and female narratives of marriage intersect:—the female narrative is voiced and the male narrative is implicated in hers.

In "A Caring Man," the female narrator addresses the reader directly—"You know how it is" (129)—which is conversational and implicates the reader into the female narrative. This causes especially the female reader to empathize with her in a common destiny of male oppression in marriage. The story is constructed around the usual framework of female narratives of betrayed love in marriage. It explores the woman as a multiple victim—of the double day (at work and at home), of the stay—young syndrome of her aging husband, of the initially-rustic-but-now-groomed house girl who becomes the husband's spice, of the wife-alienating syndrome of the mother-in-law in an oedipal relationship with her son.

The offending husband travels abroad. Often in female narratives, the journey of the male abroad on the pretext of doing business is escapist and therefore diminishing. Father Mclaid in Flora Nwapa's *One is Enough* comes readily to mind. This journey of escape inscribes the male fear of the outraged female, that prompts the running-away motif in the narrative of the randy male.

In female narratives, women's weapons of war against the treacherous male in marriage are often psycho-emotional and verbal, because man often possesses greater physical strength. And so Dani's aggrieved wife (the narrator) sheds tears of humiliation and unleashes invectives on him: "good-for-nothing adulterer," "shameless, empty gas bag," "miserable wretch" (131).

The male often constructs the female as a child in the sites of gender struggle. This is a deflationary technique that infantalizes woman. Saro-Wiwa employs this technique when he shows the offending male (Dani) winning over his angry wife with an expensive "bribe" —a Mercedes Coupe—just as a child's tantrums are soothed with gifts.

By keeping the female narrators in the major female narratives in *A Forest of Flowers* unnamed, Ken Saro-Wiwa confers on them a collective female identity. They become an "Everywoman," thus inscribing their attributes, as explored in this paper, as female gender universals. The female narratives dwell on distress and pain arising from oppressive cultural norms. The female consciousness in the stories intertextualizes the author's male consciousness and its patriarchal construction of woman, thus coloring and contouring female experience (especially in marriage) with male gender perspectives.

By constructing female pain around cultural norms that privilege the male over the female, Saro-Wiwa engages society in a discourse on change structured on our basic humanity, harmony, and a more enriching relationship between men and women in spite of gender. Saro-Wiwa employs the strategy of absence, the not-said, that speaks more powerfully than orchestration, to inscribe this message. He achieves this by inscribing the status quo and de-scribing the ideal. It is indeed a subterranean but powerful discourse on change.

# Works Cited

Clark, Katerina & M. Holquist. *Mikhail Bakhtin.* Cambridge, Mass.: Harvard University Press, 1984.

Okereke, Grace E. "Education as a Colonial Heritage and the Nigerian Woman in Literature." *Conference Proceedings of Women in Africa and the Africa Diaspora* V. (1996a):157-167.

_____. "African Gender Myths of Vocality and Gender Dialogue in African Literature." Unpublished paper, 1996b.

_____. "Language as Index of Female Space in Flora Nwapa's *One is Enough.* In *Flora Nwapa: Critical Perspectives,* ed., Ebele Eko. Calabar: University of Calabar Press, 1997.

Ruddick, Sara. "Maternal Thinking." *Feminist Studies* 6,2 (1980): 342-67.

Saro-Wiwa, Ken. A *Forest of Flowers: Short Stories.* Port Harcourt: Saros International Publishers, 1986.

Wittig, Monique. "The Mark of Gender". *The Poetics of Gender,* ed., Nancy K. Miller. New York: Columbia University Press, 1986: 63-73.

# 11

# Ethnic Minorities and the Nigerian State:
## The Ogoni Struggle After Ken Saro-Wiwa

### Felix Akpan

E thnic conflict is the fundamental reality of both domestic and international politics (and is likely to be so for the foreseeable future) because of the heterogeneous nature of nation- states. Ethnic heterogeneity has long been recognized as a pervasive feature of the contemporary world system (Jinadu 1980). Indeed, ethnic conflict is now of global concern because it is increasingly becoming difficult for polity with multiethnic groups to work together in pursuance of national goals in both developed and developing countries. According to many observers, the relationship between political unity and social diversity continues to be of central importance in many parts of the world. Thus, many multi-ethnic states have designed policy responses to the disintegrative potentiality of their heterogeneous ethnic composition.

In studies dealing with plural societies, ethnic conflicts and minority problems have been attributed to emotive power of primordial (affiliations or) cultural ties, the struggle for relative group worth, mass-based resource competition, electoral mobilization, elite manipulation, false consciousness, and/or defective political institutions and inequitable state policies. (Diamond 1987; Doornbos, 1991 [cited in Suberu, 1996:7]).

Writers and scholars agree that "the most serious challenge to the consolidation of new democracies and the health of well-established ones is posed by the problem of ethnic conflict. (Plattner and Diamond 1993:17). The growing wave of disintegration sweeping through the Eastern European countries of Yugoslavia and Czechoslovakia supply concrete examples.

With particular reference to the Third World, Diamond (1987) has aptly observed that ethnic conflicts have long been recognized as one of the more fundamental threats to institutional stability, political order, and state cohesion in the multi-ethnic societies of the Third World.

Ethnic minority problems have received extended treatment in existing literature, some of the most influential studies include Thorubery (1980), Kumoar Rupesingle (1987), Ted Rebert Gurr (1993), Welsh (1993), and, on the Nigerian experience, Okpu (1977), Nnoli (1978), Osaghae (1986, 1991), Diamond (1987), and Suberu (1996).

This paper discusses ethnic minorities and the Nigerian state in the background of the Ogoni struggle for socio-political justice and economic equity after Ken Saro-Wiwa.

The Ogoni are a small group of about half a million people and yet they have succeeded (through the effort of Ken Saro-Wiwa) in creating an awareness of their economic and political rights that is unrivalled by any other ethnic minority group in the country. Indeed, the Ogoni case has become "the paradigm of ethnic minority agitation in the Nigerian Federation today" (Suberu 1996:78). This explains why the Ogoni case remains unique and deserves an in depth and systematic study.

## II

Nigeria has been described by historians as a curious nation for obvious reasons.

> Evidence in existing literature suggests that Nigeria is made up of about 300 ethnic groups. However before colonialism, most of these groups were not conquered

or colonized by any other group in pre-colonial Nigeria. British colonialism was vehemently resisted by most
of these groups. Evidence of resistance by various ethnic nationalities to colonial rule abound. (Obaro Ikime
1976)

After the "forced unification" of some 300 ethnic groups in
1914 and the attendant animosity it generated among the ethnic nationalities, the country was divided into three major regions in the early 1940s, reflecting the three dominant ethnic
groups (Hausa-Fulani, Ibo, and Yoruba): Northern region,
Eastern region and Western region. Apart from administrative convenience, there is no other compelling argument for
this division.

Undoubtedly, each of the other 297 minority ethnic nationalities suffered considerable neglect under the respective regional governments they were forcibly consigned to throughout the colonial era. A good number of them protested against
the forced union and the consequent neglect in testimonies
and memoranda submitted individually and collectively before
the 1958 Henry Willink Commission of Inquiry Into "The
Fears of the Minorities and How to Allay Them." Rather than
mitigate the fears of the minority ethnic nationalities, the
Willink Commission Report exacerbated it by failing to recommend the creation of separate states for the minorities. In
fact, this commission effectively blocked it. The hypothetical
palliative which the commission gave was moral appeal to the
majority ethno-regional government to rule justly as if politics was played by mere appeals, especially when the economic
stakes are high, as was the case then. In addition, the Commission recommended the inclusion of a Human Rights Bill in
the Constitution, but this still did not help matters either.

The State which the British Colonial Administration left
behind in 1960 when Nigeria got its independence was a fragile rainbow coalition: people of diverse ethnic and cultural
origins were brought together by a constitutional framework
which did not provide adequately for equity and justice for all
segments of the population. This Constitution did not quite
define equity and justice in sharing political power, economic

and social development, and the enabling of each nationality or people within the Nigerian Federation to maintain and develop distinctive cultural identity. These constitutional disabilities, coupled later with the struggle for oil resources, were some of the causative factors of the Nigerian Civil War (1967-1970). The Ibo leader, Lt. Colonel Chukwuemeka Odumegwu Ojukwu, who attempted to secede from Nigeria, was partly protesting against these constitutional disabilities and partly against Hausa-Fulani hegemony at that time.

The division of the country into 12 states on the eve of the civil war (like all other subsequent ones) was not in the overall interest of the minority ethnic groups. Ken Saro-Wiwa puts it more succinctly:

> The present division of the country into a federation in which some ethnic groups are split into several states, whereas other ethnic groups are forced to remain together in a difficult unitary system inimical to the country, is a recipe for dissension and future wars. (Saro-Wiwa, 1994)

One writer aptly observed that at Independence Nigeria consisted of three regions and since then thirty six states have been created largely for the ethnic majorities who rule the country. Most of the states, including five of the six recent ones (Gombe, Nassarawa, Ekiti, Ebonyi, and Zamfara) so created are unviable, depending largely on oil wealth for survival. Whereas the demand of some ethnic minority groups for political autonomy and self-determination within the Nigerian state have been at best ignored. The feelings and grievances of these ethnic minority groups are well known:

> Generally, the oil producing communities have favoured the creation of more states and local governments in their communities as a means of enhancing the access of these communities to federal resources and of mitigating the disadvantaged political position of many smaller minority groups. These communities have, therefore, been vociferous in denouncing the present

140

tendency to use the creation of states to improve the access of ethnic majority sections to federal largess, at the expense of a more systematic attention to ethnic minority problems in the several of the minority - populated, culturally heterogeneous constituted state).(Suberu, 1996)

One noticeable trend in the preceding discussion is that in the colonial and post-colonial eras, minority ethnic groups were placed at disadvantaged positions in the restructuring of the internal territorial configuration of the Federation. This is one issue that has continued to breed discontent among the ethnic minority groups (most especially the oil-rich minority areas) in Nigeria.

One major consequence of the present Federal system is that the "nation" as a federation of some 300 ethnic groups (divided into 36 states in 1996) is not taken into consideration in formulating policies of governance. Indeed, the tyranny of the majority as reflected in the hegemonic nature of contemporary Nigerian politics is the main source of perceived feeling of marginalisation, domination, and a desire to opt out of the Federation by the dominated groups. The Ogonis have taken the lead in their struggle for socio-political justice and economic equity.

## III

Before the discovery and exploration of oil in commercial quantities in 1958, resulting in the sudden change in the economic structure of the country from cash crops to crude oil in the early 1970s, the derivative principle was the most equitable and efficient method of sharing federally-collected revenue (Okilo 1980; Oyovibaire 1978). Indeed, the derivation or original principle of distribution stipulates that a significant proportion of the revenues collected in a locality should be returned to that locality or section (Suberu 1996). But the derivation principle began to lose prominence when it became obvious that it no longer favored the ethnic majority groups in the country. As one observer notes:

The antagonists of the principle of derivation as a formula for revenue sharing have, however, forgotten that this same principle was applied religiously when groundnut, cocoa and other cash crops had relevance in foreign income earning. The following is the scenario: in 1953,100%; 1960, 50%,. 1970, 45%; 1975, 20%; 1992, 3% which is given to OMPADEC to manage. (*Vanguard*, September 1995)

One significant decision taken immediately after the military intervention in the 1960s which steadily enhanced the centralization process was the transfer of all viable sources of revenue (at this time only oil was viable) to the Federal government by the constitution (Distribution Pool Account). Decree of 1970, which repealed Decree No. 15 of 1967 relating to the allocation of federal revenue and suspended Sections 141 and 164 of the 1963 Republican constitution provided that 50 percent of federally collected revenue be retained by the Federal Government in its Consolidated Revenue Fund (CRF), while the balance be paid into the Distributed Pools Account (DPA), to be distributed on a compromise formula based on 50 percent population.

Under the new arrangement, 45 percent of mining rents and royalties from on-shore production goes to the State where the wealth is produced, while 50 percent goes to the DPA and 5 percent for the use of Federal government (Olaloku 1979). Despite the enormous resources in the hands of the Federal government, there was nothing in the Decree for the oil-producing minorities to cushion the environmental hazard that oil production has caused in the areas. Instead, the Decree considerably boosted the resources of the Federal government and the DPA to the benefit of the ethnic majority groups/states who often control the center. The DPA itself is an hegemonic apparatus which only benefits the ethnic majority groups/states in the country. Although, as Offensend (1992) has aptly pointed out, federal allocated DPA Funds (are) meant to mitigate disparities and promote national economic equality, in practice the principle of revenue sharing is based substantially on population, causing the states to rely on national wealth and resources which make the poor relatively rich, and the rich somewhat poor, thereby increasing inter-state inequalities.

It is important to note that the oil-producing states' statutory share of revenue collected by the Federal Government and the DPA since 1970 is quite phenomenal. With the exception of the three percent given to the Oil Mineral Producing Development Commission (OMPADEC) to dispense with, no serious effort was made in the past to address the environmental and socio-economic problems of oil-producing areas. This is the situation strongly detested by the Ogonis, especially under the leadership of radical leaders of MOSOP (Movement for the Survival of Ogoni People).

The restive mood of the Ogoni occasioned by the perceived differential allocation of the nation's wealth (specifically oil wealth) is perhaps the only demand in the Ogoni Bill of Rights supported by other oil-producing areas in the country. At present, inequality and injustice have become part and parcel of Nigeria's national culture. It is ironical indeed that within the country the people who are more endowed with oil minerals resource, the greatest contributor to the national economy, are denied corresponding benefit therefrom. It is in this connection that the Ogoni struggle for political and economic equity under Ken Saro-Wiwa which is examined below could be appreciated or derided depending on which side of the divide one stands—oil-producing or non-oil-producing areas of the country. Affiliation to a specific side of the divide is very important in the politics of ethnic minority in Nigeria. Ethnicity is often politics and political.

## IV

Domestically and internationally the publicity, recognition and support which the Ogoni cause has garnered has been due largely to the efforts of the late Ken Saro-Wiwa who suffered many deprivations in the process: unlawful detention, tortured harassment and intimidation. Saro-Wiwa churned out a series of literature in order to fully explain the remote and immediate causes of the Ogoni struggle. In one such publication, "The Ogoni Moment of Truth," he tells us that:

Although Shell had made more than 30 billion U.S.
dollars from oil fields in the Ogoni area since oil was
found there in 1958, the Ogoni people have received
nothing. Oil exploration has turned Ogoni into a waste-
land: lands, streams and creeks are totally and continually polluted. Acid rain, oil spillages and blow-outs have
devastated Ogoni territory. (*Newswatch*, November 13,
1995:15)

Apart from using his skill as a writer to engrave the Ogoni
cause on the minds of people, he produced a documentary on
the ecological damages in Ogoni which was well-received at
the United Nations and by Environmental and Human Right
groups in Europe and the United states. Among these groups
are the United Nations Committee for Elimination of Racial
Discrimination (CERD), the World Conference of Indigenous
Peoples, The Unrepresented Nations and Peoples Organization (UNPO), the British Parliamentary Human Rights Group
(BHRG), Amnesty International, the Greenpeace Organization, and the London Rainforest Action Group.

These organizations have played remarkable roles in support of the Ogoni cause. For example, in November 1992, the
London Rainforest Action Group organized a peaceful protest
on behalf of the Ogoni at the London premises of Shell Petroleum and was among the international observers that witnessed
the January 4, 1994 protest march organized by Movement
for the Survival of the Ogoni People (MOSOP) in Bori, the
traditional headquarter of Ogoni people. The January 4, 1994
protest march involving over 300,000 Ogoni people is a classic
example of the use of peaceful demonstration to advance the
cause of ethnic minority groups in the country. The success of
the protest march was largely due to the political education
Saro-Wiwa gave to the leaders of MOSOP. The protest march
signalled the commencement of non-violent resistance to their
denigration (and exploitation) as a people (Saro-Wiwa 1994).

The indifferent attitude of the government to Ogoni grievances and claims as contained in the Ogoni Bill of Rights presented to the government and people of Nigeria in 1990 is the
most compelling argument why the Ogonis under the leader-

ship of Saro-Wiwa embarked on disruptive activities to force the government and the oil companies to redress the 38 years of neglect the Ogoni people had suffered. For instance, disturbances in Ogoni-land between 1992 and 1993 prevented the take-off of some key oil-related projects, among them the 500-million-naira gas pipeline meant to supply natural gas to the 3-billion-naira Aluminum Smelter Project at Ikot Abasi in Akwa Ibom State.

It was in the light of these unaddressed grievances that Ken Saro-Wiwa campaigned for an Ogoni boycott of the June 12, 1993 presidential election to draw the attention of the Federal Government to the plight of the Ogoni people. In spite of his arrest and subsequent detention, the Ogonis did not participate in the presidential election. As Suberu (1996) rightly points out, the resort to attacks on oil installations has invariably provoked violent confrontations between the oil-producing communities and law enforcement agencies.

The first of such confrontation occurred on 30 April 1993, following demonstrations and protests by Ogoni farmers against the laying of an oil pipeline by Shell and its agent, Wiblboros Construction Company. According to official accounts, the Nigerian army killed one Ogoni indigene and injured eleven others in the Ogoni town of Biara. These confrontations have continued to claim lives and properties. MOSOP alleged that government's violent military actions in Ogoniland had led to the displacement of over 50,000 Ogonis (out of a total population of half-a-million people), the destruction of twenty Ogoni villages (out of a total of 126 villages), the killing of 1,000 Ogoni indigenes; and the physical assault of many more Ogonis ( *Tell*, 6 June 1994:24).

In spite of these confrontations, the rage of the Ogoni people and other oil-producing communities continues to worsen as an increasing number of communities begin to clamor for their rights: in Obagi, Rivers State, about 5,000 residents closed down the Elf facility on October 4, 1993; barely two months after the Obaji incident , more than 3,000 people in Brass demonstrated outside the Agip terminal; then, on December 4, 1993, a local Shell flow station was attacked at the Nembe Creek, Rivers State. Similarly, other communities like Igbide, Ijaw, Etche, Irri, and

Uzere have demonstrated (and are still demonstrating) against activities of oil companies *(Newswatch,* December 18, 1995:18).

At the root of the current crisis is the question of responsibilities for developing the oil-producing areas. Under Nigeria's Petroleum Laws, the Federal government appropriates the right over oil and gets all revenue accruing from its production. Thus, the primary responsibility of developing the oil-producing area is that of the Federal government. Under the same law, the oil companies do not have a legal responsibility to develop the oil- bearing areas. Their statutory obligation is to pay royalties and taxes to the Federal Government. This apparently explains Shell's indifference to the plight of Ogoni people. For instance, Shell had no appreciable community development program in all its operational areas until 1992, when protests and demonstrations in oil-producing communities spearheaded by the Ogonis threatened all its operations in the area. In Erhoike community in Ethiope East Local Government area of Delta state, where the company has been operating since 1959, the only community-development project, a 32- million Naira cottage hospital, was commissioned in 1995. In Okpare Olomu, Ughelli South, the first community project, a six classroom block and health center were commissioned in 1994, 32 years after oil exploitation started there *(Newswatch,* December 18, 1995).

At the moment, the communities do not care whose responsibility it is. As far as they are concerned, the oil companies have a responsibility to them. Indeed, only oil companies with substantial contributions to the development needs of their host communities are currently operating without disturbance in the Niger Delta region. Others have been forced to close down oil wells in many communities. While some operate under tight security provided by the Federal government (Akpan, 1996:62).

In summary, the Ogoni struggle under the late Ken Saro-Wiwa has successfully put to rest the erroneous view that the resentment of oil-producing areas cannot threaten the stability of the country. It has also successfully placed the issue of environmental degradation of the Niger Delta on the front burner of national and international politics. The highest point of it was the United Nations fact-finding team that visited the country in 1996.

## V

The idea that oil-producing communities can provide the revenue for the country and yet be denied a proper share of that revenue because it is perceived that they are few in number is the propelling force behind the Ogoni cause. As in most oil-producing areas, the anger of the Ogoni people is fuelled by the "criminal neglect" of the area. For instance, the 35-kilometer road from Port Harcourt to Bori is full of bumps and potholes; during the rains, it is unppassable. A journey which ordinarily should take forty minutes would then take two hours. Roads leading to the major towns in Ogoni, like Akpo, K-Dere, and Gokana, are untarred. Many of the Ogoni communities which have provided a major source of revenue for the country for the past 38 years still remain in darkness. There is no electricity in any of the towns and villages *(Tell,* January 31, 1994:17*)*.

It is important to note that recent efforts made by both Federal government and oil companies to alleviate the sufferings of the Ogonis appear slight against the background of protracted years of neglect. Presently in Ogoniland there is observable discontent, anger, and frustration which violent reprisals cannot defuse. In fact, contrary to the thinking in some quarters or what the government would want people to believe, the Ogoni struggle is getting even stronger than before in spite of the "judicial murder" of Ken Saro-Wiwa and eight other minority rights activists. For instance, in spite of the army of occupation stationed in Ogoni-land, the Ogonis still protest against the devastation of their environment and political marginalization. According to an eye-witness account, on January 4, 1997, the Nigerian Army killed five Ogoni indigenes and injured several others in the Ogoni town of Zaakpon. There were also causalities in other Ogoni villages. This followed demonstrations and protests by the Ogonis to mark the fourth anniversary of the Ogoni national political rally against environmental degradation and other provocative issues. The most compelling reasons for the continued agitations in Ogoniland is the awareness Saro-Wiwa created among the

Ogoni people, the associational structure established, and the domestic and international support the Ogoni cause has received.

Among the Ogoni people, everybody knows what the struggle is all about. All they want is a clean environment, respect for life and property, a fair proportion of what comes from their land, and, above all, a say in their affairs. These demands are in line with Article I (4) of the International Convention on the Elimination of All Forms of Racial Discrimination which was adopted by the United Nations in 1969:

> Special measures taken for the sole purpose of securing adequate advancement of certain racial or ethnic groups or individuals requiring such protection as may be necessary in order to ensure such groups or individuals equal enjoyment or exercise of human rights and fundamental freedoms ... and that they shall not be continued after the objectives for which they were taken have been achieved. (Article 1 (4) UN, 1969)

The Ogoni people and other disadvantaged ethnic minority groups in the country are agitating for the inclusion of these measures in the Nigerian constitution.

The Ogoni campaign has been spearheaded by the Movement for the Survival of the Ogoni People (MOSOP), formed in 1990. Other associations under the MOSOP umbrella have also featured prominently in the campaign: the Federation of Ogoni Women Association (FOWA), Conference of Ogoni Churches (COC), Ogoni Teachers Union (OTU), Council of Ogoni Professionals (COP), National Union of Ogoni Students (NUOS), Ogoni Students Union (OSU), and the National Youth Council of Ogoni People (NYCOP), widely believed to be the military wing of MOSOP. Indeed, as Suberu (1996) rightly points out, these associations individually and collectively articulate and advance the Ogoni cause using the following methods:

> Peaceful domestic demonstrations and representations, mobilization of international (and domestic) support and

violent disruption of the operations and installations of
the oil companies.

In spite of the death of Saro-Wiwa, the Ogoni position in respect of the demand for justice and environmental rehabilitation is still well articulated by Mr. Ledum Mittee, Saro-Wiwa's
deputy, now in exile, and who assumed the Leadership of
MOSOP after Saro-Wiwa's death:

> ... MOSOP is getting ever stronger than before. As for
> now, MOSOP has offices in over seven countries. And
> there are support groups in over 15 countries of the
> world that have been formed. And in Nigeria, you know
> how the security people operate, we do not intend to
> lead them to wipe out the whole of Ogoni people who
> are in the land. So, a completely new strategy has been
> adopted... This new strategy is completely strange to
> many people except those who are schooled in the poli-
> tics of non-violent struggle. ... But I can tell you that
> all the Ogoni people are still for the struggle. I am in
> constant touch with developments right in Ogoni-land.
> And the whole people are solidly behind the struggle.
> ( *Tell,* November 18, 1996:14)

This change in strategy is informed by the continued harassment, arrest, and detention of Ogoni people by security opera-
tives. Mittee explains:

> We have found that the repression is getting far more
> intense than the people ever imagined. The highest
> point of it was the United Nations fact-finding team.
> Since then, people have been brutalized, arrested and
> detained, especially those who came out in large num-
> bers to protest against what is happening to them. This
> has been brought to the attention of the United Na-
> tions Secretary General and regrettably nothing seems
> to have positively been done. These people have con-
> tinued to go through the pains. Even over the last three
> weeks (October 1996) and in my own community a spe-
> cial squad arrested ten persons and one who seriously
> panicked fell into a well. What the government has

tried to do is to persistently try to hide the facts ( *Tell*, November 18, 1996:16).

A fundamental observation concerning the Ogoni struggle that is becoming increasingly clear is that the continued used of repressive or regulatory polices by government to contain the Ogoni cause makes the struggle more vibrant and relevant, because, as Edmond Keller (1983) rightly observes, a reliance on these intimidatory or regulatory techniques not only presents the "image of a state which is low in legitimacy and desperately struggling to survive," but also "in the long run can do more to threaten state coherence than aid it." This is exactly what ethnic minority ferment in the oil-producing areas spearheaded by the Ogonis has made obvious. This point is explicit in the disaffection showed by other ethnic minority groups in the country, following the hanging of Ken Saro-Wiwa. This disaffection might be latent, but it is quite dangerous for the country given its heterogeneous nature and structural ethnic inequality.

The international support the Ogoni cause has received would continue mainly because environmental and minority rights issues are now of global concern. There are many governmental and non-governmental organizations that support and sponsor the issues that stirred the Ogoni cause. For instance, the Ogoni nation was elected into the Unrepresented Nations and Peoples Organization (UNPO) in 1994. It is on record that this Organization played a prominent role in putting the Ogoni issue on the United Nation agenda (Saro, 1994).

While the Federal government of Nigeria has been playing deaf to the cry of the Ogoni, the international community has been very supportive and there is no indication this would change with the death of Saro-Wiwa.

## Works Cited

Akpan, Felix. "The Problem of Nigerian Federalism: The Issue of Compensation to the Oil Producing Areas Through OMPADEC."

MPA Thesis, Department of Political Science, University of Calabar, 1996.

Diamond, Larry. "Ethnicity and Ethnic Conflict." *The Journal of Modern African Studies,* 25,1 (1987).

Doornbos, Martain. "Linking the Future to the Past: Ethnicity and Pluralism." *Review of African Political Economy* 50 (1991): 53-68.

Gurr, Ted Robert. *Minorities at Risk: A Global View of Ethnopolitical Conflicts.* Washington, D.C.: United States Institute of Peace Press, 1993.

Keller, Edmond J. "The State, Public Policy and the Mediation of Ethnic Conflict." *State Versus Ethnic Claims: African Policy Dilemmas.* Boulder, Colo: Boulder Press, 1968.

Nnoli, Okwudiba. *Ethnic Politics in Nigeria.* Enugu: Fourth Dimension, 1978

Obaro, Ikime. *The Groundwork of Nigerian History.* Ibadan: Univsity Press, 1986

Offensend, David. "Centralisation and Fiscal Arrangement in Nigeria". Boston: Harvard University Press, 1986.

Okilo, Melford. "The Derivation Principle and National Unity", *Daily Times,* 19 July, 1980.

Okpu, Ugbana. Ethnic Minority Problems in Nigeria Politics: 1960-1965. Uppsala, Acta Universitatis Uppsaliensis, 1977.

Olaloku, Akum. "Nigerian Federal Finances Issues and Choices." In Akinyemi, et al. eds., *Readings on Federalism.* Lagos: Nigerian Institute of International Affairs, 1979.

Osaghae, Eghosa. "Do Ethnic Minorities Still Exist in Nigeria?" *Journal of Commonwealth and Comparative Politics,* 1996.

_____. "Ethnic Minorities and Federalism in Nigeria," *African Affairs,* 1991.

Oyovbaire, S. E. "The Politics of Revenue Allocation." In Panter-Bricks, ed., *Soldiers and Oil.* London, Frank Cass, 1978.

Plattner, Mare, and Diamond Larry. "The Challenge of Ethnic Conflict." *Journal of Democracy* 4,4, (1993):17.

Rupesinghe, Kumar. "Theories of Conflict Resolution and Their Applicability to Protracted Ethnic Conflicts." *Bulletin of Peace Proposals,* 1987.

Saro-Wiwa, Ken. *A Month and Day: A Detention Diary.* London: Penguin Group, 1994.

Suberu, Rotimi. *Ethnic Minority Conflicts and Governance inNigeria.* Ibadan: Spectrum Books, 1996.

Thornby, Patrick. "Minority Rights, Human Rights and International Law." *Ethnic and Racial Studies,* 1990.

151

Welsh, David. "Domestic Politics and Ethnic Conflict," *Survival*
35, 1 (Spring 1993):63–80.
Willinks, Henry. Nigeria: Report of the Commission Appointed to
Enquire into the Fears of Minorities and the means of Allaying
Them. London, Her Majesty's Stationery Office, 1958.

# 12

# Direct Involvement and Personal Emotionalism:
## The War Poetry of Ken Saro-Wiwa

### Innocent C. K. Eyinnaya

> Silence
> The vows of silence
> They must be kept
> For you cannot speak
> While the guns roar
> And you cannot cry
> Where you'll not be heard
> For the loud resonance
> *Of one-sided truth* ...
> (Saro-Wiwa 1985:14)

The above lines from Ken Saro-Wiwa's collection about the Nigerian Civil War, *A Voice in the Wind,* vividly recreate the predicament of Nigerians on both sides of the conflict during the war. Truth, in actual fact, died in Nigeria long before the first shots were completely overwhelmed by the "the loud resonance of one-sided truth" dished out from both the Nigerian and Biafran sides. In a situation like this, the only sane option was for one to bridle one's tongue and pen. This is the pertinent point made by Ken Saro-Wiwa in his poem "Silence." The fact is that if one speaks out or cries while guns roar, one would not be heard and would even stand the risk of losing one's life.

J. P. Clark in "The Casualties" had amplified the point that when the war actually started everyone was "caught in the clash of counter claims and charges" and that the drum (the propaganda) overwhelmed the guns (Clark 1980). There were on both sides of the hostilities people who could have spoken out against the goings-on but kept silent for fear of being silenced forever, thereby keeping the vows of silence.

Silenced recently by the government of Nigeria, Ken Saro-Wiwa was a sensitive poet whose poems articulate the muzzled voice of one entrapped in what used to be called the "rebel enclave." He was from Ogoni, an oil-rich riverine area of the East, now Rivers State, which at one point during the crisis became the bone of contention and the indigenes became the beautiful bride to be wooed. The Biafran side was bent on controlling this area if not for any other reason but to deprive the Federal side of the rich oil fields of the area. When secession was contemplated the rich oil fields were seen as a gold mine to be exploited by the new nation of Biafra. Realizing that Nigeria would be a huge but poor nation without the oil-rich fields, Lagos used all the forces at her disposal as well as coercion and propaganda to wring out the riverine areas from Biafra. To achieve this, the Federal side fought hard to win the support of the Rivers people, especially the enlightened ones among them, some of whom even before the hostilities started were already disenchanted with Biafra. (Before the dream of Biafra, some of them led by Isaac Adaka Boro had attempted to pull their people out of the then Eastern Nigeria and were subsequently charged with treason.) Ken Saro-Wiwa was a young lecturer at the University of Nigeria, Nsukka before the war but he escaped to Lagos in September 1967 and was subsequently appointed Administrator for Bonny by the Federal Government.

The synthesis of Ken Saro-Wiwa's poetry is that there were voices of dissent within the Biafran enclave but they dared not bare their mind. To such people "the vows of silence" became very sacrosanct and "must be kept/or else . . . they will be where silence will be kept" forever. It would be foolhardy on

154

the part of any sane person to speak to a regime that was utterly averse to any form of criticism.

"Silence" recaptures the mood of the time when people gagged their mouths to avoid the wrath of the roaring guns. The poem "Silence" is epigrammatic; it says much in a few words. The structure is such that the first three lines and the last five lines complement each other. The first and tenth lines are one-word lines indicating "silence" and each ends with a period. Apart from the first line—"where silence will be kept"—which also reinforces the first and tenth lines, no other line in the poem ends with a period. The poem appeals to the auricular through words like speak, roar, cry, heard, and loud resonance and the import of the word "silence" becomes more pungent in the midst of these words of action.

The second of Saro-Wiwa's seven poems, "Voices," speaks of the issues that claimed the attention of the dramatic personae in both Nigeria and Biafra—taxes and royalties, oil, power, honor, pride of tribe, war and its implements. In the face of all these, the poet in line with "the vows of silence," does not only uses the unidentified "they" but also withdraws completely to talk of love only.

> They speak of tanks
> And putrid human flesh
> I sing my love
> for Maria (13).

The poet's resignation and indifference in the face of the impending carnage when people speak "of war . . . of tanks and putrid flesh" is worse than the entry into a church of Mtshali's persona on seeing his brother being clobbered "like a victim of slaughter" by the dark forces of oppression in South Africa (Mtshali 1972). This selfish alienation puts Saro-Wiwa on a different level from, say, Christopher Okigbo, whose own last testament is devoid of any personal consideration but instead like a sacrificial lamb offers "the ram's ultimate prayer to the tether"—which is his own life. While Okigbo would warn against the impending danger, Saro-Wiwa would keep silent and instead sing of love. Saro-Wiwa characteristically visual-

155

izes the more troubled times ahead as he admits in "Invitation" that "surely, the doom is near." But he is incensed by what he calls:

> the lack of vision
> of greed and mad ambition
> That stones the mind and stops the
> heart from beating a rhythm of love.

As he attests in this poem, "love and truth are strangers here."

In this poem, the poet invites his friend to come and sing with him but more importantly he wants to enjoy life before the darkness falls.

> Let me love and sing and dance
> Let me dance and sing and love
> Before the doom engulfs.

Though Saro-Wiwa wishes to live and sing love, "Invitation" is more of nostalgic lament of a lover of peace who sings of "times that were and are no more," one who is grieved that the greed and mad ambition of a few individuals "stones the mind and stops the heart/from beating a rhythm of love." What he sees as the lack of vision leaves a hole in his heart and one feels that his desire to sing and dance is only perfunctory since he anticipates an engulfing doom.

"Night Encounter" presages the bloody months ahead as the poet encounters a soldier "One dark night, I met him one with the darkness" (16). The atmosphere is murky as "the skies wept heavy tears." The tone is laden with pity for the would-be victims of the carnage, "the soldier on patrol duty/The man who was about to die."

It is very pertinent to observe that the lines of "Night Encounter" were written at Nsukka near the border about a month before the university town became a war theater. Saro-Wiwa's effort to foreshadow the "dying sun riddled with bullets," the "harsh boots on stones," and "the curse of doom" is very noteworthy. The uneasiness at Nsukka, the border town which at this time seemed to be stifling people's lives, and the uneasy

calm of the nights as "the clang and clangour snap the silence/
(and) sap the soul" are all vividly recreated in another poem in
the sequence, "Near the Border," which Saro-Wiwa in his later
collection *Songs in a Time of War* (1986), re-titled "Near the
Front." The "metal doors banging" and the harsh boots grat-
ing on stones as well as the "clang and clangour" that not only
"snap the silence of the still world but snaps the soul at "bush
of night" recreate the pathetic predicament and suffering of
the apartheid victims of "Night Fall in Soweto" (Mtshali 1972).
This poem vividly shows the apprehension of insecurity that
was the lot of the inhabitants of Nsukka where the poet was at
that time.

One peculiar quality of Ken Saro-Wiwa's poetry is the ability to provoke the mind to thought. The poems set the mind
wondering, questioning, drawing conclusions. This is achieved
through Saro-Wiwa's terseness and precision in the use of
words.

This quality is everywhere in the very intense poems. From
"Silence," the lines:

> And the vows of silence
> Must be kept
> Or else . . .
> Where silence will be kept

set the mind wondering on and conjecturing the consequences
of the foolhardiness if one raising a contrary view or an opposite voice here where the guns roar, where one daily hears "the
curse of doom" ("Near the Border"), where people "speak of
tanks and putrid human flesh." The same control of language
is also seen in "Voices," where the two-line stanzas vividly articulate what occupy people's minds. The language of the poems is quite simple but pithy and the poet's attitude could be
said to be cynical. This attitude is the treacherous reaction of
one who witnessed all the preparations, sang about "the lack
of vision/or greed and mad ambition" but deflected for fear of
being "the man who was about to die."

Ken Saro-Wiwa later enlarged his war poems and published
them under the title, *Songs in a Time of War*. Some of the po-

ems in this collection make quite interesting reading. One can say that in most of these poems borne out of real war experiences he no longer can afford to sing of his love for Maria when others speak of war and of bows and arrows. The time lapse between the poems in the sequence "A Voice in the Wind" and some of the poems in this book (which one might describe as the actual war poems because they were probably written at the time of hostilities) is seen in the poem titled "Corpses Have Grown." The war is raging and the "the bumping thud of bombs has driven ancestral spirits way from home", and what is more, "the orphaned land weeps." The poem, "Corpses Have Grown," conjures a lot of pathos. The land, the poet observes, is festered with cadavers and life has ground to a halt as "the xylophone of the deceased chief/is still" (18). As the ancestral spirits of the land, "driven from home/walk tearful abroad," the people squat before the shrines with bleeding knees in pain, offering prayers that are never answered.

> The morning libation is vain
> In vain the loud name-call . . .
> The sacrificial cocks are dumb.

The uncertainty of the times and the bleak future are recreated by the new year which ". . . unheralded/By shouts of laughing children" seeps sadly into empty homes. The dominant imagery here is one of emptiness or void, numbness and silence on the part of women and animals. Corpses have covered the land. The xylophone, a traditional musical instrument symbolic of activity, is still. "The sacrificial cocks are dumb." The homes and the bridal chambers are all empty, their inmates having been driven away by the horrors of war. "The old year is dead" and the new year is engulfed in silences. He notices that the only sounds that fill the earth are those of devastation and death.

> Earth echoes with alien sounds -
> Shatering rifles, weird moans-
> And the harsh face of war
> Fills the land with abomination.(18)

Faced with these harsh realities of war away from "home" and with the "horizon taut with uncertainty," Saro-wiwa had no alternative than to plan an escape from Biafra. "The Escape," a sort of poetic travelogue, recaptures the adventurous escape wading through storms on the Andoni River to Bonny through Escravos Bay to the safe sands of Lagos. The poem begins with the plight of refugees who have fled their homes, the memories of which were gradually being obliterated from their mind. "The dwelling in the village/Faded out of sight and mind" (p. 19). The bleakness of the days was unending, "It was like the rainy season in Bane/It lingered and lingered so." This comparison of the suffering with the never-ending rain that fall in "sheets" in this rain forest region is spectacular and the future that faced the victims was only "a drawn-out horizon taut with uncertainly."

> At dawn, instead of the expected sun
> Sheets of rain began to fall
> The evil wild storm lasted so long
> We thought it would never end.

With this fear of the unending "evil wild storm," which is symbolic of their sufferings, the only alternative for them is to move and with this movement on the Andoni River came some brightness. The poet expresses this glimmer of hope in these enchanting lines:

> Swimming on beyond the canoe
> A lone fish dived and resurfaced
> Leading on, so it seemed
> To the realms of peace. (19)

The "lone fish" diving, resurfacing and leading the way acts like the star to the Magi. The silent birds standing on stumps watching the sojourners are all in sympathy with man. The poet vividly expresses the sojourners' internal emotional reaction, their fears and their hopes.

We sat at the bottom of the dug-out
Fear stirring our hearts
Hope lighting our way
As we fled from the stink of war
The stain of greed and bitterness. (20)

The risk these voyagers were taking was adequately compensated by the consolation that they were fleeing from "the stink
of war," a war that was an aftermath of greed and rancor. This
feeling of safety in the end is the hope that lighted their way.
Their arrival in Bonny 'at sundown/through the snaky creeks'
is blessed by the setting sun which 'lit (them) a spangled way.'
One notices the very effective use of personification in this
verse. Nature and animals are in sympathy with the escapees.
At Bane, a lone fish showed them the way and birds silently
stood and watched them as they fleed. At Bony, 'the dying sun
lit a spangled way' for them and to crown it all, the river welcome them.

We arrived at sundown
And before dusk the Bonny river
Roared us a throaty welcome

The picture of Bonny is one of deep reverence and though the
guns boom here the poet has some respite and is more relaxed
as he can now exchange cigar with the soldier "in a trench."
Bonny, "this ancient isle," has always witnessed the boomings
of naval guns but this time "the issues are far greater." Saro-
Wiwa's precision in language is well illustrated in this stanza.

On this ancient isle
Washed by the deep blue sea
Naval guns boom as at yore
Only the issues are far greater. (20)

Here the poet has succinctly given the history of Bonny, its
geographical location by the Atlantic Ocean (the deep blue
sea), the fact that Bonny has for a long time witnessed the
booming of naval guns but this time the reasons for the guns,
"the issues"— are not only different but "are far greater." The

third part of the poem titled "Escravos Bay," starts with apos-
trophes. The poet hails the bay and this shows the excitement
on sighting the Escravos Bay. The lyricism here is exquisite as
the diction mirrors the joy of the persona in beholding "the
gentle lap-lapping of wavelets." This excitement is, however,
tinged with sad memories of the slave trade:

> The Bay of Slaves! Escravos! Escravos!
> Nature's own beauty!

But the arrival here seems to offer the same relief that the
freed slaves might have found in the emergent city-states of
the Delta at the abolition of the Slave Trade in the first decades of the nineteenth century. The poet's reference to "the
ruin of the old" suggests the disquiet that was Bonny's following the rivalry of the "Houses" and the intervention of the
British Counsul Beecroft, who in 1854 deported King Pepple
V of Bonny. (Anene, 1969: 306) What the poet calls "joy on
wrong" in this poem immediately gives way to uncertainty and
weeping: "All night we dreamt of horror and death/ . . . And
we wept," (21). The liveliness of the bay, "The bright morning
sun" and the refreshing wind would have been comforting
enough but for the sad reminders of the bloody times symbolized by "the dawn beyond the bay all red/like a bloodbath" and
the "khaki-decked soldiers/rifles slung" who are awaiting the
arrival of the escapees in the barge "drawling like a crab." The
consolation is that they have arrived at "the welcome shores"
but because they are aware that the danger is not over, they
lay half awake and still prayed for peace. The arrival of the
escapees to "the sands of Lagos," it appears, is shrouded in
doubts and uncertainty. The poet seems to be unsure if Lagos
would really provide the much needed peace.

> . . . After the storm-tossed night
> The sands of Lagos
> And cohorts of bathers
> Peace? (21)

More correctly, perhaps, this rhetorical question which ends this poem may be expressing the poet's unbelief at the apparently peaceful Lagos with people relaxed, quite oblivious of what others are suffering somewhere within the same country. Elechi Amadi, a Nigerian novelist, also from Rivers State as Ken Saro-Wiwa, makes the same astonishing discovery of the unperturbed life in Lagos during the war in his novel *Sunset in Biafra*. (Amadi 1973:169)

The perfect art of disinformation (or is it propaganda?) whose resonance sounded louder than the guns, is taken up again in the next poem. The poet seems to be addressing the people who were easily gulled by the propaganda and could smile at the false "radio account/of victories and smashed battalions." The poet says if such people had witnessed the firing and seen the victims of the "balls of fire," their reaction would have been different:

> Were you there to see sticking out
> Of the shallow sandy grave
> As though in supplication
> The bony palms of the bombed soldier.

The poem achieves effect through the poet's use of suspense. This suspense is illustrated firstly by the quoted lines above, where the structural ordering of the lines leaves the direct object of what to see till the last line. Above all, in the poem the conditions the poet gives (were you there) are piled up in three stanzas of eleven lines till the last stanza of two lines when the poet completes the propositions.

> You would not smile at the radio account.
> Of victories and smashed battalions. (22)

The constant evocation of visual images in the three stanzas ("Were you there to see . . .") keeps the gory sights of war hanging like a pendulum before the reader's eyes. The image of the "shallow sandy grave," of "the bombed soldiers" whose bony palms stick out as "though in supplication," does not only arouses pathos but also shows the extent to which life has been

162

devalued. This image of violence is complemented by the picture of the lean dog reaping human skulls in a shallow gutter in another poem, "Ogale—An Evacuated Town" (29).

The thoughts of the carnage give the poet sleepless nights hence in "Midnight" he becomes envious of the young "brown eyes" who "can laugh and sing/And sleep in bliss," while he is "storm-tossed/in tormenting billows" (23) that buffet him "from shore to shore." Now "a listless insomniac," he is all-prayer for the tender child so that he does not suffer his own fate.

> May you always laugh and sing
> Young innocence, e'en when storms
> Towering high wash me down. (23)

One peculiarity of these poems is their personalized dimension or rather tone. This makes the experiences very touching and one sees the communal sufferings through the poetry. The voice is the "I" or "We" and the experiences are "my" or "our."

> How I envy you . . .
> While I, I'm storm-tossed . . .
> My smile a quickish mirthless grin
> My sleep a garish closing of the eyes (p. 23)
> We drank in long draughts . . . (p. 19)
> We arrived at sundown . . . (p. 20)
> And we wept. (p. 21).

The poet/persona is a participant. One notices that in most of these poems the most grueling agony of the poet is the constant thought of the present that was bleak and hopeless and the futureless future. Faced with this predicament the poet in "Thoughts in Time of War" waits endlessly for music to soothe his "troubled soul". Instead what jars his ears are "the monotonous rhythm of rain' and "the bumping thud of bombs." This death din sets the "troubled soul" thinking firstly of the young men who at the front "clubber one another" and "groan painfully and die/for a cause they barely understand."(24) Secondly, the poet thinks of those victims and wonders if they must die so that others might live. Thirdly, in "Thoughts of Time of War", the poet reminisces on patriotism and "that honour and sweet we preach/To them that are to die" and seems to abhor "the famous lie about the sweat and honour/that lie in dying for one's country" (p. 24). The allusion to "sweat and honour" reminds one of Wilfred Owen's poem "Dulce et Decorum Est" which apparently provided Saro-Wiwa the idea of "the old lie." (Owen 1974:558) The poet finally calls on the panel-beaters of truth, those who through their lies lead the unwary young men to their death and asks how they can untell the lies that have led many to their grave.

> Ye bakers and hawkers of lies
> Who bare your jaws and call for wars,
> Inviting the lame, the blind and the deaf
> To the merry ways of guns
> Where shall you find the lotion,
> The balm to heal their wonds? (24)

The diction of this poem is quite intriguing, as one can see from the above lines how the poet (through the assonance of) in ". . . your jaws and call for wars" seems to mirror the gaping mouths of these "bakers and hawkers of lies."

The ultimate stand the poet seems to hold is that it is more honorable for one to live than to die for one's country for he insists that it is only the living who can know what is happening since all consciousness is denied the dead.

> The death is a taskmaster
> And only the living can know
> That honour and sweat we preach
> To them that are to die . . .

"Thoughts in Time of War" reminds one of J. P. Clark's "The Casualties" and Domkat Bali's "Propaganda," all of which call attention to the powerful effect of propaganda which leads many young men to early death.

"Ogale—An Evacuated Town" paints the dismal picture of a town that has been a war theatre, saturated with cannibalized and amputated cars lying abandoned by the wayside. The second stanza of this poem shows the extent to which life has been debased: dogs forage and reap human skulls.

> A lone lean dog
> Scrounging for food
> Reaps human skulls
> In a shallow gutter (29)

The picture is that of devastation, defilement, and mourning. Ogale, the town which is probably bisected by a tarred road, mourns the loss of her sons and daughters whose wails the poet hears.

> Ogale lies in broken images
> Across the narrow tarmac
> Mourning insensate
> His lost sons and daughters
> Whose wails I hear
> This eerie night (p. 29).

These sons and daughters no doubt have either died or are languishing somewhere as refugees. The image of Ogale as "a ravished woman," "a cheap prostitute...utterly exposed," is very striking. The vulgarity shows the destruction of the sacredness of life and there is a tinge of wickedness attributed to the perpetrator of the evil on Ogale.

> For Ogale out in the dreary rain
> Her legs apart like a cheap prostitute
> Exposed, utterly exposed
> Ogale is a ravished woman.

The "wet angry skies" to which the roofless broken houses "gape forlorn" shows the extent to which nature is angry with the horrible devastation. One immediately sees the very epigrammatic picture of the desolate and empty village.

> Cars cannibalized
> Amputated

Lie by the roadside
Abandoned
Forgotten.

The arrangement of the lines with the words "amputated," "abandoned," and "forgotten" indented and each taking one line depict the prevailing disorder. The lines themselves appear amputated and abandoned. The arrangement of those lines further shows the poet's sadness at the annoying vandalistic traces the poet sees and this sadness is again complemented by the picture of the lone lean dog scrounging for food and defiling God's noble creation. A comparison of this poem with a similar one by Domkat Bali, "The Deserted Town," shows that while Saro-Wiwa's is pungent with sustained imagery, Bali's does not go beyond the commonplace and lacks poetic merit (Bali 1974:22-23).

The poem, "To Sarogua, Rain Maker" is both a lament and a prayer of people who have returned from the bloody war completely disoriented. Like the voice in Lenrie Peters' "We Have Come Home," these people have returned with sunken hearts. The difference here is that the war they have returned from, unlike Lenrie Peters', is "The thunderstorm raising blood." The apostrophe to Sarogua and the hyperbole show "the extraordinary mighty one/whose wink brings rain."(30) The war has caused a lot of damage, hence the poet laments that they did not ask for war and swears that they will no more do anything that will bring war.

We'll speak no more
Of coups and colonels
And raids at dead of night.

The voice pleads with Sarogua "the mighty one" to "wash the stain of strife away." The rain the poet asks for is "a cleansing shower" for both the people and the land. The implication is that the people have soiled their hands and the land has been defiled and all need cleansing. This is the poet's confession and prayer.

We did not pray for war
Wash the stain of strife away . . .
Receive us, mighty one
With a cleansing shower. (30)

Another poem, "Epitaph for Biafra" is an indictment on the people of Biafra who believed in the invincibility of the young nation and pitched their puny strength against the Federal might. The poem is in four sections. The first section asks two questions that seem to blame Biafrans for their insistence on the war in which many

. . . young men lost their bones
In lonely trenches
In a plain of agony. (33)

The poet's voice is that of an enraged Nigerian at the end of the war asking "Where will they (Biafrans) go now?" This question, no doubt, is borne out of the orchestrated Biafran propaganda that impressed on all that Nigeria was not a healthy and safe place for Biafrans. The second section focuses attention on the sufferings, resourcefulness, and ingenuity of the people who during the hostilities were forced by circumstances to have "snakes for lunch/and lizards for breakfast." The survival game which they played successfully is praiseworthy, though the poet seems to deride them as he says they will have toads for supper. Toads for supper may be an allusion to Chukwumeka Ike's novel of that title. In the third section the poet seems to be incensed with Biafrans for playing at "rebels and vandals" who, having failed in their secession bid, will now

. . . return as agents
And angels
Laughing and weeping and begging
For minor mercies.

This follows the recriminatory utterances of many highly placed people on the Biafran side who in an attempt to exonerate themselves at the end of the war blamed one another for the intransigence. These blames and counter-blames annoy this bemused poet who in the last stanza of the poem warns that "they should stop their foul breath/From infecting God's good air." (p. 34).

The fourth section asks three rhetorical questions that seem very pertinent. Did the Biafrans not know that fighting leads to death? Why did they not test their military strength before marching it against a superior force? The analogy of the fragility of an egg and the hardness of a rock standing for the weakness of Biafra and the might of Nigeria, respectively, is very striking.

> Didn't they test the hardness of the egg
> On the skin of their teeth
> Before dashing it against the rocks?
> Didn't they know that water turned wine
> But once in days of yore?

From all indications this poem, "Epitaph for Biafra," was probably written immediately after the war and seems to portray the minds of those "renegades" who defected to the Nigerian side during the war and now saw themselves as the wise and foresighted ones. To such people the Federal Government's policy of "No victor no vanquished" after the war did not receive full blessing. Biafra was dead and they were happy it died; hence the epitaph.

The disillusionment with Nigeria which the poet poignantly expresses in the pidgin poem "Dis Nigeria Sef" (36-44) completely erases the supposedly good sentiment towards her expressed in "Epitaph for Biafra." The Nigeria which in "Epitaph for Biafra" was presented as a country where one breeds good air now stinks. The decadence to which Nigeria has sunk makes her irretrievable.

> Nigeria don spoil
> Water wey dey boil
> No hot like this Nigeria
> Pot sef wey don black propa        ·
> Dem fit wash am till 'e clear

No be so for this Nigeria
De more you wash, de more 'e soil. (36)

The poet expressed frustration with the country, Nigeria, which is full of confusion and defies all attempts to make her change. The poem catalogues most of the ills in the country—the phones that never work, the hospital where "all de medicine is out of stock," the Nigerian Airways whose flights are constantly cancelled, the train system that delays for a week, and the boss who is forever dodging his duty. The poem "Dis Nigeria Sef" is a complete vindication of the Biafran stand and assessment of Nigeria shortly before the hostilities.

This rottenness of Nigeria, its confusion, and the lack of a sense of direction are all shown in the scatological imagery in the fourth and fifth stanzas of the poem "Dis Nigeria Sef." The odor of the nation is now more nauseating than the stench of a decomposing body.

Person wey don quench sef no go smell so
Poto poto for gutter, latrine for road,
Shit for bucket, yeye don de smell
Cow and goat dey block road for motor.

Nigeria, the poet insists, is an embodiment of confusion where "chop and drink dey mix with shit" and in utter exasperation the poet asks Nigeria: "Why all your ting na soso confusion?" The houses that cannot stand the rains show how unpatriotic Nigerians are in executing national projects. Nigeria, according to the poem, is an opposite country where soldiers shoot their brothers instead of the enemy and the Nigeria Police is an embodiment of corruption.

For yonder soza dey shoot him enemy
Nigeria soza dey shoot him broder
Oder people police na gentleman propa
Nigeria Police na wuruwuru wayo tief.

The poet does not leave out Nigerians' penchant for useless titles and names. He lashes at the Muslim who glories in the

out-of-content title "Alhaji," reserved for strangers in Saudi
Arabia as well as the country that has over two hundred languages.

> You no see as him dey proud
> Him be alhaji, double alhaji
> Dey put gold for all him teeth
> Sake of him don go mecca return.

Nigeria is bitterly castigated for borrowing everything from
language to clothes, money, automobile, names and food and
is condemned for confusing whatever it comes in contact with.

> You dey borrow chop, you borrow drink
> Sotey you borrow anoder man language
> Begin confuse am with your confusion
> Anytin you borrow you do confuse am to nonsense.
> (98-101)

The poet is incensed at the way Nigerians adopt foreign names
without pausing to look at the meaning of such Moslem or
Christian names.

> You no dey tink, you no dey shame . . .
> Name sef you no get, Peter, Paul
> Nincompoop . . . Pepper Excreta . . .
> Abdullahi Hussein Muhamadu Haba!
> Common name you must borrow borrow.

The poet's disgust and anger are shown in the inclusion of
such things as "Excreta," "Pepper," and "Nincompoop" in the
litany of useless names Nigerians adopt. The civil servant who
loafs about, embezzles the nation's money to build his personal house, the half-baked technicians who are incapable of
inventing anything new, and the half-educated man who ter-
rorizes his towns people in the village, do not escape the poet's
hammer.

> Person wey say him get money
> Or like him sabi small book

No for him village 'e go run go
begin de confuse people with goat and kaikai
Push-me-I-push-you say him be chief
Chief tief, chief doctor, doctor debtor. (11.151-6)

In the same vein, the poet is bitter with the "fine fine gals dem
sef" who have no healthy means of livelihood but "paint their
mouth and nails" and put on very costly dresses. He labels all
of them prostitutes and asks them: "Abi you no sabi say ashawo
no be work?" To vividly portray his anger with these loose
girls the poet borrows from a popular Nigerian Highlife music
of the 1960s titled "Baby Pancake" which castigated Nigerian
girls, of that period for their obscene but elaborate facial make-
ups. The poem says "Baby Pancake: Iyawo pancake, una too
rub (11.163-170).

The poet's tone changes from line 179 where the poet pipes
down as if he has suddenly realized that he has been too sarcastic at the expense of the nation. The point here is that the
poet realizes that Nigeria does not welcome criticism and will
easily use its forces to silence any critic.

... I know as you dey do your own
You no dey like make person talk true
Small time now you fit send your pickin
Weder soza police or kotuma ash bottom
Make dem wahala my life small
Come lock me for one dirty shit prison.
(11.182-7)

These lines no doubt allude to the coercive military regimes
which can muzzle a man for speaking the truth. The poet wants
to escape being a victim of military harassment by identifying
himself with the country's problems as he says:

Nigeria and myself na one belly
If 'e get bellyache, me I get bellyache
If 'e no get to chop, me I go hungry qua
Nigeria and myself we be prick and blokkus.
(11.196-99)

The poet goes on to highlight some of the potentialities the country has—her beautiful citizens from both the North and the South—some who are very hardworking and some who live honest lives.

> Which one again go fine like your face?
> Look dose Fulani gals, fine calabash
> Come slender like palm tree
> See the waterside gals like mami water
> See as dem dey smile, dey waka with style.

The poet, however, seeks this amalgam of the good and the bad in Nigeria as an index of her confusion which nauseates the poet hence he exclaims, "Dis Nigeria Sef,/You too bring confusion" (11.264-5).

"Dis Nigeria Sef" is a poem that catalogues the ills inherent in the Nigerian nation and is born out of disappointment and frustrated hopes of a nation that has lost valuable chances of improving herself.

The tone is bitter, though the poet midway tries to attenuate this bitterness by trying to pander to the powers-that-be. This sudden switch in tone mars the style and detracts from the original and intended impact of the poem. By this act the poet, a moral force, chickens out of a laudable crusade by giving in to the force of armament. Though one may not fully endorse the poet's dirty language in some parts of the poem, one realizes, however, that it is the voice of a person disgusted with a system or a country that has defied efforts for improvement and that the language employed here is part of that very decay which he deploys.

Ken Saro-Wiwa uses his own language—"Rotten English"—which is neither standard English nor pure pidgin and this is quite intriguing. According to Ken Saro-Wiwa in *Sozaboy:*

> Rotten English is a mixture of Nigerian
> pidgin English, broken English and
> occasional flashes of good, even idiomatic
> English. This language is disordered and
> disorderly. (Author's Note, *Sozaboy*)

There is evidence of the poet's use of the phonetic defects of some Nigerians in the pronunciation of such words as "Soza" for "soldier" instead of "soja" in pidgin and "aks" for "ask." Some examples are the use of typical Nigerian pidgin words like "wahala" for "trouble," "hala" for "shout," "oga" or "sah" for "master," "potopoto" for "filth," or "mud," "wetin" for "what," "wuruwuru" for "dishonesty" and "intrigue," "push-me-I-push-you" or "kai kai" for locally brewed gin, "kotuma ash bottom" for court bailif. In his classic novel, *Things Fall Apart*, Chinua Achebe uses "kotuma ash buttocks" (1967:158). The use of 'bottom' by Saro-Wiwa shows the low level of the language which matches the tone of the poem. The words "whosai" for "where" and "sidon" for "sit down," call for mention as these give the poem a hilarious texture. The poet also uses local words used in many parts of the country like "agaracha," a word which came into Igbo vocabulary during the war to stand for either the deserter or the exile, "ashawo," Yoruba for prostitute, "oyibo"—an Igbo word for whiteman, "iyawo"—a Yoruba word for woman or wife, and "haba"—a typical Hausa exclamation for "why". These words make the language of the poem appeal to a cross section of the country. The poet also uses local onomatopoeic words like: "wuruwuru" and "potopoto" to highlight the negative aspects of the country.

"Dis Nigeria Sef" is Saro-Wiwa's post-mortem of the nation years after the war and brings out very vividly the degeneration in the country as well as the poet's disappointment with the country for its failure to improve itself. The decadence and lethargy of the Nigerian nation is portrayed through the images of dirt, disorder, confusion, and indiscipline. Even though it was written years after the war, there are in the poem traces of the war. The soldiers who shoot their brothers, the "wuruwuru wayo tief police" and the "agaracha" are all products of the war.

Saro-Wiwa's war poems are full of emotions emanating from the poet's participation in the war. This involvement tended to give some of the poems a bias narrative texture. By articulating the almost suffocating voice of the silent minority in the then Biafran enclave in his poetry, Ken Saro-Wiwa enriched Nigerian Civil War poetry in a special way. It is unfortunate and ironical that this prolific writer who sacrificed so much and alienated himself from friends and colleagues and working assiduously for the survival of the Nigerian nation should so end fighting for his ethnic minority.

## Works Cited

Amadi, Amadi. *Sunset in Biafra*. Ibadan: Heinemann, 1973:169.

Anene, J. C., "Benin, Niger Delta, Ibo and Ibibio Peoples' in the Nineteenth Century." In *A Thousand Years of African History*, ed., J. F. Ajayi and Ian Espie. Ibadan: University Press, 1969: 306

Bali, Domkat. *War Cries*. Lagos: Civiletis Nigeria, 1984: 22-23.

Chinua Achebe *Things Fall Apart*. London: Heinemann, 1967:158.

Clark, J. P. *A Decade of Tongues*. London: Longmans, 1980.

Mtshali, Oswald. *Sounds of A Cowhide Drum*. London: Oxford University Press, 1972: 56.

Owen, Wildred. "Dulce et Decorum Est." In Laurence Perrine, *Literature: Structure, Sound, and Sense*. New York: Harcourt Brace, 1974: 558.

Saro-Wiwa, Ken. *Songs in a Time of War*. Port Harcourt: Saros International Publishers, 1985: 14.

Saro-Wiwa, Ken. *Sozaboy*. Port Harcourt: Saros International Publishers, 1985. Author's Note.

## 13

# Ken Saro-Wiwa:
## Poetic Craft, Prophetic Calling

### Titi Adepitan

The post-structuralist humanist crisis in the arts may yet redress itself after all. It does seem mankind may never succeed in finding a replacement for itself as subject and object of artistic pursuits, and no matter how long we wander far afield in the pursuit of signs and other faddisms of the technologization of letters by the West, man has only to butt his toe against a stump, score another victory over his environment, or take a long, invigorating walk in the early morning mists of dawn to realize that deconstruction may not be what the arts, particularly literature, are all about. The very best and most salient of our literature must still return to a conscious address of its provenance, the state of being of humanity, in order to compel our attention.

Distinctions between art and artifice, craft and calling, are inevitable in discussing the writings of Ken Saro-Wiwa. An Indian critic, C. D. Narasimhaiah deposes in his essay, "What have the Arts in Common?" as follows: "If what goes out as sympathy to an individual retains its creative edge, it can, when the social concern is directed to a large group and becomes general, degenerate into social realism, protest literature and protest art . . . Enter protest, exit literature!" Narasimhaiah makes his argument for the essentiality of the arts against a formidable background of evidence from both the literary traditions of the West and Bhuddist thought, liberally cluttered with the cabbalisms of oriental discourse. There is need to "recuperate" the writings of Saro-Wiwa as much from the excessive formalism of the West as from the divine conception of art and the deification of genius to which oriental reflections on art are prone.

The significance of Ken Saro-Wiwa as a writer should become increasingly clear now, after his death and the circumstances leading to it. There is a prophetic, all-embracing commitment to a depiction of the reality of his Ogoni people in his works about which he seems helpless. In other writers for whom literature has served as an organ of expression for minorities or the under-privileged, such as J. M. Synge or Ngugi wa Thiong'o, the same earnestness is present, but perhaps not the same near-total withdrawal into the W*eltanschauung* of a minority; like other writers in whom the first-person narrator frequently functions as a statement of the innocence and naivéty of youth, irrespective of the distance from authorial personality, as V. S. Naipaul or William Saroyan, there is the same customary wild-eyed innocence, cynicism, or occasional bafflement of traditional life, but not the dark, pervasive suggestion of authorial immolation which has finally found grim consummation in Saro-Wiwa's final encounter with Nigeria's bizarre politics of nation-building. Saro-Wiwa's career is a refutation of notions of the significance of the literary enterprise outside the matrix of communal aspirations and populist beliefs.

Saro-Wiwa will endure for long in the consciousness of the world because his writings are an expression of faith in literature's boundless humanist possibilities; they are likely to win their appeal and attention as much by the facilities of good style and sundry pre-occupations of technique which Saro-Wiwa also quite legitimately possessed or cultivated as by their relentless focus on the tribulations and anxieties of the Ogoni homeland. No doubt Nigerians will wake up one day to discover that in the small man from Ogoniland, more remembered for his pipe and the timbre of his laughter, Nigeria pro-

duced, without being aware of the fact, one of the major literary voices of the contemporary world whose ideas will surely
catch on.

To suggest a relationship of the prophet between Saro-
Wiwa and his writing may not be an exaggeration. For that
matter there is in his career something of an overloading of
"avocations" (his word) and responsibilities variously devolv-
ing on the ethnographer, the creative writer, the polemicist,
the politician, and the activist leader. And the sum of his out-
put in the larger Nigerian literary and socio-political contexts
has to be seen in terms of Saro-Wiwa's self-perception of his
responsibilities and affiliations in these roles. He deserves to
be called a prophet, a Moses of his people, to the extent that
his exertions in our political and socio-economic culture, backed
up by a programmatic approach to the vocation of letters, were
all meant as strategies for constructing a secure niche for the
Ogoni in the Nigerian political and economic equations and
winning some respectability in the larger world.

I have argued in another paper that part of the mystique
which African and Third World literature and writers in general hold for their contemporaries in the West is the enduring
salience of their concerns and the force of their moral authority. The Japanese-born British novelist, Kazuo Ishiguro, for
instance, laments that "the front line" in the commitment of
literature to popular struggle "somehow seems to be" in "places
like Africa, or Eastern Europe, or Latin America." Writers from
Western Europe, according to Ishiguro, "in the latter part of
the twentieth century . . . are writing from somewhere very
far away from where the main events are taking place, and we
somehow lack the natural authority of writers who are living
in Czechoslovakia, or East Germany, or Africa, or India, or
Israel, or the Arab countries." Ishiguro is himself not a member of the hapless breed whose fate he laments in a European
literary relevance gone *passe*. He is able to carve new areas of
concern and pertinence for himself in his fiction; in the first
two novels, especially *A Pale View of Hills* and *An Artist of the
Floating World*, Ishiguro succeeds in re-prioritizing the values
and other cultural habits of his Japanese people, as a way of
exploding some of the Western myths about the race.

Saro-Wiwa's faith in the instrumentality of literature for the transformation or radicalization of culture puts him in the distinguished company of the likes of Ishiguro, for whom literature as art is the voice of the voiceless, the badge of identity that otherwise anonymous persons, cultures, and societies carry in order to stand up and be counted in the civilized world. In Saro-Wiwa's writings there is a relentless effort to project the Ogoni viewpoint, especially through the little joys and the several disappointments and frustrations which define the existence of the people. If the fictive medium of the stories and novels somehow obstructs a full appreciation of his metier as a writer, Saro-Wiwa's essays in the "Similia" column in the *Sunday Times* lend the requisite bite to his perception of national politics. The social, crusading basis of his writings on behalf of minority rights has to be seen as a life-time project in the name of his people; and his cynical readers may yet be humbled by the prophetic resonance, the candor and vitality of his writings and, above all, the writers' all-consuming attempt to make the culture and beliefs of the Ogoni available to the reading public.

This latter concern pervades *The Singing Anthills: Ogoni Folktales*, a series of fables dominated by the wily and ubiquitous Kuru, the Tortoise. As in fables from other societies with which some of the tales in *The Singing Anthill* share character, tone, and moral perspective, the Tortoise is invariably the *enfant terrible* and *agent provocateur* of folk life rolled into one, and the repository of lore sacred, profane, devious, and self-serving; the animals simply take turns succumbing to the superior machinations of the ever-resourceful Tortoise.

In the first tale, "The Promise," clearly the masterpiece of the collection, Kuru the Tortoise and Kue the Leopard hit upon a plan to go hunting in a season of drought. It is decided that Kue, notorious for his predatory excess before the other animals, should play dead in a canoe while Kuru, busy at the oars, exults over the fallen nuisance before his erstwhile hapless victims. The first animal they meet is an antelope who soon falls for the ruse; she steps into the canoe to take a swipe at Kue, and in a second she lies "at the bottom of the canoe, dead." She is followed by a rabbit, a hippo, and a sea-lion. But Kue the leopard can't have enough; he would not mind monkey meat. In no time Kuru and Kue find one and step into their routine. The monkey tells Kuru to please wait; he wouldn't mind stepping into the canoe to give the dead Kue a punch in the nose. He hops from tree to tree, branch to branch, keeping the dissimulators waiting. Something whooshes the treetops into the canoe, a coconut hits Kue flush in the face and he tumbles over into the river, spluttering. Kuru is the first to burst into laughter, "Wha! wha! wha! wha!" while "Whe! whe! whe! whe!" the monkey joins in.

Saro-Wiwa's authorial presence is heavy in all the tales, and the sundry lessons which he routinely attaches to each at the end may have derived from a notion of children's tales which may not be complete unless clinched at the end with a moral. Nonetheless, his interpretation of the moral of such tales sometimes appears defective, perhaps because they are superimposed by an ethnographer trying to articulate a world-view for his people. Many of the tales are etiological. "A Mother in the Sky" concludes with the moral, "it is believed that had not Kuru hidden his mother successfully at that time, people would today kill their mothers in times of stress." Hardly the appropriate moral to explain why a particular animal chose to hide his mother in the sky while others served up theirs for food in a time of famine. But there is a twist in Saro-Wiwa's version of the tale right from the beginning. The clever animal is Kuru the Tortoise and not the dog of the more familiar versions. In the latter the Tortoise is the interloper, and when the besieged mother of Dog cuts the rope, Tortoise barely survives the crash, his shell a mighty wreck which one of his detractors only succeeds in patching up crudely.

The authorial presence is more pronounced in the earlier collection of short stories, *Adaku and Other Stories*. The stories in this collection are racy and it is obvious there is a problem with control of language. It is not unlikely that some of the stories were written at a younger age. This need not be taken as a criticism; one of the finest stories in the collection, "Ave, Ave, Sathanas!!" was first published in *The Umuahian*, a magazine of Government College, Umuahia, in 1961. The prevailing temper in some of the stories is almost unbridled in its endorsement of all forms of libertinage, as in the stories "The Empire Builders" and "Cross-Pollination." Of course, there is the reassurance of the comic dramatist trying to employ the medium of fiction for a full belly-laugh in the background; in the main, though, the greater risk is of a trivialization of the point of view.

Saro-Wiwa's experimentations with the form also start here. The title story opens with a bird's eye view of Enugu, "This is rolling country . . .." But there is an unmistakable gap between the evocation of environment and atmosphere and the authorial temper. The latter is always restless, flip-flopping between tenses and perspective, trying to co-ordinate the progress of the narrative. It is in "Africa Kills Her Sun" that the future Ken Saro-Wiwa comes into his own. In the story, Bana, one of three condemned robbers, writes a final letter to his girl-friend, and rounds off by choosing an epitaph for himself: "Africa Kills Her Sun," a borrowing from a mythical African leader who stood on the grave of a dead lieutenant and through his tears said: "Africa kills her sons." If the story carries a frightening ring of prophecy, it is not on account of its title alone. Somewhere in it the narrator recalls the story of another condemned man whose one request at the point of death was that his heirloom walking stick be buried with him. Not quite long ago, we need to recall, another man requested that a heirloom pipe be sent to his father.

*A Forest of Flowers*, another collection of short stories, is very accomplished. The first part, consisting of eight stories, is devoted to folk life in Dukana. Aspects of traditional Ogoni life are captured in snapshots and vignettes of emblematic events and incidents told through the eyes of Mene, the narrator, who does not become fully identified along with his complement of freaks and hoboes, almost in the manner of Naipaul's early characters, until *Sozaboy*. These characters, Chief Birabee, Duzia, Bom, Terr Kole, Zaza, Mene, and "Progress" (the ramshackle lorry which services the needs of the village) define a fictive universe for Saro-Wiwa's evocations of Ogoni traditional life in ways that recall similar narrative strategies in the novels of Thomas Hardy.

The second part of the collection, devoted to the larger Nigerian society, is more cosmopolitan in character, and affords the story writer the opportunity of critiquing the national life: the libertinage of city life ("High Life"); police corruption ("Case No. 100"); religious fanaticism and ethnic bigotry ("Garga"); and marital infidelity ("A Caring Man"). The stories in this latter section lend a wider latitude to Saro-Wiwa's finest range and facilitates graces as a writer. Here also the artistic temper is in greater repose, and there is less of the narrative flourishes of *The Singing Anthill* and *Adaku* which tend to insist on the stamp of juvenilia. This is curious, considering that the more reticent of these books are not the most recent in publication.

*Sozaboy* is better known as "a novel in rotten English." Its true significance should derive more properly from its attempt to capture through a commensurate linguistic medium the level of consciousness of characters defined both by social class and rural placing. Certainly, the experiment is not as neat as it is in the shorter forms, as in the stories "Die—A Tribe" (*Adaku and Other Stories*) and "High Life" (*A Forest of Flowers*). No doubt the novel "throbs vibrantly enough and communicates effectively," to borrow Saro-Wiwa's expression in the "Author's Note," but the monotony and the lack of sublimity in the language are major impediments in the way of a successful experiment. The major triumph of the linguistic medium in *Sozaboy* is the way it familiarizes to the reader the eye of innocence through which the story is told and the brash, pragmatic, loquacious but nonetheless plaintive tone which underscores the experiences of a hapless recruit caught up in the counter-claims and cross-fires of somebody's war.

Above all else, Ken Saro-Wiwa will be remembered as a polemicist. *Similia*, a collection of his newspaper articles under a column of that title, is arguably the most poised, the most distinguished and the most wide-ranging body of such opinions we are likely to have in the country in a long while. Saro-Wiwa's views on Nigerian politics and national life are enhanced by his familiarity with crucial personages and their ideas and viewpoints in Nigeria's contemporary history, his own chequered careers in public, business, and social life and a privileged education which lends an appropriate muscularity to his thoughts and elegance to his language.

Those of his critics who picked bones with him on his views on the Yoruba, the question of minorities, and sundry shibboleths of our national life generally missed the point: Saro-Wiwa was hardly ever wrong. In addition, he carried the grievances of a whole community of people who believed rightly that their patrimony was being haggled over and shared out by neighbors and nudniks who had little or no thought for their welfare. If his tone is remorsely acerbic in the newspaper articles, the reason has less to do with the lack of merit of his cause than with the passion with which they are expressed.

There is another lesson we have to imbibe from Saro-Wiwa's political thought. This is our inability to empathize with people in distress simply because the truth which they wail about seems to put our own cranked-up reality in jeopardy. The politics of juggernaut capital and multinational business interests aside, the Ogoni cause which defined the overall perception of Nigeria's power equations by Saro-Wiwa ought to have served as an excellent example of our structural inadequacies without a resolution of which we are not likely to ever know peace. Well, those who knew better finally shouted him to silence.

The dialogue has hardly begun with Ken Saro-Wiwa's writings; acceptance of the value and significance of his ideas will come later as a matter of course

## Works Cited

Ishiguro, Kazuo. *Artist of the Floating World.* London: Faber and Faber, 1986.

————. *A Pale View of Hills.* New York: Vintage, 1990.

————. *Similia: Essays on Anomic Nigeria.* London: Saros International Publishers, 1991.

————. *The Singing Anthills: Ogoni Folktales.* London: Saros International Publishers, 1991.

Saro-Wiwa, Ken. *The Singing Anthills: Ogoni Folktale.* Port Harcourt: Saros International Publishers, 1991.

_____. *Adaku and other Stories*. Port Harcourt: Saros International Publishers, 1989.

_____. *A Forest of Flowers*. Port Harcourt: Saros International Publishers, 1989.

_____.*Sozaboy: A Novel in Rotten English*. Port Harcourt: Saros International Publishers, 1986.

# 14

# The Fictionalist as a Journalist:
## Literary Reportage in Ken Saro-Wiwa's
### *Sozaboy* and *A Forest of Flowers*

Diri I. Telilanyo

(The Writer) may... Propose that he is discovering
*something which the act of writing is reporting.*
(Omotoso 1979:4)

## I

T he aim of this essay is to highlight the overlap that some
times obtains between fictional composition and journalistic reports and to demonstrate this with two works by the
late Nigerian writer, Ken Saro-Wiwa: his novel in "rotten English," *Sozaboy,* and his collection of short stories, *A Forest of
Flowers.*

Fiction is conceived here first in the broad sense as literature, as imaginative composition in language creating beauty
through excellence of form and expression and conveying ideas,
events, and feelings that are of permanent and universal significance. In the restricted sense, it is seen as prose-fiction,
including the novel, the novella, and the short story. The notion of journalism adopted here is that which emphasizes the

collection and periodical publication of current news. It is also recognized that journalism may go beyond the gathering and reporting of events to include analytical journalism or commentary and investigative journalism. The latter two are, however, secondary.

This essay proceeds through four stages: fiction and journalism, Saro-Wiwa's journalistic fiction, the fictionality of fiction, and realism in fiction.

## II

Initially it would appear to be an over-ambitious and futile, if not utterly impossible or irrational, exercise to attempt equating or bringing under the same umbrella literature and journalism. For one is primarily concerned with the presentation of facts and empirical reality and the other is almost always fictional, conceding only "unreal reality"; one is objective in reportage and public-information-oriented, the other is usually a subjective activity full of individual sensibilities and emotions.

At a second look, however, we find that both are art forms and both use primarily language (although journalism now also uses pictures and the cinema) in the search for truth. Thus, the difference gradually evaporates.

This essay has made some underlying assumptions. First the utilitarian function of literature (and art as a whole) is preferred to the purely aesthetic function in its extreme as art-for-art's sake, as in Macleiah's famous line that "A poem should not mean but be." Since its beginning, literature has been functional in reflecting and reshaping empirical reality. Thus epic poetry often uses real-life history as its raw material: the history is merely recollected and recast through the idiosyncratic sensibility and interpretation of the author. Thus, Homer's *Iliad* is known to be an artist's retelling of a series of wars fought between the Greeks and the Trojans. The South African *Chaka the Zulu* and *Sundiata: Epic of Old Mali* are representations of legendary heroes that actually lived in flesh and blood. Renaissance dramatists adopted the histories of classical Greece and Rome for their plots.

Related to the above is the assumption that most of Africa's literature is socially committed. The idea of commitment is clearly expressed by Chinweizu, Jemie, and Madubuike (1980:252-254):

> Artistic commitment, as we see it, is therefore a matter of orientation, a matter of perceiving social realities and making those perceptions available in works of art in order to help promote understanding and preservation of, or change in, the society's values and norms . . . For the function of the artist in Africa in keeping with our traditions and needs, demands that the writer, as a public voice assure a responsibility to reflect public concerns in his writings, and not preoccupy himself with his puny ego. Because in Africa we recognize that art is the public domain, a sense of social commitment is mandatory upon the artist. It also demands that his theme be germane to the concerns of his community.

Thus, the subject matters and techniques (especially language) of African artist's themselves often reflect the concerns and life patterns of the continent.

Wellek and Warren (1963:94), while being cautious of such commitment, admit that "Literature is a social institution... a social creation." The proponents of "art-for-art's sake" condemn such commitment as the didactic heresy (Edgar Alan Poe) and would fastidiously shun matters of contemporary concern to their community as topical, journalistic, sociological, ephemeral. Chinweizu *et al.* (1980:252) condemn such opinions as "sheer humbug."

It tallies with such social relevance that African writers take most of their subjects from contemporary historical events. To Thomas Warton, literature has the "peculiar merit of faithfully recording the features of the representation of manners" (Wellek and Warren 1963:102). To Kole Omotoso (1979:v), "What goes into a novel changes with history". In this way, the artist also becomes a chronicler.

It is when this recasting of history becomes apparent and immediate that literature becomes associated with journalism. Hence, the development of African literature and that of African journalism have always moved *pari-passu* and both have had identical concerns. In the colonial period, the nationalistic and cultural journalism (as in *The West Africa Pilot*) had its ally in the cultural nationalism in literature (as in Achebe's *Things Fall Apart* and Camara Laye's *The African Child*, both defending African culture and pursuing independence. Africa is now in an age of social reconstruction where both fiction and journalism agitate for positive social change.

The overlap between journalism and fiction is brought out very clearly by Obiechina (1973). He has shown that the Onitsha Market pamphleteers adopted most of their fictional themes from newspaper and television reports and the cinema. Thus, African nationalists like Nnamdi Azikiwe, Kwame Nkrumah, Patrice Lummumba were read about in the papers and then were turned into protagonists in fictional prose, drama, and poetry. The subject matter is from the media and stock phrases and cliches were freely lifted from the papers into the literature. Love plots and language patterns were freely adopted and developed from romance cinema.

The operative faculty here is that of imagination. According to Coleridge (1817) imagination "dissolves, diffuses, dissipates, in order to recreate." Hence, the literary artist assimilates and synthesizes the most disparate elements of historical events into an organic whole. Unlike pure journalism, whose reports may stand in their different bits, the literary artist organizes his reports into "a generated unity, constituted by the living interdependence of parts whose identity cannot survive their removal from the whole" (Abrams 1981:60).

While literature has become journalistic on the one hand, journalism has also recently become literary on the other. This literary journalism is noticed in what is called "New Journalism," a term made popular by American journalist, Tom Wolfe. According to Dan Agbese (1992), the term is used "to describe an emerging new style in the American press, a new news reporting and literary technique that blurred the distinction between news reporting, feature writing and fiction", while "some of these people easily crossed the thin, dividing line between journalism and fiction and became novelists." This journalism is marked by artistic ornamentation and embellishment, giving life and vividness through detailed description, each description capable of being "a paragraph from a novel." This new journalism has also come to Africa.

The identity between journalism and literature is brought to a height by Charles Okigbo (1984) in his article "Chris Okigbo: Portrait of the Poet as a Journalist." In it, he portrays the late poet Okigbo's recording of the Nigerian Civil War as it rages on to be journalistic. Therefore Charles Okigbo, a cousin to the poet, gives Okigbo the poet the appellation of a "REPORTER" (that is a poet-reporter or reporter-poet), a term coined by James Murphy to designate a person who maintains his status as a literary artist while at the same time journalizing and reporting. This work is embraced by scholars of New Journalism and in argument seems to be that there is only a thin line of demarcation between works of literature and those of journalism.

It is also noteworthy that many of the world's best novelists have passed through the mass media. We recall Daniel Defoe (Note his *A Journal of the Plague Year,* which is history and journalism turned into literature.) Others include Charles Dickens, Chinua Achebe and Cyprian Ekwensi.

### III

As Chidi Amuta has observed (1988), "To be familiar with the Nigerian literature in the period between 1970 and the present is to be conversant with one dominant and recurrent area of social concern: the Nigerian Civil War (1967-1970)," because this war has become the subject matter for the composition of much of the recent literature in Nigeria.

Ken Saro-Wiwa's *Sozaboy* is based on this event, and the accounts in the novel could be gathered to some extent from a good journalism of the war. What we see is a chronological account of the war. The author, therefore, actually *journalizes* on the activities; and he could verily have adapted his story from newspapers, had he not been present. However, Saro-Wiwa was an eye-witness and could merely have embellished his diary of the period with linguistic artistry and given it a fictional touch. At least we see the novel as a journalistic review or documentary.

189

The difference is that the reportage has been ornamented and subjectivized through the observation of an individual in a particular community of the embattled society. The journalistic character in the novel is observed also in the pattern of narration. The writer reports on each stage of the war, albeit as an individual undergoes the experience of it. Here the author surrenders his journalism to the protagonist who reports. The important thing is that much as a neutral journalist gives his report in as objective and unbiased a form as possible, the naiveté of the narrator gives us the benefit of receiving reports of the war:

> So as we were still looking at the plan as it came to pass round and round the camp, I saw that plane drop something. 'E dey me like say the plane de shit and I begin laugh. But my laugh no reach my belly because that thing from the plane just land near we camp and I hear very very big noise which come carry me for air throway for ground. Then I hear Bullet shouting "Bomb! Bomb! Take cover! Take cover! (138)

In chronology and in style, there is little difference between *Sozaboy* and Domkat Bali's collection of poetry *War Cries* also recounting the same war:

> I was gripped with fear as the
> H-hour drew near,
> And I began to shiver and perspire;
> 'You must control yourself,' I thought in despair
> As I issued orders that were unclear...
>
> Rat-tat-tat-tat-boom-boom-boom,
> Rent the air as our guns released the bombs
> To herald H-hour and spell doom
> To whoever dared to be in the path. (p10)

It is significant that there is no omniscient judgement in *Sozaboy*; we only see the report as the event comes, and whatever judgement we make is not because of the eponymous narrator's opinions. (In fact, there are some events he reports

190

which he himself does not understand, as we do, until much later.) Rather, we judge the events based on what Carl Jung calls the "collective unconscious" which we share with the author and the events. We are not bound to accept the narrator's opinions or those of others. The journalist merely reports, for example, what Chief Birabee does and what others say about him. If we consider Birabee to be the epitome of corruption and betrayal of trust in the traditional institutions, it is our own judgement imposed upon a journalist's report.

When Zaza talks about his military "prowess" in Burma, we understand the falsehood in the story, long before Sozaboy realizes it. When we are taken into the battle fields and streets and villages and cities, we are given objective cinematographic accounts of the happenings. It is in our own *collective unconscious* that we evaluate the events and say that the war was a waste, that it was a situation in which there is no difference between a friend and a foe (notice Sozaboy and Manmuswak), that war turns a dear friend to a dreadful foe, that the masses suffer untold hardship and death from a war about which they know little and that there is nothing heroic about two brothers, two black races, or two sections of the nation fighting each other.

Therefore, when divested of the private emotions and idiosyncrasies, the novel amounts to a news magazine's or film documentary on the war.

This journalism is sustained and even reinforced in the collection of short stories ironically titled *A Forest of Flowers*. The continuity in characterization and setting from the novel through the first part of the short stories is significant. What we find is a journalist, a community chronicler, prepared to give a total coverage of the war in the community. The aftermath of the war—the under-privileged suffering for the ravages of battles, the influenza and cholera epidemics, and the environmentally degrading exploration of petroleum—are reported to complete the war documentary (in "The Inspector Calls" and "Night Ride"). Saro-Wiwa's work as Administrator of Bonny shortly after its liberation (Irele 1988:366) reinforces this journalism.

The journalistic quality in the short stories is notable. In this volume of short stories, there is little or no evaluation, no editorial commentary on the events. The barbarisms in the village cultures are presented as they are seen for an unedited record for a pin-hole camera. Thus, the killing of twins and the ostracizing of their mother ("Hoe, Sweet Home"), the murder of a man by his family who do not want to bear the burden of the disgrace brought by his insanity ("A Family Affair"), the incineration of a man unconvincingly and maybe innocently accused of witchcraft ("The Bonfire"), the devaluation of womanhood to the status of a procreation machine and the hypocrisy, and the failure of both churches and traditional medicine to meet expectations—and all these stories are told with neither approval nor disapproval. One would expect that like other writers, there would be some condemnatory attitude to these practices. But that is not the primary function of the journalist; his duty is to report the event as it happened. It is the audience's duty to make deductions from the reportage.

The rest of the short stories present the author *journalizing* on other socio-cultural ills. In Part Two, the setting moves to the urban center and what we find is a series of satires on the ills prevalent in the cities. "High Life" presents the city in its good light, with its horde of impostors. The corruption and gross inefficiency of the police ("Case No. 100"), the typical swindler ("Acapulco Motel"); the animosity between members of the same clan and the religious bigotry ("Garga") and the miserly trader ("The Shopkeeper and the Beggar") are individuals and events we witness in everyday life, presented here in the impersonal fashion of journalistic reportage. The commonplace stories of the suspicious wife ("Love Song of a Housewife") and the gullible and materialistic wife ("A Caring Man") are identical with the romance stories we read in soft-sell magazines, newspapers, romance novels, and the famous but moribound Onitsha market literature.

Indeed, these stories take the form of individual portraits of characters who are the varied embodiments of contemporary Nigerian experience (Irele 1988:342). Irele was unconsciously observing the journalistic narrative method of these stories when he observed that "The remarkable thing about

these stories is the total absence of any kind of romantic involvement on the part of the author with the world he presents," and the stories share with the author's poems, *Songs In
a Time of War*, in the "mental record of a momentous collective
drama."

While the purely socio-political journalist can *journalize* only
on people and events that actually exist physically, the literary
journalist is capable also of *journalizing* minds (thoughts and
feels) as we observe in *Sozaboy* and the protagonist in "Night
Ride."

## IV

*He may not indeed destroy the framework of the received
legends .... but he ought to show invention of his own, and
skillfully handle the traditional material.*
                    —Aristotle, *Poetics* XIV

The above section might seem to suggest that there is no difference between fiction and journalism or history or sociology, in Africa. But it is not so. Fiction remains fiction, an
imaginative creation of the individual artist, a product of invention. Thus, there may be no village called Dukana or a
particularly identifiable individual Mene or Sozaboy or any
other characters for that matter, there may not have been any
of the actions and events in the exact form as they are presented in the novel and the short stories. All may have come
from the imagination of the author. What may have happened
is that the author has assimilated a collective history, and his
fictional world of subject and technique has come to have a
parallel with the imagination.

It is also conceded that history or sociology will not be able
to capture the emotional overtones of the historical events.
The universality and permanence of literature is noted because
each of the fictional works discussed has a universal relevance,
cutting across time, place, and action. The events have resemblances in several other parts of the world and have all-time
relevance. People in all places and all times will always identify with literature, and the actions and events are not just

what was or is but also what could be or could have been. As many writers have argued, literature is more philosophical and more universal than history.

## V

Social realism is the meeting point between the history and the fiction of these works and their crystallization as *repoetry* or literary journalism. By realism is meant the similarity, the similitude and verisimilitude between fiction and reality. The central idea here is imitation, literature as an imitation of life. This imitation has different ranges of closeness to reality and life experiences. The fictional may be remotely related to empirical reality as in romance, fairly close as in purely imaginative novels, or very directly related as a socially committed and historical fiction (Stevick 1967:370).

The closest realism is observed when we are able to make a one-to-one correlation between the fiction and social reality. Therefore, the fiction goes beyond direct imitation, even beyond adaptation to direct adoption of historical fact to which artistic adornment is given. This correspondence is observed in subject matter, in setting, in character, and in other aspects of technique.

Fiction becomes journalistic or *repoetic* when we can pick a precise event in real life and say "This is what the author is talking about." For we can say with a measure of exactitude that Okigbo talks about the First Republic and the impending civil war in Nigeria in his series of poems *Path of Thunder*. We have no doubts claiming that Saro-Wiwa's *Sozaboy* is an account of the Nigerian Civil War; we hardly consider it to be about another war (in another place). These identifications are acknowledged by both reader and writer. Saro-Wiwa concedes this much in his interview with me in 1992 when he said that "I was fully involved in the war. So there is much of that experience in the story" (Telilanyo, forthcoming).

Historical realism is also observed at the level of setting. Although we may not have any Dukana, we know that Ken Saro-Wiwa's is from the Khana-speaking area of Ogoniland, with a community called Gokana. Dukana and Gokana suggest each other. In his interviews with me Saro-Wiwa said "Dukana actually means Khana Market." We know that

"Pitakwa" is a popular pidgin corruption of "Port Harcourt."

Similarly, correlation is observed at the level of characterization. The naming of characters, their speech and action echo socially identifiable names and behavior. Birabee is the name of a royal family in Ogoni-land. Thus, there is a direct transfer from real life into fiction, from *home sapiens* to *home fictus* (Omotoso 1979:5,6).

Narrative technique would play an important part in this realism. The plot is usually linear, as a journalist documentary should be. The point of view is often varied—from third person omniscient (in some of the short stories) to first person innocent protagonist (in *Sozaboy*). The most journalistic point of view would be "the camera" which would take the form of passive recording, without a narrative voice, the "ultimate of authorial exclusion" (Friedman 1955:1178-1179).

The importance of language in such reportage is unique. Thus, Saro-Wiwa's language, like Okara's in *The Voice*, suits the aim, not only to "capture the authentic feel of life at the level of society of which the language of his novel functions as the regular medium of communication ... the register of existence which it explores ... the disordered and disorderly" experience (Irele 1988: 337,339). It is also the register which the protagonist-journalist has at his disposal to *journalize*.

This method of fictional composition, then, is remarkable for its double function. The style towers above ordinary news report or the purely imaginative novel. Whereas a news report becomes history as soon as it is published, and the ordinary fiction fulfills a purely literary role, fictional journalism or *repoetry* cuts across the two domains to give socially salient "reportage" that is at the same time fictional. This is what has sometimes been called "faction"—fact plus fiction. Thus, history, fiction, realism, and style all "conspire" to make the writer the conscience or intellect of society, tasking him with compounded social responsibility—he becomes a fictional journalist and his writing becomes fictional journalism or literary reportage.

# Works Cited

Abrams, M.H. *A Glossary of Literary Terms.* New York: Holt, Rinehart Winston, 1981

Agbese, Dan. "The New Journalism in Nigeria." Unpublished 1st Kapuswatch Inaugural Lecture Series, University of Benin, Benin City, February 28, 1992.

Amuta, Chidi. "Literature of the Nigerian Civil War." In *Perspective on Nigerian Literature,* Vol. 1. Lagos: Guardian Books, 1988:85-92.

Bali, D. Y. *War Cries,* Lagos: Civiletis, 1984.

Chinweizu, Jemie, and Madubuike. *Toward the Decolonization of African Literature.* Enugu: Fourth Dimension, 1980.

Coleridge, Samuel Taylor. *Biographia Literaria,* 1817.

Friedman, Norman. "Point of View in Fiction, The Development of a Critical Concept." *PMLA* LXX, 5 (Dec.1955):1160-1184.

Irele, Abiola. "Ken Saro-Wiwa." In Yei Ogunbiyi, ed., *Perspectives on Nigerian Literature.* Vol. 2, Lagos: Guardian Books, 1988:333-344

Obiechia, Emmanuel. *An African Popular Literature,* Cambridge: The University Press, 1973.

Okigbo, Charles. "Chris Okigbo: Portrait of the Poet as a Journalist" *Sunday Concord,* January 22, 1984, MX.

Omotoso, Kole. *The Form of the African Novel.* Akure: Fagbamigbe, 1979.

Saro-Wiwa, Ken. *Sozaboy.* Port Harcourt: Saros International Publishers, 1985.

_____. *A Forest of Flowers.* Port Harcourt: Saros International Publishers, 1986.

Stevick, Philip. (ed). *The Theory of the Novel.* New York: The Free Press, 1967.

Teilanyo, Diri I. "English is the Hero: Interview with Ken Saro-Wiwa". *Matatu* (forthcoming).

Wellek, Rene & Warren Austin. *Theory of Literature.* New York: Penguin Books, 1963.

# 15

# The Fear of Colonization: Reading Ken Saro-Wiwa's Political Thoughts In Nigeria's Political Public

## Onookome Okome

### I

Quoting from the popular saying of a newspaper of the 1960s, the respected Nigerian historian, Michael Crowder, represent the fact of Nigeria's political history this way: "Nigerians seem to have perfected the art of walking to the brink of disaster without falling in"(1978). In the years leading to and shortly after the death of General Sanni Abacha, Nigeria moved yet again towards that direction. The "divine intervention" which led to the death of the General, the hated dictator of Nigeria's recent history, once again pushed this country a few steps away from that great pit which may eventually happen if the words of the late Ken Saro-Wiwa are not heeded in the true process of creating a federation of ethnic nations.

It is not clear what the consequences of a break-up of this country will entail, but the very prospect of this cataclysm which Saro-Wiwa hinted at is enormous, not only for Nigeria but for the whole of the continent. If we go by the examples in Soviet Russia and now in the Balkans, the chaos can only then be imagined. But once more, Nigeria has been spared the spectre of disintegration. The slow but sure and measured attitude to public life, politics and social realignment which the successor to General Sanni Abacha has assumed since the death of his predecessor is certainly dousing angers and the prospect of national disintegration. The new General is certainly dousing flames of anger and protestation from different sections of the community, yet inside each community (and there are many in Nigeria, ranging from ethnic communities to social and class communities) not very far from the surface of things, there still remain those social facts that made General Abacha's regime of violence, intimidation and arbitrary incarceration, the most hateful and despised so far in the political history of this nation. It was this General who, relying on trumped-up and unverified charges, murdered Ken Saro-Wiwa, the environmental rights activist from the Ogoni people of the Niger Delta area, one among the many micro-minorities in that part of the country. This is the area that produces the crude oil wealth upon which parts of the arid country depends.

At exactly 11:30 am. in a Port Harcourt prison, southeast Nigeria, Ken Saro-Wiwa and eight other Ogoni environmental activists were hanged on November 10, 1995. This act was the culmination of the eroding evil of the Abacha dictatorship. The nation was saved just in time—but it was in the form of a "divine intervention,"[1] not the concerted and orchestrated act of the people upon which the General unleashed his unexplained wrath.

While the troubles which led to the hanging of the Ogoni nine is tied to the Abacha Regime, the reading of what happened before and after the death of Ken Saro-Wiwa reveals a larger picture of a nation in turmoil. It further reveals a political system without rules, without faith in its own very being. Ken Saro-Wiwa's criticism of this nation in this palous condition was not welcomed at all. Indeed they were not to be tolerated. But he questioned the treatment of ethnic minorities, detailing in the popular mass media the very dicey position which they sit in the nation's politics. He talked and wrote about the state of the nation's economy; about oil-exploration and more importantly about his own minority, the Ogoni people of the Niger Delta, explaining the problems it faces in the era of oil mining in that area. All of this brought him into direct contact with General Sanni Abacha who became the final and decisive intervention in Saro-Wiwa's life and the goals of social justice which Saro-Wiwa spent the last years of his life propagating. The General did everything within his powers to subjugate and then kill the man and his dreams. The man, Ken Saro-Wiwa died, but not his dreams.

The tales coming out of the Niger Delta are not evidence of dead dreams. Rather, they are examples of dreams which the suffering people are trying to make into reality.The remote causes of the problems which confronted the General as a result of the activities of Ken Saro-Wiwa and the Movement for the Survival of Ogoni People (MOSOP) can be located in the history of the Union of Nigeria. According to Michael Crowder:

> Any country is, in a sense, an artificial creation. In the case of Nigeria, however, union was so sudden, and included such widely differing groups of peoples that not only the people, who created it, but the inhabitants themselves, have often doubted whether it could survive as a political entity. On 1st October 1960, despite many difficulties, focusing mainly on the differences among its various component groups, Nigeria became a sovereign federation and has survived intact despite a civil war (12).

Ken Saro-Wiwa wrote profusely about the survival pattern of this nation and the victims, the ethnic minorities, who are the puns spread out in the gamble-game of this survival bid. He documented this in his controversial books, *On a Darkling Plain: An Account of the Nigerian Civil War* and the posthumously published *A Month and a Day: A Detention Diary*. It is in these books that we reconstruct the political ideas of Ken Saro-Wiwa and the debates about ethnic minorities in the politics of oil exploration and the economic problems which the major ethnic groups have always overlooked in the history of his country.

Certainly, Saro-Wiwa was a witness to the many twists and turns of Nigeria towards disintegration. A keen observer of history, he said these words to the executioners, "You can kill the messenger, you cannot kill the message, you cannot kill the message." (*Africa Today*, November 9, 1998:9) implying that his political thoughts about his place as a spokesperson for the Ogoni and the marginalization of ethnic minorities were crucial debates for the Union and that they cannot be an individual choice of political dissent. Even in that final moment, he was sure of a "moral victory" for his project of redefining a place for his Ogoni micro-minority, one of the examples of cheated ethnic minorities on whose land the nation's wealth is mined. His death, which came shortly after the annulled June 12, 1993 presidential election, was to be the final movement towards the "brink of disaster" which Michael Crowder wrote about.

From the public debates about contemporary Nigeria, no one is left in doubt as to why Ken Saro-Wiwa and the other eight Ogoni environmental and political activists were judiciously murdered inspite of what the General and his numerous "supporters" contested in this public. The sum of the discourse which these "supporters" sought to push into the centre of the debate of public matters during and after the death of Saro-Wiwa was that the activities of the Ogoni people amounted to sheer lawlessness and that indeed Saro-Wiwa actually took laws into his own hands when he ordered or caused to happen the murder of four pro-Abacha Ogoni chiefs who were meeting in Giokoo, Ogoniland. This was the picture which government painted to the public, yet it was very obvious that Saro-Wiwa was killed for the increasing political successes of his utterances and for his resolute desire to redefine and place the issues of ethnic minorities marginalization at the centre of national debate. In this regard, it is important to recap that his sudden and brutal death did not eradicate the problems which ethnic minorities face. If anything, this death has heightened the apprehension which ethnic people feel towards a government controlled by the bigger ethnic groups in Nigeria. Not long after his death, the "moral victory" which Saro-Wiwa spoke of has been yielding fruits. According to one report published in the *Nigerian Punch,*

Urhobo elder in Delta State are currently locked in a
tug-of-war with the aggrieved youths of the area who
are planning to join their kith and kin in Ijaw and Isoko,
to militantly press for the realization of the Kiama Declaration[2] (January 29, 1993:3).

The youth are demanding, among other things, "the creation
of a state for Urhobo,[3] creation of twenty additional local government areas, making Urhobo company-leaders in their dis-
tricts, paying compensation to victims of the October fire disaster at Jesse[4]" (13). This catalogue of request would not have
been possible without the trail blazed by the martyred Saro-
Wiwa. The persistent struggle, even after the death of this
man, has led to calls for the government and oil companies to
rethink their roles in the life of ethnic minorities of the Niger
Delta, signifying that the problems of the Niger Delta are far
from over. While it is not clear why the "Urhobo chiefs" were
calling for a truce to a war that is yet to be declared, what
seems obvious is that the Urhobo youth are determined not to
allow gullible elders to hijack the process of redressing some
of the telling consequences of oil exploration in the area. It is
also important to point out that the youth may just be react-
ing to a similar problem which Ken Saro-Wiwa faced with the
Ogoni elders as he tried to combat the insensitivity of the governments of Generals Babangida and Abacha over the Ogoni
issue. The youth recognize that the elders have often placed
themselves between the people and government and that more
often than not, government officials, acting on *directives* from
*above,* often dolled out generous gift packages to these chiefs.
Bribed into a difficult position, these chiefs then assume conciliatory roles, pleading with the more militant and radical
youth to be patient. This is one of the factors that has made
the struggle of the Niger Delta a very difficult one. Successive
governments have often used to their advantage a divided
house.

It is equally important for us to recognize what is referred
to in this report as the Kiama Declaration in the post Saro–

Wiwa militancy of the Niger Delta youth and its significance to the struggle of the Niger Delta people. This Declaration took place when a group of youth gathered together over the grave of the Niger Delta separatist, Isaac Adaka Boro, in the small town of Kiama, about 80 kilometers from Port Harcourt, to declare solidarity for the ideas which Boro stood and died for in the 1960s. It was Isaac Adaka Boro, the policeman from Kiama, who unilaterally declared a Niger Delta Republic in 1967. He was quickly rounded up and tried by the then Eastern Regional Government, was found guilty in the court of law and was sentenced to death. He became the first official casualty of the war of attrition against minorities who spoke out against the appalling situation of the Niger Delta. The story of Boro is well known and respected by the youth of the Niger Delta, therefore the symbolism of the Kiama Declaration was not lost to the journalist who reported this matter. This symbolism was not lost to the government either.

Indeed Ken Saro-Wiwa was very aware of the role and significance of people like Isaac Adaka Boro. Saro-Wiwa mentions him in *On a Darkling Plain* where he reports the circumstances that led Boro to declare war against the Federal Government of General Aguyi Irousi in the late 1960s. This was after the first failed coup attempt which sacked the civilian government of Alhaji Tafawa Balewa. Hopefully idealist, Saro-Wiwa tells us that Isaac Boro's aim was to take the Niger Delta area away from the Federation at that time "into a nation and strive to maintain it." The authorial intervention in Saro-Wiwa's narrative of this action gives us a clue to his position in this matter. According to him, "The Ironsi regime moved in against Boro and quickly captured him before any further harm could be done" (31). The harm that Saro-Wiwa refers to here is that which the ethnic minority risks when he tries to question the logic of rulers who come from the majority ethnic groups. Boro fell into harm's way and was summarily sentenced to death although he was to die in a different circumstances later in the Nigerian civil war which raged on from 1967 to 1970.

Saro-Wiwa's conclusion in this connection is of course important both for his own political activities as well as for those who will take up the ethnic minority fight soon after. Viewed in the background of the Nigerian civil war, Ken Saro-Wiwa saw that it was not possible for the minorities to win any battle against aggression and marginalization without a change of strategy, but he also recognized from the Boro case that it was important to position the problems of the area in a very eloquent manner, soliciting help from everybody who cared to be sympathetic to the cause. These problems are very well articulated in Boro's posthumously published *The Twelve-Day Revolution,* (1982) one of which was the overbearing presence and might of the ethnic majority groups in the Federation and their strong inordinate desire to keep the polity in their own image by any means possible. According to Boro, "A Niger Delta state is a clear case as the people concerned have a distinct historical silhouette," threatening that "If Nigerian governments refuse to do something drastic to improve the lot of the people, inevitably a point of no-return will be reached; then evil was afoot" (30). Evil was indeed afoot but it was not upon the brows of those who wielded political power at the time. It fell squarely on Isaac Adaka Boro, first true martyr of the cause of the Niger Delta. The Kiama Declaration was therefore both a symbolic and physical call to continue the struggle.

It is now obvious that Saro-Wiwa was acutely aware of the precarious position of the minority activist because we know from his accounts in *On A Darkling Plain* and *A Month and A Day* that he took steps to overcome them. He moved quickly to solicit support as he befriended national and international presses and then allied the Ogoni cause to international and national human, ethnic and civil rights movements. He constructed a fairly well defined intellectual codes of reference with which he tried to understand the psychology of the rulers of Nigeria in his time, coming out just in time before his death with the theory of *domestic colonialism* which was first mentioned in *On A Darkling Plain* and then given greater emphasis in *A Month and A Day.* Like no writer before him, Ken Saro-Wiwa constructed the "literature of commitment in expressly environmental terms." (Rob Nixon 51.) Ethnic marginalization or *domestic colonialism* was perhaps one of the major trajectory of Ken Saro-Wiwa's political thoughts on the state of Nigeria.

## II

It is true as many notable historians have pointed out that "Nigeria was the most artificial creation in the course of European occupation of Africa" (Lord Malcolm Hailey, qt in Nixon 40-41) but this fact alone cannot adequately answer the questions that have bedeviled the country 30 years after independence. In any case, there are examples of pluri-ethnic nations that have successfully existed in some measure of stability in Africa and outside the continent as nation-states. More precisely the problems which Nigeria faces at crucial points and turns of its history are created by a group of self-seeking pseudo-patriots who have effectively but dubiously redefined what the idea of nation means in their own image, social and economic aspirations. This is partly what Ken Saro-Wiwa discusses at length in two of his books dealing with political thoughts.

However, these issues have always been discussed as part of the political debates in Nigeria and even more recently Soyinka tackles these issues in the face of a looming call to arm during the Abacha regime in a recently published book, *The Open Sore of A Continent: A Personal Narrative of the Nigerian Crisis.* In it, Soyinka seeks to rethink the whole idea of *nation* and *nationhood.* This did not come as a surprise. The endless transition which military dictatorship since the duo of Generals Buhari and Idiagbon had instituted culminated in the ferocious and merciless dictatorship of General Abacha, who together with his former master and collaborator, General Ibrahim Babangida, annulled the June 12, 1993 election considered to be the fairest in the history of political elections in Nigeria. The man poised to win that election was a Southwesterner, the rich Chief, M. K. O. Abiola. The annulment caused a lot of trouble, rekindling hopes that after all this nation-state of ethnic nations should not be together.

The essays in the *Open Sore of A Continent* attempt to understand the nation-state at this point of its life. More precisely they attempt to intellectually examine the idea of "when is a nation?" Certainly the events leading to the annulment of the 1993 elections were traumatic for the nation, but the events after that were even more so. What comes out clear in Soyinka's polemical interrogation of the Nigerian nation-state during this period is that "The truth is, some conceive of a nation almost in terms of gross national product," while "others conceive of the nation as an expression of divine will whose active processes, from private conduct to the art, from fiscal policies to architectural designs, must be governed by the desire to win the approbation of and/or reflect and glorify the omnipotence and grandeur of the invincible presence" (111).

Of course Soyinka's position here is not a new one. This position is pretty well known to those who live the capricious political existence of this world. But it is important for us to note that those who merely think about the complex and complicated issues of nation, nationhood and ethnicity which the events leading up to the annulment made obvious, cannot be said to be the active participants in this dubious and self-serving definition of the nation-state in Nigeria. It is only when this thinking is backed up by the force of economic strength defined by the primary access to the gross national product, that this idea is activated.

Since independence, the force which this economic means granted to the idea of the nation-state in Nigeria has been squarely in the hands of the big ethnic groups. And since then too, the major ethnic groups have viciously sought to hold on to it in one way or the other, in one form of political repression of dissents or the other. Since it is these major ethnic groups, Hausa-Fulani in the north, Igbo in the southeast and Yoruba in the southwest, that have the democratic upperhand in number, over the years, probably long before independence, they have moved into the big areas of nation life-military, commerce, administration etc. And since democratic principles on the surface favors number, they have remained at the head of the army. Inevitably, when political power shifted to the army through the brash use of the gun in the 1960s, governance was once more put in their hands.

Ken Saro-Wiwa was interested in intellectualizing these problems in so far as it will help the cause of his Ogoni people. Although he was somewhat philosophical in his writings and in his approach to the problems facing his Ogoni nation, he tackled his philosophy of marginalization and ethnic difference by dealing with problems arising headlong in the field of his activities. In this sense, he was a philosopher-fighter who waged two kinds of war: the philosophical war in which he attempts to come to terms with the wretched conditions of existence in the oil-rich region of which he was part and the physical war to resist the overlords, the domestic colonialists, from slowly killing the people and environment of the Niger Delta.

## III

The first real sustained discussion of the ethnic composition in the Nigerian Federation by Ken Saro-Wiwa is in On *A Darkling Plain*, a book of political narrative, of which the author tells us in *A Month and A Day*, was written "during the most impressionable years of my life, but which nonetheless 'was a controversial book.'" (*A Month and A Day* 15) Ken Saro-Wiwa was well aware that this book would generate a lot of hate-debates, but he was out to prove that there existed a different form of colonialism in Nigeria perpetuated by the ethnic majority groups on the ethnic minorities. As he himself puts it, "I do not expect the book to please anyone; I expect it to provoke debate and thought, to add to the corpus of view on the civil war and to help chart a new course in the political thinking of Nigeria" (*A Month and A Day* 62). There is no doubting the fact that Saro-Wiwa's aim of contributing to the debate is important. What we cannot also doubt is the fact that this book did not please everyone, yet the ideas which Ken Saro-Wiwa put forward here are crucial to the survival of the nation and important to the restitution of the place of ethnic minorities.

The discourse of ethnic relations opens this book and Saro-Wiwa lets us into his life as a child in the heartland of the Igbo country. He was then in Government School, Umuahia, just before the civil war which broke out in 1967. It was here, soon after the elections of 1966 that the young Ken first recognized that he was different from the cooks who served him food at the refectory. He was jeered at and called *foolish* because his Ogoni people had refused to vote for the Igbo politicians in the then Eastern Nigerian House. According to him, this was a very sad moment. It was a moment when he also suddenly realized his *ethnic difference.* He realized too that each ethnic group was out to keep its hold on the others and that since there was the number-game that each ethnicity played, he reckoned that it will be a difficult task for this small Ogoni minority to mean much in this political chessboard. But this experience, according to him, ignited very deep concern in him; the concern for his own people in the face of obvious marginalization in political, social and economic affairs.

The Umuahia incident is of course narrated in the backdrop of the political upheavals of the 1960s when Saro-Wiwa had moved to the University of Ibadan, so that his childhood experience was in a sense a narrative digression, the aim of which is to cut clearly the picture of ethnic colonialism, a form of cultural and political subjugation against his own people. More importantly, both narratives of Nigeria's political life and the place of the individual who comes from an ethnic minority depict vividly the relationship that existed between the big ethnicities and the small ones. It is important to note how Saro-Wiwa managed to prefigure his place and that of his Ogoni people in the political reading of that time by providing very vivid and captivating pictures of true experiences. In his own words, "I am afraid that the incident in the dining hall at Umuahia made me rather conscious of Ogoni people. When I narrated it to my father, he told me to forget it."

The bit about narrating this story to his father is also important. The consciousness of the young Saro-Wiwa about his ethnicity was further charged by the deliberate silence which the father's (non)response inscribed in the larger narrative of ethnic relation in the region. The author's father's reading of the situation was a cool and calm responce to marginalization; it was a resignation. This consciousness led Saro-Wiwa to conclude that "I had to be involved in mobilizing the Ogoni people for progress and against indigenous colonization" (*On A Dar-*

*kling Plain* 46). Indeed this book is essentially about stories of how Saro-Wiwa tried to describe the debilitating effects of domestic (indigenous) colonization by the majority Igbo neighbors on his Ogoni minority and as he rightly predicted, the ideas in the book were not pleasing to many of those who belong to this ethnic majority of the southeastern part of Nigeria.

In *On A Darkling Plain*, Ken Saro-Wiwa frequently hammers on the idea that the notion that "Nigeria consists of three ethnic groups is at the center of the nation's malaise" (147). This is the favorite theme of his political thought which is also well represented in *A Month and A Day*. He argues that "Surely the answer to Nigeria's problems is the evolution of a more equal society, based on the ethnic nationalities," (147) rather than the divide and rule tactics which the ethnic majority groups have instituted since the attainment of independence. Saro-Wiwa believed initially that ethnic equality was attainable and did everything within his powers to support any genuine move towards that goal. When civil war broke out in 1967, Saro-Wiwa was caught up in his Ogoniland. He reviewed the situations leading up to the war and concluded that once more this was a war that had nothing to do with his ethnicity. If anything it was a war fought over the control of oil that was mined from the land of his Ogoni people and that the Igbo went into it believing that;

> Eastern Nigeria blessed as it was with oil wealth and "sophisticated" Ibo manpower, could make a success of nationhood. Such a nation could be more successful if the drawback of the "North" was removed for all times (*On A Darkling Plain* 35).

This, according to Saro-Wiwa, was the thinking of Igbo intellectuals of that time. He believed that the war was conceived and prosecuted as a means of gaining control of the oil wealth of the Niger Delta. He did not want any of this. He also believed that the result of the parliamentary elections to the Eastern House just before the war broke out had left the Ogoni people on the bad side of their Igbo neighbors. Therefore the prospect of a Biafran nation in which the Ogoni would be part was a nightmare. Armed with the history of the Willink Commission which did nothing to allay minorities' fears of marginalization and subjugation, Ken Saro-Wiwa and the Ogoni people knew that to agree to a new form of colonialism, indigenous colonialism, was asking for something worse than death. Neighborly relations had not been good for some time and the question of who owned and ran Port Harcourt, the big town of commerce and prosperity, was still a nagging one. The Igbo claimed it and as Saro-Wiwa reports in his account of this struggle, the Igbo insisted that Port Harcourt must not be included in the new Rivers State that was agitated for from the 1960s and which continued well into the 1970s.

Situated at a strategic location in the Niger Delta, Port Harcourt belonged to the Ijaw and Ekwerre people. Saro-Wiwa's picture of the tussle for Port-Harcout is one that suggests a process of reclamation from the Igbo who had built an enviable commercial success of this town on the coast. He argues in *On A The Darkling Plain* that the Igbo were unwilling to give it up and had gone to a great length to persuade the political figurehead at that time, Chief (Dr.) Nnamdi Azikiwe, not to include Port Harcourt in the new state that was agitated for by some indigenes of the Niger Delta. The agitation for a new state was itself a result of the fear of domination by the smaller ethnic compositions in the area. It was against this background that Ken Saro-Wiwa opposed the civil war and fled to Lagos to join the Federal side. From Lagos, together with other Ogoni patriots and people from the Niger Delta ethnicities of Ijaw and Ekwerre people, he was able to influence the creation of Rivers State in which Port Harcourt became the headquarters. According to his account, once in Lagos, Saro-Wiwa made contact with the Federal Government and was nominated the first administrator of Bonny. This is what he made of the situation at the time of his appointment.

> I examined the issue a bit more closely. In the first
> place, I had escaped from biafra (*his babylon*) because I
> did not believe in secession, and I thought I should be

contributing in a positive way to the birth of a new
Nigeria (my emphasis) (150).

Ken Saro-Wiwa was soon to learn that the new Nigeria of his
dream was indeed a pipe dream.

Ken Saro-Wiwa dealt extensively with the case of Biafra,
the new nation, which was the aim of the successionist Igbo
people in this controversial book. In his portrayal of the remote causes of this war, Ken Saro-Wiwa left no one in doubt
about his position. He stated in no uncertain terms in *On A
Darkling Plain* that this war was fought by the three major
ethnic groups, Yoruba, Hausa-Fulani and Igbo because they
were interested in the huge oil reserves of the Niger Delta. In
the heat of the moment and in the hope that the victory of the
Federal forces will assure his people a fairer deal in a true fed-
eration-a new nation, Ken Saro-Wiwa opted for the lesser evil.
But he realized soon enough the futility of his position. One
way or the other, he remained the *indigenous colonial.* He was
until his death the indigenous colonized subject because the
political equation remained the way it was when he was hanged.
The civil war had come and gone, but the coalition of the three
major ethnic groups still managed to ride the storm of dissents at crucial junctions in the history of Nigeria. The numerical strength of the three major groups has made the domination over 300 other ethnic groups inevitable. Even though
Saro-Wiwa did not like it, there was little else he could do. Of
course he protested but this led him elsewhere—the grave.

Soon after the war, and tired of the politics of the times,
Ken Saro-Wiwa was to engage in writing creative works as
well as political commentaries in the popular press where he
launched yet another form of protest against the injustice of
this ethnic equation. In both forms of writing, it is clear that
Saro-Wiwa argues eloquently the plight of all minority people.
To this extent Saro-Wiwa saw both forms of literature in purely
political terms. Saro-Wiwa believed that literature must be
put to the service of human actions. In other words, Ken Saro-
Wiwa engaged the problems of the minorities in Nigeria in
clearly a partisan perspective and his *grand narrative, the* cause
of the minorities, was engineered primarily from the perspec-

tive of the oppressed. It is for this reason that Azubike Ileoje[5] remarks that;

> ...the significance of *On A Darkling Plain* can be grasped only if it is understood that he (Saro-Wiwa) was an outsider constantly in search of an alternative context that would convert him into an insider. (85)

This is an argument that those who oppose Ken Saro-Wiwa often put forward, especially people from the Igbo ethnicity who find him pertulent. However, this argument is a part of the larger canvas of the opposition to the ideas of Saro-Wiwa. As would be imagined, the spectrum of the opposition to Saro-Wiwa is wide.

In any case, if we take a critical look at the literary works as well as the political writings of Saro-Wiwa, we would immediately grasp the singular fact that Ken Saro-Wiwa was every inch an insider of his culture and of the political landscape (landmine?) of Nigeria, therefore he didn't need to get inside any of these two at all: he was always inside. Even the vehement pro-government pamphlet, *The Ogoni Question in Nigeria, MOSOP and NYCOP: The Reality of the Situation* recognizes this point. Indeed it states this point equally. It may then be a matter of putting the cart before the horse if Ileoje concludes that Saro-Wiwa was like the "ignorant armies" in Arnold's "Dove Beach." While Ileoje's position may seem partisan, perhaps as partisan as that of Saro-Wiwa himself in certain respects, his essay provides the critical summation of what Saro-Wiwa often referred to in his writing as Igbo-domination.

It is true to say that Saro-Wiwa was sometimes paranoid about the idea of Igbo-domination. On *A Darkling Plain* is a coherent, albeit flamboyant narrative of the relationships of his Ogoni minority with the Igbo majority. But if Ileoje's essay attempts to minimize the role of Ken Saro-Wiwa, it cannot however hope to wish away the huge and unmitigated injustices meted out to ethnic minorities that live on the Delta coast line where oil is indiscriminately mined and for which this country had gone to war. Indeed there are few people, if any, who would doubt, let alone minimize, the place of Saro-Wiwa in the debate about ethnicity and nation-building. This includes Azubike Ileoje. As the anthropologist, Eliott Skinner, puts it, until there is a "compromise that would ensure ethnic justice, neither the so-called liberal democracy nor any other species of government would succeed in Africa." (1)

It is clear from what is set down in *On A Darkling Plain* and *A Month and A Day*, (the latter being the emphatic replay of the former) that Ken Saro-Wiwa believed in the idea of the Nigerian nation. He spoke and wrote about this belief in both books with equal passion. He did not do so as an outsider, but as an insider who once believed that the political incongruous of the 1960s will eventually give way for a greater Nigerian nation when the military is forced to give up power to a democratically elected civilian administration. He truly believed in a true federation of the many ethnic nations of Nigeria into a plural polity in which respect for each other's cultural specificities are taken into account. According to him: "It is equally important that the relationship between all ethnic nationalities are built on solid foundations, on the principle that both the hawk and the eagle may perch." (*On A Darkling Plain* 1). But Ken Saro-Wiwa also recognized "that all fingers are not equal" as the saying goes here and that in the political life in Nigeria, the *more equal* people let you know this fact brazenly. Indeed even now some are more equal than the others. This realization was hard for him to take. He did not accept it throughout his lifetime.

While it is evident that Ken Saro-Wiwa gave a lot of time and literary space to the issues of ethnic composition and the politics of ethnicity, he never once spoke or wrote about the need for the break-up of the Federation. He maintained that while the problems associated with ethnicity cannot be merely wished away, he suggested the "make-up of the Federation of 300 ethnic groups be taken into account in formulating policies of governance." (*A Month and A Day* 63.) It is only through this way that the fears of the minorities would be allayed. This point is very important in the political thought of Saro-Wiwa because it was his idea that if this imbalance in ethnic representation in political and social life was not adequately ad-

212

dressed, there would arise what he referred to as *domestic colonization*—a situation in which the big ethnic groups will perpetually eliminate the smaller ones in all aspects of national life. This kind of situation he said, was bound to lead to chaos, dissent and even another war. According to Saro-Wiwa, the Ogoni people have had to put up with both British colonialism and *domestic (internal) colonization.* He loathed both forms of colonialism and thought the time was now to fight them.

Saro-Wiwa saw the Federal Government as the prime symbol of the subjugation of the Ogoni people. It was the Federal Government who confiscated Ogoni land and blatantly refused to pay royalties for the oil excavated from it. Although the Federal Government has changed hands over the years, Saro-Wiwa maintains that civilian or military, the aim of every successive government in Nigeria has always been to take from the minorities, impoverish them and their land and deny them their due in national life. Since independence in 1960, the three big ethnic groups have controlled the government at the centre and have constantly put the minorities at the grey edges of national life.

Ken Saro-Wiwa goes back in history in both books to tell us the kinds of difficult colonial subjugation that the Ogoni people have had to endure on the pain of death. British colonial history in Ogoniland was one of intimidation and irrational treatment of the Ogoni people. In 1958, the Willink Commission of Inquiry into the fears of the minorities was set up to find solutions to the unrest and protests from the minorities as they were forced into local political authority of unequal ethnic representation. In the eastern part of Nigeria, the Ogoni people together with Ikwerre and Ijaw leaders, opted for a Rivers State out of the then Eastern State dominated by the Igbo ethnic group. The fear of domestic (internal colonization) which began the agitation was soon realized when the civil war broke out. For Ken Saro-Wiwa, the Willink Commission's failure to recommend a River State and the granting of independence to Nigeria in 1960 exacerbated the plight of the Ogoni people. The discovery and exploration of oil in large quantity in Bomu, an Ogoni territory, in 1958 sealed the hopes of the Ogoni people. Ogoniland and people became,

in the ensuing years, pawns in the power-play by the larger
ethnic groups to gain access to the wealth resulting from oil
exploration.

Indeed the physical and brutal colonization of land and
people had peaked. According to Ken Saro-Wiwa, where Biafra
left off, the military oligarchy, compromising all three major
ethnic groups took over. Playing the role of the passive arbi-
ter in the melée that ensued in the confrontation between the
Ogoni community and the Federal Government is Shell, the
multinational oil company that has the largest stake in Nigeria's
oil industry. Shell was to feature prominently in the problems
and social upheavals that consumed the Ogoni communities in
the early 1990s. But while Saro-Wiwa contested the subjugation of the Ogoni people, unlike his earlier compatriot, Isaac
Adaka Boro, he knew the need of the nation and made it abun-
dantly clear that the Ogoni people do not wish to break away
from the Nigerian nation, at least this is what is stated in both
books. This position taken and clearly stated in the Ogoni Bill
of Rights was in *difference* to the pain of internal (domestic)
and external slavery which the Ogoni people had faced in their
history in the Union.

In the Ogoni Bill of Right which was presented to the Federal Government during the reign of General Ibrahim
Babangida, the point is made clear: "our (Ogoni) wish is to
remain a part of the Federal Republic of Nigeria," stressing in
subsequent sections the need and urgency for the Federal
Government to allow the Ogoni "the right to the control and
use of a fair proportion of Ogoni economic resources for Ogoni
development" (*A Month and A Day* 69). Saro-Wiwa argues
here that this is the only way that the Ogoni people could be
delivered from slavery. After all, he argues further, there is
also the need for a Crude Oil House, an obvious reference to
the Cocoa House in Ibadan, Western Nigeria, built in the hey-
days of the boom in cocoa trade boom. Today Cocoa House
stands as a monument to that period of prosperity in the Yoruba
country. There is no monument yet to show for oil prosperity
in the Niger Delta, except of course the loss of arable farmland in the Niger Delta.

## IV

On the part of the Federal Government of Nigeria and its ally, Shell Petroleum Development Company, Nigeria, the "sins" of Ken Saro-Wiwa were many. There was no denying the fact that Saro-Wiwa knew that he was going to "pay" for these "sins." The evidence was *writ large* on the walls of the uneven political situation of his time, yet he couldn't help himself. In the heat of the situation, he wrote to his friend and writer, William Boyd and the comments are typical of what Saro-Wiwa read of the political temperament of his time, "I am mentally prepared for the worst, but hopeful for the best. I think I have the moral victory." (55). Evidently Saro-Wiwa could not help his activism as he witnessed the huge degradation of life and environment in his homeland. Like the great thinkers and activist before him, especially Mahatma Ghandi of whom he made several references to in *A Month and A Day*, he chose the path of the people, believing that he will triumph in the knowledge of truth. He did but without his life.

One of the many "sins" of Saro-Wiwa was that he dared take the case of the Ogoni people to the parliament of the Unrepresented Nations and Peoples Organization (UNPO), during which he detailed the cost of oil exploitation of Shell on the life and environment of Ogoniland in particular and the Niger Delta in general. As would be expected, this did not go down well with the authorities of Shell (Nigeria) and Shell (International.) It did not go down well with the Federal Government either who, in any case, has been implicated in the complacency of Shell towards the life and well-being of the local people who live in the areas where Shell prospects for and mines crude oil.

According to Ken Saro-Wiwa, the UNPO was to play a very crucial role in the affairs of the MOSOP. Known for its secrecy in matters concerning its operations in Nigeria, Shell was obviously alarmed that Saro-Wiwa was able to internationalize the problems of oil pollution in the Niger Delta. Shell, through its spokesperson, agreed in one of its briefings during this period of uncertainty in the Niger Delta, that "Oil, as Nigeria's main source of revenue, is a highly political subject" and that "The country had suffered serious economic difficulties since the oil price collapse in the mid-1980s (*A Month and A Day* 163)." He also expressed sympathy for some of the people and communities of the area, agreeing that they "are not getting a fair share of the oil revenues" (163) but Shell insists that the blame should be located elsewhere: the Nigerian government which has denied the area of the right amount of assistance.

However while Shell was putting up this soft and conciliatory posture, behind the scene, it was putting pressure on the Federal Government to do something to solve the "ethnic" problems in the Niger Delta. The Government reacted promptly to Saro-Wiwa's "sin" of internationalizing the Ogoni crisis: an army of occupation was led into the area, killing at random, maiming and looting the area. The infamous Treason and Treasonable Felony Decree was then quickly promulgated. In July of 1999, the year of the infamous decree, Saro-Wiwa was arrested and kept in prison at different locations in the country in sordid inhuman conditions. He was treated as a common criminal. According to Saro-Wiwa, the ordeal which he went through taught him the extent that the Government was ready to go in order to do him in.

Arrested in Port Harcourt in July, 1993, he was first taken to Lagos and then back to Port Harcourt through Owerri for trial. One of his offenses was that he and some unnamed people assembled at an Ogoni village to plan some actions inimical to the "progress" of the nation, actions which were tantamount to the breach of peace. Another offense for which he was charged was that he designed an Ogoni flag and wrote an Ogoni anthem, charges which the State Secret Service (SSS) officer, one Mr. Terebor, had outlined to him months earlier. (*A Month and A Day*, 154) In all, the charges came to six-counts, all of which amounted to "sedition and unlawful assembly" (219). It is on record that Shell did not intervene during the travails of Saro-Wiwa. The manner of the trial was itself a farce. The trial judge, one "Mrs. D," was obviously ill-disposed to Saro-Wiwa and was more interested in putting him in prison so that she enjoyed her holiday than to listen to the defense which Saro-Wiwa's lawyers put up.

The "sin" committed against Shell was grievous but not grievous enough to send him to the point of no-return: death. For the brutal Nigerian government at the time, the UNPO could only bark, it cannot involve itself in the affairs of a sovereign nation. Thus far the Nigerian Government was willing to accept. But for Shell, the man was a real danger, an upstart who could tarnish the international image of Shell. So he must be properly tamed. Meanwhile Shell's drilling sites in Ogoniland were abandoned. Saro-Wiwa knew that trouble was not far away.

The "sins" of designing a flag and composing a national anthem were serious, but it was clear at this point that Saro-Wiwa's was still a mile or so out of harm's way. At the Port Harcourt hearing, this offense was reduced to a six-month punishment in prison but because the trial judge was not ready to follow proper legal procedure, having made up her mind to "deal with Saro-Wiwa," the case was dismissed after an order came from higher quarters in government.

Ken Saro-Wiwa did not deny that he was actually privy to the designing of a flag. Indeed in *A Month and A Day*, while in prison in Port Harcourt, as he reviewed the struggle so far, he revealed that Edward Kobani's son, "Tombari had designed the MOSOP flag" (205). There is no mention of an Ogoni flag. Even at that Saro-Wiwa did nothing to clarify this point in all his writings except to say that "Mr. Terebor, the director or misdirector, of the SSS, questioned me about an Ogoni flag, an Ogoni National Anthem, the UNPO, and so on and so forth." Soon after he drops the matter, unexplained. This seems a trivialization of a serious and deadly issue.

The "sins" associated with the Ogoni flag and anthem were to reoccur frequently at strategic points of government propaganda against Ken Saro-Wiwa and the MOSOP. One such example was the pro-government inspired pamphlet, *The Ogoni Question Nigeria, MOSOP and NYCOP: The Reality of the Situation*. With no clear authorship, the evidence is that this pamphlet was hurriedly written. Its pages are littered with grammar and typographic errors, not to talk of the deliberate factual errors. Obviously published to counter the intellectual position to the Ogoni crisis which MOSOP presented, it reads like a bad solicitor's outline to squash MOSOP's argument. The anonymously written book lists many of the "sins" of Saro-Wiwa after he assumed the position of President of the movement. He is accused of turning the movement into a "gestapo organization" with NYCOP (National Youth Council of Ogoni People), the youth wing of MOSOP, as the hit squard for his personal ambitions. According to this source, "While Ogoni burnt, while the Ogonis have surrounded themselves with hostile neighbors due to Ken Saro-Wiwa's expansionist program for his pet Ogoni Kingdom, Ken Saro-Wiwa was busy perfecting plans for declaration of the Ogoni nation at the end of 1993" (30). This was to take place on January 4, 1994 "following the end of the Ogoni week celebration" (31). Fortunately for the Ogoni people, "The plan however was preempted by the security agents which (SIC) banned public gatherings on the fatefully awaited day" (31).

As I have pointed out before Ken Saro-Wiwa took the issues of the Ogoni anthem and flag very lightly. This was probably because before these issues became public, he had made public the Ogoni Bill of Right which is very clear about these matters. This is what he refers to when, soon after his encounter with Mr. Terebor, who accuses him of these offenses, he writes in *A Month and A Day* that "He was obviously trying to establish a case for treason" (154), arguing a little later that "there was nothing treasonable in the Ogoni demands. The Ogoni Bill of Rights had expressly stated as follows: now, therefore, while reaffirming our wish to remain part of the Federal Republic of Nigeria we make demand upon the republic as follows..." (154). The Ogoni Bill of Rights is therefore clear on these matters.

It was inconceivable that Ogoni was to declare a war of secession from the Federation. If Isaac Adaka Boro had eleven soldiers on his side when he declared his "revolution," Ken Saro-Wiwa did not have a soldier. He depended more on the triumph of moral and ethical values than on physical violence. He professed nonviolence.

The final and deadly "sin" committed by Saro-Wiwa for which he was vilified and hanged was the "murder" of the four Ogoni Chiefs-Albert Badey, Edward Kobani, Samuel Orage and his brother, Theophilus Orage, illustrious sons of Ogoniland. Ken Saro-Wiwa denies any involvement in these murders, arguing that he was miles away from the murder scene when they occurred. But his fate seemed to have been sealed forever. His luck with the Abacha Regime had run out. A tribunal was quickly set up, Saro-Wiwa and eight other Ogoni activists were arraigned before it and on November 10, 1995, he was hanged in a Port Harcourt prison, together with the eight Ogoni accused with him. Finally, Shell had the last laugh and in a show of some concern after these deaths, Shell came out in public to say that it condemned the execution of these men, a position which was totally belated and directly opposite to the action which reported Shell to have provided "guns for the special police forces which they requested that the Nigerian Government deploy to protect their oil installation against sabotage" (*The Guardian*, 28 January, 1996:1). It was for his people's sake that he died but it was the "vultures," those Ogoni whom he often referred to as the Ogoni sell-outs, that finally sealed his hopes of moving the struggle beyond where it is today.

Since his death, the struggle has gone on, but without the bite which Saro-Wiwa put into it. Today, even the most apolitical person from the Niger Delta and elsewhere can tell that the issues which Saro-Wiwa raised are far from resolved. The Niger Delta area still boils and it won't be for too long before another man of Saro-Wiwa's status and coordination gets up to challenge the government of the day. We can only hope that when it occurs this time, a more positive line of action would be arrived at, bringing the fresh air of political life which the two prominent Delta martyrs, Isaac Adaka Boro and Ken Saro-Wiwa, always hoped for. Saro-Wiwa's "sins" are after all the "sins" associated with opposing a reckless Federal system of government which continuously marginalizes the minorities of oil-bearing Niger Delta. While the metaphor of the Kiama Declaration lingers on, the "moral victory" which Saro-Wiwa started will continue to hunt the political landscape of Nigeria. So for now, let us simply say that the Niger Delta has been "sold for a song," and by this action the country is denied the pitiable and irreversible move towards the brink of disaster. But the real crucial question that we should ask and which ought to prick our minds is this: if the Niger Delta ethnicities face these problems at a time of huge oil revenue, what would happen to them when this source of revenue dries up if the federated ethnic nations of Nigeria remain in this form?

# Notes

1. This was how the cynical and oppositional Nigerian daily newspapers describe the sudden death of General Sani Abacha. Against all codes of African decorum for the dead, the General's death was openly celebrated in Lagos streets in the Southwest of Nigeria as well as in Kano in the North, the General's home town. The newspapers were hysterical as well as jubilant.
2. The Kiama Declaration occurred after the death of Ken Saro-Wiwa and it is significant that it marks an important step towards the continuation of the struggle by the youth of the Niger Delta after the death of Ken Saro-Wiwa.
3. The Urhobo ethnic group which share certain affinities with the Ogoni people has about 5 million people, most of whom live on the Niger Delta coastline. This group, like those of Ijaw and Itsekiri, has seen more than enough of oil spills on their farmland and their fishing ports.
4. The Jesse fire victims were some of the most graphic human pictures of the carelessness of the oil industries in the Niger Delta. It was estimated that more than 1,000 people died when a petroleum-bearing pipe going over Jesse, north of Warri, in Delta State burst open and indigenes rushed to the site to scoop the black gold which was a scarce commodity in Nigeria at that time. Somewhere in the melée someone lit a fire and the rest is a sad tale of charred bodies.
5. Azubike Ileoje argues in his essay *On The Darkling Plain: The Darksome Lyrics of An Outsider* that Saro-Wiwa was basically an outsider to what happened during the course of the war and therefore could not provide an unbiased view of the situation in his book on the subject.

# Works Cited

Boyd, William. "Death of a Waiter." *The New Yorker.* November 27, 1995. 51-5.

Boro, Isaac Adaka. *The Twelve-Day Revolution.* Benin: Idodo Umeh Publishers, 1998.

Crowder, Michael. *The Story of Nigeria.* London: Faber and Faber, 1978.

Ileoje,Azubike. *On A Darkling Plain: The Darksome Lyrics of An Outsider. Before I am Hanged.*New Jersey: African World Press,1999.

Nixon, Rob. "Pipe Dreams: Ken Saro-Wiwa, Environmental Justice, and Minority Rights." *Black Renaissance.* 1/1, 1996:39-55.

Okome, Onookome. "Ken Saro-Wiwa, A Man of Many Tall Parts: Literature, Nationhood and Dissent." *Before I Am Hanged.* (ed) New Jersey:Africa World Press, 1999. (Forthcoming)

Skinner, Elliott P. "African Political Cultures and the Problems of Government." *African Studies Quarterly.* 2/3, 1998:1-8.

Skugly, Sigrun I. "Complexities in Human Rights Protection: Actors and Rights Involved in the Ogoni Conflicts in Nigeria." *Netherland Quarterly of Human Rights.* 15/1, 1997:47-60.

Saro-Wiwa, Ken. *On A Darkling Plain: An Account of The Nigerian Civil War.* London/Port Harcourt: Saros International Publishers, 1989.

_____. *Nigeria: The Brink of Disaster.* Lagos/London: Saro International Publishers, 1991.

_____. *A Month and A Day: A Detention Diary.* London: Penguin Books, 1995.

*The Ogoni Question in Nigeria, MOSOP and NYCOP: The Reality of the Situation.* Port Harcourt: Marine Communications Limited, 1995.

Usen, Aniete. "To Set the Captive Free." *Africa Today.* November 1998: 11.

# Notes on Contributors

**Titi Adepitan** teaches at the Ago Iwoye University, Ago Iwoye, Nigeria.

**Amen Ahunuwangho** teaches at the Edo State University, Ekpoma, Nigeria.

**Felix Akpan** teaches Ethnic and Federal Character Politics at the University of Calabar, Nigeria.

**Francis Unimna Angrey** teaches French Literature at the University of Calabar, Nigeria.

**Innnocent C.K. Eginnaya** teaches at the Alvan Ikoku College of Education, Owerri, Nigeria.

**Solomon Ediri Ejeke** is a Ph.D candidate at the Department of Theatre Arts, University of Calabara, Nigeria. His dissertation is on the Nigerian theatre director and playwright, Ola Rotimi.

**David Eka** is a language specialist. He teaches at the Department of English at the University of Uyo, Akwa Ibom State, Nigeria.

**Imo Ben Eshiet** teaches Caribbean and African dramas in the Department of English and Literary Studies, University of Calabar, Nigeria. His scholarly interest is mainly focused on aesthetics and structure of African drama, oral and written. He is currently preparing a Ph.D. dissertation in this area.

**Harry Garuba** teaches Caribbean and African Literature in the Department of English at the University of Ibadan Nigeria. He is interested in postmodernship scholarship, authorship and authority in postcolonial literature and has published widely in these areas.

**Azubuike Ileoje** teaches African-American Literature at the Department of English and Literary Studies, University of Calabar, Nigeria. He has published many essays on the Igbo novels, especially those of Chinua Achebe.

**Obododimma Oha** teaches Language and Literature at the Department of English, University of Ibadan, Nigeria. Recently his essay on women and social discourse in contemporary Nigeria appeared in *Mosaic*.

**Grace Eche Okereke** teaches Literature at the University of Calabar, Nigeria.

**Onookome Okome** teaches Cinema and Theatre Studies at the University of Calabar, Nigeria. With Jonathan Haynes, he published *Cinema and Social Change in West Africa* (1995; 1997 second Edition), and with Hyginius Ekwazi et al, he published *Studies in Film and Television* (1994). He has editied a volume of essays on the subject of sound in cinema and theater production, *The Sight of Sound: Sound in the Media and Theater*. He recently made a selection of the poems of the Nigerian born British poet, Femi Oyebode for Kraft Books, Lagos. He has published essays in *IRIS*, *Ufahamu*, *Ase*, *Glendora*, *After Image* and *World Literature Today*. He currently edits *Ase: Journal of Nigerian Life and Literature*.

**Oshita O. Oshita** teaches philosophy at the Department of Philosophy and Religion at the University of Calabar, Nigeria.

**Diri I. Telilanyo** teaches at the University of Benin, Ugbowo Campus, Benin City, Nigeria.